The
Global Politics *of*
Educational
Borrowing *and*
Lending

The GLOBAL POLITICS *of* EDUCATIONAL BORROWING *and* LENDING

Edited by

Gita Steiner-Khamsi

Foreword by

Thomas S. Popkewitz

Teachers College, Columbia University
New York and London

Published by Teachers College Press, 1234 Amsterdam Avenue, New York, NY 10027

Library of Congress Cataloging-in-Publication Data

The global politics of educational borrowing and lending / Gita Steiner-Khamsi, editor ; foreword by Thomas S. Popkewitz.
   p. cm.
 Includes bibliographical references and index.
 ISBN 0-8077-4493-X (pbk.)
   1. Educational planning—Cross-cultural studies. 2. Education—Social aspects—Cross-cultural series. 3. Education and state—Cross-cultural studies. 4. Globalization—Cross-cultural studies. I. Steiner-Khamsi, Gita.
 LC71.2.G56 2004
 379. l—dc22   2004047995

ISBN 0-8077-4493-X (paper)

Printed on acid-free paper

Manufactured in the United States of America

11   10   09   08   07   06   05   04   8   7   6   5   4   3   2   1

Contents

Foreword

Globalization is the type of phrase that Antonio Nóvoa (2002) calls *planet speak*. It is a ubiquitous word that travels across the media, academic literatures, and the local bars as something that everyone "knows" and that seems to need no author. Yet globalization is an empty signifier whose spaces are filled continually with multiple and differentiated meanings. It is a name to signal the fulfillment of the progress that modernity was to bring, spoken about with a reference once reserved for the worldwide Church's redemption of the soul. But globalization also produces talk about the degeneration of culture, the erosion of national identity, and the end of diversity in an increasingly standardized world. While globalization appears ubiquitous, it often is treated ahistorically. It is made to seem as a condition that encapsulates contemporary life, one that, if I use a recent comparative study of schooling in Europe, is accepted almost fatalistically.

This planet speak raises the question of understanding the things happening in the world that make the talk of globalization possible. That is, while the talk of globalization may function as an empty signifier, there are things happening in the world for which the word acts as a convenient fiction. The intellectual problem is how to interpret these phenomena of the world. Gita Steiner-Khamsi and the scholars she has invited to contribute to this book take up one such phenomenon—educational borrowing— and explore its historical and contextual dimensions in their national and transnational studies. They note that globalization, like policy borrowing, is not a new phenomenon but rather speaks to anxieties, or celebrations, regarding the rationalities and systems of knowledge governing the social and the individual in contemporary reforms.

If globalization is not a new historical phenomenon, the question is how to account for the present. Most of the literature on contemporary globalization takes the economic characteristics as central for investigating the changes occurring. Such discussions often focus on, for example, the movement from Fordist to post-Fordist economies as evidence of greater global differentiation in changing both cultural and social patterns. Some literature focuses more directly on the cultural phenomena of globalization as an area to be studied in its own right. This latter literature considers, for example, the spread of fast foods or the global village produced through television and now the Internet.

Globalization as economic and social changes, however, leaves unexamined particular and distinctive patterns of knowledge. One of the distinctive qualities of the modernities that begin to emerge from the seventeenth century onward is a particular secular knowledge of the self in which the individual becomes an actor and agent of change. Yet when one examines the globalization literature, that knowledge is investigated as an epiphenomenon to the materiality of the world. Knowledge is treated as something that is used by causal agents of change, reflecting the purpose and social interest of different social groups of actors, institutions, or social forces. Knowledge is placed as the outcome of material forces of production/reproduction rather than investigated as a productive object or "social fact" in constituting the world in which we live.

Ignoring the central role of knowledge in globalization is an odd omission in contemporary studies. I say that it is odd because one of the central foci of modernity is what Max Weber called the disenchantment of the world. The rationality of science replaces the magic and spirituality of prior periods to offer a particular reflectivity. "Thought," reason, and rationality are treated as the secular salvation themes of modernity. They are viewed as expressing the norms of a global humanity that brings change, progress, and individual self-betterment. The phrases of "democracy" and "empowerment," the entrepreneurial "spirit" of capitalism, and the notion of the patrimony of the state embody these salvation themes of reason. The salvation narrative relies on the expertise of rational knowledge to administer the rules and standards of social interactions and conduct. Theories of the family, the child, and the citizen order the "reason" and knowledge of the individual in the name of universal values of humanity that are seemingly to replace particular contexts and communal constraints.

I pose globalization in these terms as projects of a modern mind that knows itself through particular expert systems of knowledge as it brings to the fore the studies presented in this book. The case studies follow the flows, networks, assemblages, connections, and reconnections in which the knowledge of educational reform, especially educational borrowing, occurs. And as I suggest later, the placement of schooling and educational policy are pivotal to these investigations. The school is the major institution in which the circulation of knowledge about the modern self is positioned; yet it often is assumed to be peripheral, if considered at all. In what follows, I outline briefly certain paths taken by the contributors to this volume, and the theoretical and empirical contributions to issues of globalization, education, and comparative studies made by the book as a whole.

First, there is a focus on knowledge that enables one to consider distinctive qualities of current patterns of globalization. This concern with knowledge stands as part of a complex assemblage of institutions and structure, but I will focus for the moment on the question of knowledge and its investigation. At least since the northern European Enlightenment at the end of the eighteenth century, principles of reason and rationality have functioned as global principles by which to govern. The idea of the Enlightenment's rule by reason was formed in relation to religious, national, and colonial projects. But more important, *thought* became something calculable, administrable, and reformable in the making of the citizen that is essential to the conditions of different modernities. The idea that reason could be ordered, classified as inner qualities of the mind, was essential as state planning became prominent. The Enlightenment attitude about reason and knowledge still pervades contemporary thought, although with different configurations and contours to assemble social planning and individual thought. A central contour is not only institutional change, but the linking of collective rationalities with the individual who, as several contributors note, is to become a participatory citizen in "civil society."

Two, this book provides important empirical examinations of the nodes and networks in which the flows of knowledge circulate in social systems (local and worldwide) and institutions. The notions of borrowing, lending, and convergences of knowledge are central concepts to give attention to complex interweaving of practices. It is important to note that borrowing is not copying but rather, as the authors illustrate, provides a concept to examine how patterns of thought move through and are transmuted in different layers of the local and global systems.

Third, these studies give attention to the school and to the policies by which it is constituted as a central place to examine how the local and the global play out. The school is the premier institutional site of modernity, intervening in the thought of the child who is to be the future citizen. The child, family, and community have been sites of school reform from the late eighteenth century to the present, and they are increasingly regulated subjects as the development of the rationally ordered life of the child and family becomes linked with the "political will" and progress of the nation. Recent educational reforms do not forgo this function, as illustrated in the chapters on parent–teacher associations as INGOs in Bosnia-Herzegovina and schooling in Latvia. School reform is one of the central intellectual techniques to render the child and family as visible and amenable to government.

Fourth, the various case studies in this volume place knowledge within an assemblage that examines international agencies, national projects, and local schools. This is one of the ways in which the concept of lending is theoretically helpful. The chapters, for example, provide specific case studies in which to consider which actors "lend" ideas for circulation. These external agencies range from quasi-governmental agencies (e.g., the World Bank and UN) to nongovernmental organizations, such as the Soros Foundation and Save the Children. These analyses enable consideration of the relation of multiple agencies that overlap with national systems of education in producing the governing of education.

Fifth, the book brings together an array of disciplinary fields for the study of globalization itself—from educational studies to historical and comparative studies concerned with understanding the changes occurring in contemporary life. The studies in this book call upon different disciplinary fields to explore the changes—from sociology, anthropology, history, and economics as they intersect with the worldwide phenomenon of schooling.

Sixth, the case studies give systematic and historically specific explorations of the relation of the global in local situations. From Eastern and central Europe, the Mideast, Africa, and South America, the chapters explore the complex impact of policy borrowing and lending on local educational reforms. The studies help readers to understand the relations between what circulates internationally as "reforms" and the processes and the actors that move and translate such practices into local context. Further, the studies continually place the centrality of expert knowledge in the understanding of globalization.

Seventh, this particular theoretical intervention of studying "lessons from elsewhere" provides innovative ways to think about comparative research that is not normative. I say that because the field of comparative education often is designed around developing ameliorative models for the "transferring" of ideas and practices. In this respect, the concept of externalization is especially useful in these studies to explore how and why particular nations use foreign or global policies to justify and legitimate what is being done locally. This notion of externalization, for example, enables us to consider how Tanzania or South Africa turned to other places for educational and health models, illustrating how external references or referent society is used in particular social and cultural contexts, and how international convergence and divergence occur.

Through the concept of externalization we also can consider the idea of neoliberalism that floats through much of contemporary comparative analysis. It appears most often as an external policy inserted into national policies through the global dominance of particular Western nations and economic rationalities. Yet the analyses in the book provide a way to understand how the internal politics of a nation draw upon such neoliberal policies for myriad reasons. Neoliberalism may appear the same in name, but its cultural points of reference involve a hybridity as new assemblages and connections are made in educational policies of reform.

In conclusion, this volume provides an important contribution to comparative studies of education and educational politics. The case studies enable us to consider the flows and networks in which particular educational knowledges circulate in different national systems. In addition, important key concepts are provided to theorize about distinctions and convergences in comparative studies of educational systems.

—Thomas S. Popkewitz

REFERENCE

Nóvoa, A. (2002). Ways of thinking about education in Europe. In A. Nóvoa & M. Lawn (Eds.), *Fabricating Europe: The formation of an education space* (pp. 131–156). Dordrecht, Netherlands: Kluwer.

Acknowledgments

I owe this book to my doctoral students at Teachers College, Columbia University. Together, we delved into exploring why politicians and policy makers systematically refer to educational reform in other countries. Is it really only about learning from reform experiences taking place elsewhere, or is there more to the story of policy borrowing and lending, or educational import and export, that might not seem apparent at first sight? The trend of cross-national policy attraction has increased dramatically since we first began to marvel these questions 5 years ago.

In addition to the students at Teachers College, two grand scholars in comparative education stretched my thinking on these issues. During the preparation of the book outline, I was invited to spend my sabbatical year at the international comparative education programs of Stanford University and Humboldt University in Berlin. I was fortunate to be hosted by two scholars, Francisco O. Ramirez (Stanford) and Jürgen Schriewer (Humboldt), who for the last couple of years have had an inspiring intellectual disagreement on cross-national policy attraction and globalization in education.

My son Manu deserves special mention here. He watched for years as I became completely absorbed with issues of policy borrowing and lending. One day in the spring of 2003, he astutely asked me how I could possibly deal with the topic without analyzing the institutional and social networks that disseminate ideas and innovations in education on a global scale. At the time he was taking a class on social network analysis and small world research. On his next visit, he discreetly left a few texts behind, sparking my interest in these areas ever since.

I am tremendously grateful to Thomas Luschei (Stanford University School of Education) and Nicole Angotti (Teachers College, Columbia University) who helped me with editing and preparing the final manuscript. I also want to extend my sincere gratitude to the Dean and Vice President of Academic Affairs of Teachers College, Darlyne Bailey, and to my colleagues in the Department of International and Transcultural Studies who, in various ways, have actively supported our research in this area.

The
GLOBAL POLITICS *of*
EDUCATIONAL
BORROWING *and*
LENDING

Globalization in Education: Real or Imagined?

Gita Steiner-Khamsi

When researchers study privatization, decentralization, choice, and standards in education, they often point to the international dimension of these particular school reform movements. For many experts in domestic policy and school reform studies, an international perspective is now considered indispensable. Their particular interest lies in borrowing or "learning from elsewhere" (Phillips, 2000). This book responds to the global trend of transnational borrowing and lending in education. While some of the authors seek to explain why educational policies increasingly are imported or exported, others describe how they are locally adapted once they have been transferred from one context to another.

In comparative education a large rift yawns between those implementing and those studying educational borrowing and lending. A common misconception among practitioners holds that comparative researchers compare educational systems and selectively borrow or lend what "works," transferring it from one system to another. Consistent with this view, policy analysts, for example, believe that the advantage of comparative studies often lies in learning from elsewhere. This normative, ameliorative approach toward comparative studies—extracting models that are perceived as effective from other systems—holds huge appeal. In fact, it has generated a tremendous interest in comparative studies that is uncanny to comparativists.

In contrast to the normative endeavor that seeks to impart an understanding of what can be learned and imported from elsewhere (borrowing), as well as what can be taught and exported to elsewhere (lending), contributors to this book describe, analyze, and attempt to understand in detail the impact of policy borrowing and lending on local educational reform. In so doing, they examine the politics of educational borrowing and lending ("why"), the process ("how"), and the agents of transfer ("who"). In addressing these issues, this book applies comparative methods to study the phenomena of transnational transfer, globalization, and international convergence in education.

Every now and then epidemics emerge in educational research that feverishly spread into every discipline and professional field. They start out with a few scholars who are the first to become infected with a new theme; the virus then circulates within the scholarly community, eventually burgeoning into an epidemic when each and every author feels compelled to at least briefly comment on the theme. The contagion is under control only when a saturation point is reached. Beyond such a point, authors writing in a frenzy on the topic merely recycle old publications, providing neither new "data" nor a new interpretive framework for a concept that has become increasingly shallow. As an example, with a mass of writers joining the debate on "civil society," the concept became elusive; manifestations of "civil society" were seen wherever more than two individuals gathered in pursuit of a common goal. With the topic having become increasingly broad and nebulous, scholars in the late 1990s scurried to provide a simple, lasting explanation for the differences between the "old" and "new" democracies of the early 1990s that would resonate over time; in the process, however, they left the original context (the transition from planned to market economies) behind. In addition to the previously discussed features of thematic epidemics—that is, their contagious nature as well as the attempt by scholars to provide simple explanations for complex issues—the context in which epidemics emerge, matters a great deal (Gladwell, 2002). When the context is lost to academic exhaustion and oversimplification, the contagion of an epidemic weakens to such a degree that it is almost entirely eradicated.

Undoubtedly, "globalization" has grown into an epidemic. What simple explanation have scholars generated for globalization that has transformed it from a virus to an epidemic? With the globalization epidemic lasting for quite some time now, there exist a few. Many cultural anthropologists, for example, tend to explore why globalization plays out differently in different cultural contexts (e.g., Comaroff & Comaroff, 2001), whereas historians seem to be interested mostly in identifying the differences between globalization and earlier forms of transnational and transregional dependencies (e.g., Hopkins, 2002). Clearly, researchers do not operate in a vacuum; they build on and respond to existing scholarship in their own field. When their object of study is considered superfluous, they understandably exhibit feelings of loss. Appadurai (2000) identifies globalization as such a "source of anxiety" in the U.S. academic world.

> Social scientists (especially economists) worry about whether markets and deregulation produce greater wealth at the price of increased inequality. Political scientists worry that their field might vanish along with their favorite object, the nation-state, if globalization truly creates a "world without borders." . . . And everyone in the academy is anxious to avoid seeming to be a mere publicist of the gigantic corporate machineries that celebrate globalization. Product differentiation is as important for (and within) the academy as it is for the corporations academics love to hate. (p. 1)

What is the pet idea that educational researchers and practitioners fear to lose in the wake of globalization? Judging from publications in educational research, it is the idea that we are abandoning our idiosyncratic conceptions of "good education" or "effective school reform," and are gradually converging toward an "international model of education." One of the most frequently given explanations for such a fear is the following: Once the barriers for global trade are eliminated, we will import and export anything, including education. Such an assumption also holds that only a small number of school reform models are traded, typically those that are high in demand, that is, those considered to be most effective. Such an explanation might appear commonsensical, but it is erroneous. Nevertheless, the idea of *education sans frontières* mystifies many scholars, and the study of the international convergence of national educational systems has drawn considerable attention in journals of comparative education since the late 1990s.[1]

One is tempted to believe that the saturation point for the globalization epidemic is in sight. Before highlighting yet another topic in this field, for example, many authors recently have introduced their interest in globalization studies with an apologetic note for amassing scholarship in this over-studied subject. Clearly, some aspects of globalization are more examined than others. As Carnoy and Rhoten (2002) note in their introduction to the most recent issue on globalization in education, "the notion that economic and social change affect educational structures and content is old hat" (p. 1). Thus, any study dealing with globalization in education needs to move beyond confirming the intimate relationship between the increased transnational flow of goods, finance, communication, people and ideas (globalization), and changes in national educational systems.

Without anxieties or apologies, this book addresses globalization in education, and attempts to introduce both a historical and a contextual dimension that we find lacking in the ongoing debate. Studies on how and why educational reforms are transplanted from one context to another, whether borrowing is ever wholesale or by design selective, and, finally, the interest in understanding the relation between transnational policy borrowing and international convergence, have a long-standing research tradition in comparative education. It is only in the past few years, however, that this well-established niche in comparative education has drawn academic curiosity and practical interest from other researchers and practitioners.

The authors of this book take the process of globalization for granted, but have serious doubts about whether globalization necessarily leads to a "world culture," "internationality," or "internationalism" in education, that is, to an international model of education. They neither share the enthusiasm for an emerging international model that is supposedly more just and equal than previous models, nor fully embrace the fears that many scholars in the field are experiencing. Some such scholars fear a hybrid international model of education that is composed of borrowed bits and pieces from various high-income educational systems, whereas others fear, more specifically, a complete Americanization of educational reforms in the rest of the world.

Rather than fueling existing anxieties about an emerging international model of education, several authors of this book observe that domestic policy makers, researchers, and practitioners tend to resort to "globalization" and refer to reform experiences only in particular policy contexts. Guided by an interpretive framework that seeks to understand how decision makers justify reforms to an informed and interested public, they find that references to "lessons from elsewhere" often provide a much-needed justification for introducing and accelerating fundamental educational reforms at home. The likelihood for policy borrowing increases when incremental reforms fail, leaving policy makers with a protracted policy conflict that brings any further attempts at reform to an impasse. In such moments of protracted policy conflict, they construct an "absent other" by resorting to an imagined world culture in education *as if* there exists an international agreement on how reforms in education are supposed to unfold. In other words, the authors of this book think that globalization is for *real*, but the international community of experts agreeing on a common (international) model of education is *imagined*.

That said, it is necessary to emphasize that "invented communities," even though they are imagined, are still real in their impact. They have proved to be very effective policy manipulation tools both in the past (Anderson, 1983) and in the present. In recent years, the proliferation of references to "globalization," made by both lenders and borrowers, is striking. The "semantics of globalization" (Schriewer, 2000, p. 330) has generated tremendous political and economic pressure to compare educational systems and to mutually "learn" or borrow from them. Implicitly, the semantics of globalization promotes de-territorialization and de-contextualization of reform, and challenges the past conception of education as a culturally bounded system. The semantics of globalization has been so effective that policy analysts and practitioners often defer to a new sort of patriotism, one that claims that the nation-state must transcend national boundaries in order to survive, economically and politically, in today's "global village" (Jones, 1998). As Schriewer (2000) and Mundy and Murphy (2000) have demonstrated, "global civil society" and other international agents acting on behalf of globalization have contributed considerably to constructing an international model of education at a discursive level. In low-income countries, the external pressure to reform in certain ways, and the reference to an international community that exerts such a pressure, are not self-induced as in economically developed countries. On the contrary, the pressure from the international community on low-income countries in the form of international agreements (e.g., Education for All, Millennium Development Goals, Fast Track Initiative, etc.) is real, and will be addressed in the last part of this book. Whether and how these externally induced reforms are locally implemented is an issue of great importance. Borrowing is not copying. It draws our attention to processes of local adaptation, modification, and resistance to global forces in education.

From a historical perspective, the current semantics of globalization is reminiscent of earlier expansionist, transnational agendas. Earlier discursive educational campaigns such as the semantics of progress, democratization, modernization, and development each had an impact similar to that of globalization. From a critical perspective, the semantics of globalization may be regarded as yet another "education for" campaign (Steiner-Khamsi, 2000, p. 180). As was the case with its predecessors, it places external political pressure on local educational reform. Hence, there may be greater convergence among the voices of policy analysts and researchers justifying their models, than among the educational reforms themselves.

The remainder of this book is divided into three parts. Part I includes three chapters that provide an interpretive and methodological framework for the study of transnational policy borrowing and lending. The remaining two parts offer numerous examples and applications. The seven chapters in Part II focus on the politics of policy borrowing. In Part III two chapters offer examples of policy lending. In the Conclusion, I reflect on how research on policy borrowing and lending contributes to policy studies in education.

NOTE

1. I am referring here specifically to the following journals: *Compare, Comparative Education, Comparative Education Review, Prospects,* and *International Journal of Educational Development.*

REFERENCES

Anderson, B. (1983). *Imagined communities: Reflections on the origins and spread of nationalism.* London: Verso.

Appadurai, A. (2000). Grassroots globalization and the research imagination. *Public Culture, 12*(1), 1–19.

Carnoy, M., & Rhoten, D. (2002). What does globalization mean to educational change? A comparative approach. *Comparative Education Review, 46*(1), 1–9.

Comaroff, J., & Comaroff, J. L. (2001). Millennial capitalism: First thoughts on a second coming. In J. Comaroff & J. L. Comaroff (Eds.), *Millennial capitalism and the culture of neoliberalism* (pp. 1–56). Durham, NC: Duke University Press.

Gladwell, M. (2002). *The tipping point* (2nd ed.). Boston: Little, Brown.

Hopkins, A. G. (2002). *Globalization in world history.* London: Verso.

Jones, P. (1998). Globalisation and internationalism: Democratic prospects for world education. *Comparative Education, 35*(2), 143–155.

Mundy, K., & Murphy, L. (2000). Transnational advocacy, global civil society? Emerging evidence from the field of education. *Comparative Education Review, 45*(1), 85–126.

Phillips, D. (2000). Learning from elsewhere in education: Some perennial problems revisited with reference to British interest in Germany. *Comparative Education, 36*(3), 297–307.

Schriewer, J. (2000). World system and interrelationship networks: The internationalization of education and the role of comparative inquiry. In T. S. Popkewitz (Ed.), *Educational knowledge: Changing relationships between the state, civil society, and the educational community* (pp. 305–343). Albany: State University of New York Press.

Steiner-Khamsi, G. (2000). Transferring education, displacing reforms. In J. Schriewer (Ed.), *Discourse formation in comparative education* (pp. 155–187). Frankfurt/M, Germany: Lang.

Globalization, Internationality, and Cross-National Policy Attraction

The chapters in Part I are written by scholars in comparative studies who have visibly informed research on policy borrowing and lending in education. Their interpretive frameworks frequently are used as a foundation to anchor this particular research field of comparative policy studies in the larger arena of social research. Chapters 1 and 2 are designed to complement each other by reflecting on the distinction between *real globalization* (also referred to as "internationalization") and *imagined globalization* ("internationality"). Charles Tilly in Chapter 1 focuses on real globalization, whereas Jürgen Schriewer and Carlos Martinez in Chapter 2 examine internationality in educational knowledge. In Chapter 3 David Phillips concludes this part of the book by presenting a comprehensive methodological framework in which to analyze borrowing and lending in education.

Charles Tilly, internationally known as a scholar in comparative sociology and history, has deeply influenced research on transnational interactions, including comparative education research on transnational policy borrowing and lending. For example, his comparison of several European "revolutionary situations" in the early 1990s, and his corresponding discussion of the different political "outcomes" in these central and Eastern European countries, is only one of his myriad methodological masterpieces that combine cross-national comparison with contextual analysis (Tilly, 1993). For many researchers of policy borrowing and lending, Tilly's focus on transnational interaction has helped in understanding why, in a given context, one policy solution is selected over another, and how external factors influence and are integrated into local politics.

Tilly's contribution to this book sets the stage for our reflections on globalization. He contends that globalization *per se* is not a new phenomenon or, in his own powerful words, "humanity has globalized repeatedly." What differentiates the three most recent waves of globalization between the fifteenth and twentieth centuries is, according to Tilly, "their relative emphasis on commerce, commitment, and coercion." His statistical material from 2000 and his numerous examples of growing inequalities among countries, in brief, the "darker sides of globalization," are particularly important for researchers and practitioners in education. For many of us, our attention span for statistics is confined to reading educational statistics of various countries (e.g., gross enrollment ratios, dropout rates, public expenditures for education as a percentage of GNP, teacher student ratios, etc.), and when curiosity confronts us, we look up indicators from the adjacent social sector. Often, we forget the larger social context for existing inequalities and globalization that Tilly's chapter provides.

In Chapter 2, Jürgen Schriewer and Carlos Martinez make a case against the international convergence of educational knowledge. As measures of "educational knowledge," they use a set of national education journals from Spain, Russia/Soviet Union, and China and compare these three variations of "national educational knowledge" with "international educational knowledge" as represented in the 1985 and 1994 editions of the *International Encyclopedia of Education*. In policy borrowing research, we frequently use the term "references" or "reception" to denote instances in which policy makers, researchers, or practitioners explicitly mention "lessons from elsewhere." We also use the term "reference societies," albeit less frequently, to classify those educational systems that are regarded as exemplary and worth borrowing from.[1] In their analysis of national educational knowledge(s) and international educational knowledge, Schriewer and Martinez use the term "references" literally, that is, they analyze the bibliographies from both the journal articles as well as the encyclopedias, and then count the number of references made to authors from other countries. Next, they interpret the type of references made.

Their study covers a period of approximately 70 years, from the early 1920s until the mid-1990s. If we were to assume that educational knowledge in all three national contexts is gradually converging toward an internationally shared version of educational knowledge, then we would expect to find the authors in these three countries, as well as the authors represented in the encyclopedias, referring to the same group of authors in their published works. In other words, proponents of the international convergence thesis would believe that there is an increasingly (internationally) shared understanding of what constitutes educational knowledge. Schriewer and Martinez's empirical analysis, however, does not support such a claim. There is no evidence to suggest that we are increasingly reading the same books and journals in different parts of the world, that is, that we are sharing the same knowledge on education. What they find, rather, is a close correspondence between references and political developments in each country.

The introductory section of Chapter 2 also provides a glimpse into a dynamic debate that comparative education researchers at Humboldt University (Berlin) and Stanford University are currently heading. This debate deserves special mention, given that we rarely find scholars in educational research who engage in a passionate debate on theories. At one side of the debate stands the neo-institutionalist approach to the study of globalization processes, advanced by John Meyer and Francisco Ramirez at Stanford University. At the opposing end is the work of Jürgen Schriewer at Humboldt University in Berlin, who draws from the theory of self-referential systems (Luhmann, 1990) in order to distinguish between globalization/internationalization (real) and internationality (imagined). Since the selection of chapters for this book is purposefully biased, leaning toward an interpretive framework that applies system theory to policy studies (Luhmann, 1990; Schriewer, 1990), it is recommended that readers also learn about the other side of the debate.[2]

In Chapter 3, David Phillips, one of the first scholars to pioneer research on the politics of educational policy borrowing, presents a conceptual framework for studying cross-national "policy attraction" in education. He seeks to explain the sustained interest of policy analysts of one educational system in the educational provisions, reform strategies, and other institutional features of another. Directing attention to educational reform models and policy solutions of other countries is by no means a new phenomenon. By observing the British interest in German educational provision over a sustained period of time, he finds that the same educational system can be an object of attraction for different reasons. Specifically, he traces a consistent line of interest in educational provision at all system levels in Germany on the part of British educationists and policy makers. The focus, starting in the early nineteenth century, has been on the nature of schooling, on styles of teaching and learning, on the structure of vocational and technical education, as well as on the German model of a modern university.

Phillips's chapter provides a much-needed conceptual framework for studying policy borrowing. The framework not only is cognizant of different policy contexts, identifying different "foci of attraction," but also acknowledges that educational borrowing is a process involving several policy stages: cross-national attraction, decision to borrow, implementation, and internalization or indigenization. How exactly globalization of the economy and communication functions as a "catalyst for change" at the national level, and whether globalization increases cross-national policy attraction, are important issues that researchers on borrowing are only beginning to grasp. As previously discussed, depending on the theoretical framework that one is applying, cross-national attraction can be interpreted as an act of international cooperation advancing convergence (neo-institutionalist approach) or as an act of inter-state competition strengthening divergence (system theory).

NOTES

1. For example, in *A Nation at Risk* (National Commission on Excellence in Education, 1983), Japan and Germany were used as reference societies for U.S. educational researchers and policy analysts.

2. The first chapter of *Constructing World Culture: International Nongovernmental Organizations Since 1875* (Boli & Thomas, 1999) provides an impressive account of the main intellectual positions in this research area. Another recently published book, *Constructing Education for Development: International Organizations and Education for All* (Chabbott, 2003), applies neo-institutionalist theory to prove the international convergence of discourse and programs in development as reflected in the "Education for All" campaign. John Meyer and Francisco Ramirez have published on this theme for more than 30 years. One of their earlier texts (Meyer, Ramirez, Rubinson & Boli-Bennett, 1977) and a few recent publications (Meyer & Ramirez, 2000; Ramirez & Meyer, 2002), in which they explicitly address the debate between neo-institutionalist theory and system theory, might provide the reader with at least an idea of their main line of argumentation.

REFERENCES

Boli, J., & Thomas, G. M. (1999). INGOs and the organization of world culture. In J. Boli & G. M. Thomas (Eds.), *Constructing world culture: International nongovernmental organizations since 1875* (pp. 13–49). Stanford: Stanford University Press.

Chabbott, C. (2003). *Constructing education for development: International organizations and Education for All.* New York: RoutledgeFalmer.

Luhmann, N. (1990). *Essays on self-reference.* New York: Columbia University Press.

Meyer, J. W., & Ramirez, F. O. (2000). The world institutionalization of education—origins and implications. In J. Schriewer (Ed.), *Discourse formation in comparative education* (pp. 111–132). Frankfurt/M, Germany: Lang.

Meyer, J. W., Ramirez, F. O., Rubinson, R., & Boli-Bennett, J. (1977). The world educational revolution, 1950–1970. *Sociology of Education, 50*(4), 242–258.

National Commission on Excellence in Education. (1983). *A nation at risk: The imperative for educational reform.* Washington, DC: U.S. Department of Education.

Ramirez, F. O., & Meyer, J. W. (2002). National curricula: World models and national historical legacies. In M. Caruso & H.–E. Tenorth (Eds.), *Internationalisierung—Internationalisation* (pp. 91–107). Frankfurt/M, Germany: Lang.

Schriewer, J. (1990). The method of comparison and the need for externalization: Methodological criteria and sociological concepts. In J. Schriewer (Ed.) in cooperation with B. Holmes, *Theories and methods in comparative education* (pp. 25–83). Frankfurt/M, Germany: Lang.

Tilly, C. (1993). *European revolutions 1492–1992.* Oxford & Cambridge: Blackwell.

Chapter 1

Past, Present, and Future Globalizations

Charles Tilly

Since the movement of humans out of Africa some 40,000 years ago, humanity has globalized repeatedly. Any time a distinctive set of social connections and practices expands from a regional to a transcontinental scale, some globalization is occurring. Each time an existing transcontinental set of social connections and practices fragments, disintegrates, or vanishes, some de-globalization occurs. Only when the first sort of process is far outrunning the second, does it clarify matters to say that humanity as a whole is globalizing. On balance, the period since World War II qualifies. Despite some localizing countertrends, internationalization of capital, trade, industrial organization, communications, political institutions, science, disease, atmospheric pollution, vindictive violence, and organized crime has been producing a net movement toward globalization since the middle of the twentieth century.

GLOBAL FLOWS

Over the long run of human history, globalization has taken three related forms: first, migration of specific connected populations, with their particular ways of life, across the globe; second, spread of ideas, techniques, and forms of organization from one population and place to another; and third, increased coordination and interdependence of important activities at a world scale. In the first regard, for example, the initial migration of humans from Africa into Eurasia, and thence into the rest of the world, constituted the first great wave of globalization. In the second regard, consider rapid conversion of millions to Christianity, Buddhism, Islam, and other religions as priests and proselytizers traveled across the worlds accessible to them. In the third, Mongol empires covered much of their known world (if not Africa, the Pacific, or the Americas) during the thirteenth and fourteenth centuries CE. To detect globalization deeply involving all the world's major populated regions, however, we must move forward to European-Ottoman colonization and conquest after 1500.

Globalizing processes vary in their relative emphasis on commerce, commitment, and coercion. Trading populations such as Chinese, Armenians, Jews, and India's Gujaratis often have built world-spanning commercial networks bound internally by strong personal commitments, without creating big political structures to back them. Expansion of religious faiths sometimes has occurred by the sword, but often has happened through the substitution of one set of commitment mechanisms for another. Europeans, Ottomans, and Mongols used large concentrations of coercion to spread their influence. In their purest forms, commercial globalization produces markets and merchants, commitment-based globalization produces cultural communities, and coercive globalization produces empires. Of course, all major surges of globalization involved at least some of each, but in varying proportions.

During the half-millennium since 1500, three main waves of globalization have occurred. The first arrived right around 1500. It resulted from the rapidly spreading influence of Europe, growth of the Ottoman Empire, and parallel expansions of Chinese and Arab merchants into the Indian Ocean and Pacific. The Ottomans extended their control into southern Europe, northern Africa, and the Near East, while Western Europeans were building commercial and territorial empires in Africa, the Pacific, and the Americas. Meanwhile, seafaring Muslim merchants (most of them not Ottoman) continued to connect Africa, the Near East, and Indian Ocean ports. In Asia, European and Muslim commercial activity interacted with China's energetic expansion into Pacific trade under the Ming Empire (1368–1644 CE). Ottoman expansion ended in the nineteenth century. Europeans then partly displaced Muslim merchants across the Indian Ocean and the Pacific. But Europeans and Chinese continued their shares of the first post-1500 globalizing process into the twentieth century. Europeans began colonizing the more temperate zones of their empires in Africa, the Americas, and the Pacific. Chinese migrants by the millions likewise moved into Southeast Asia and the Pacific. Here is one sign of the world's increasing connectedness: By the seventeenth century large amounts of silver mined in South America were ending up in Chinese treasuries.

The second major wave after 1500 overlapped with the first. Consider the flurry of long-distance migration between 1850 and World War I: 3 million Indians, 9 million Japanese, 10 million Russians, 20 million Chinese, and 33 million Europeans. During this period, international trade and capital flows reached previously unmatched heights, especially across the Atlantic. Improvements in transportation and communication such as railroads, steamships, telephone, and telegraph lowered the costs of those flows and speeded them up. Massive movements of labor, goods, and capital made prices of traded goods more uniform across the world and reduced wage gaps among countries that were heavily involved in those flows. The chief beneficiaries included Japan, Western Europe, and the richer countries of North and South America. For the world as a whole, globalization's second wave increased disparities in wealth and well-being between those beneficiaries and everyone else. Except for settler colonies such as Australia and coastal South America, European colonies generally did not share in the prosperity.

Migration, trade, and capital flows slowed between the two world wars. But as Europe and Japan recovered from World War II, a third post-1500 surge of globalization began. This time intercontinental migration accelerated less than between 1850 and 1914. Fewer economies felt acute labor shortages, and labor organized more effectively to bar immigrant competition. As a consequence, long-distance migration bifurcated into relatively small streams of professional and technical workers on one side, and vast numbers of servants and general laborers on the other. Because differences in wealth and security between rich and poor countries were widening visibly, potential workers from poor countries made desperate attempts to migrate into richer countries, either permanently or long enough to earn substantial money for their return home. Whole industries grew up around the facilitation of illegal, semilegal, and legal but brutal forms of migration into richer countries.

Flows of goods and capital accelerated even beyond nineteenth-century levels. Many of those flows occurred within firms, as multinational companies spanned markets, manufacturing sites, headquarters, and sources of raw materials in different countries. But international trade among countries and firms also accelerated. Goods produced in East Asia, Western Europe, and North America became available almost everywhere in the world. At the same time, political institutions, communications systems, technology, science, disease, pollution, and criminal activity all took on increasingly international scales. The third wave of post-1500 globalization is now moving ahead with full force.

The waves of 1850–1914 and of today differ conspicuously. Despite imperial outreach and the rising importance of Japan, nineteenth-century expansion centered on the Atlantic, first benefiting the major European states, then increasingly favoring North America. Its twentieth- and twenty-first-century counterpart involved Asia much more heavily. As sites of production, as objects of investment, and increasingly as markets, China, Japan, Korea, Taiwan, India, Pakistan, Bangladesh, Indonesia, Malaysia, Singapore, Thailand, the Philippines, and other Asian countries participated extensively in global growth.

Another difference: During the wave of 1850–1914, economic expansion depended heavily on coal and iron. As a consequence, capital and workers flowed especially to a limited number of smokestack regions, producing the characteristic grimy concentrations of industrial cities along waterways and rail lines. By the late twentieth century, oil, natural gas, hydroelectric generators, and nuclear reactors had largely displaced coal as sources of power in the world's richer regions. Post-1945 globalization featured such high-tech industries as electronics and pharmaceuticals. Those industries depended on important clusters of scientific and technical expertise such as Paris-Sud and Silicon Valley, California. But with goods of high value and relatively low transport cost, they could easily subdivide production according to the availability of labor and markets. Service and information industries pushed even farther in the same direction: Low-wage, data-processing clerks in Southern India, for example, processed information for firms based in New York and London, with fiber-optic cable and satellite connections transmitting data instantly in both directions.

Globalization in its nineteenth-century version consolidated states. It augmented their control over resources, activities, and people within their boundaries as it increased their regulation of flows across those boundaries. In the process, uneasy but effective working agreements emerged among governments, capital, and labor at the national scale. Organized labor, organized capital, organized political parties, and organized bureaucrats fought hard, but made deals. Those bargains eventually turned states from free trade toward protection of industries that combined large labor forces with extensive fixed capital. Chemicals, steel, and metal-processing industries led the way. The twentieth/twenty-first-century variety of globalization, in dramatic contrast, undermined the central power of most states, freeing capital to move rapidly from country to country as opportunities for profit arose. Post-1945 states also lost effectiveness when it came to containing accelerated flows of communication, scientific knowledge, drugs, arms, gems, or migrants across their borders.

At the same time, nongovernmental and super-governmental organizations escaped at least partially from control by any particular state. Newly powerful nonstate organizations included multinational corporations, world financial institutions, the United Nations, political compacts such as the European Union, military alliances such as the North Atlantic Treaty Organization (NATO), and international activist groups such as Doctors Without Borders. An irony appears: The United States sponsored or at least supported the initial formation of many such transnational organizations, and in their early phases often bent them to its national interests. Yet as the twenty-first century began, even the United States, the world's greatest financial and military power, could not simply order these organizations around.

POVERTY AND INEQUALITY

As of 2000, the world economy displayed startling inequalities. North America had only 5% of the world's population but 30% of the world's industrial production. At the other extreme, Africa had 13% of world population and a mere 2% of industrial production. Asia (including the rich economies of Japan, South Korea, Taiwan, and Singapore) stood in between, with a full 61% of world population and only 26% of industrial production ("Bilan du Monde," 2001, p. 22). If we compared these figures with an even worldwide distribution of wealth, they would mean that inhabitants of North America had six times their share of the wealth, Asians less than half their share, and Africans less than a sixth of their share.

Country-by-country disparities, of course, ran even larger. National income per capita is a peculiar statistic for three reasons: First, it averages over the entire population—men, women, and children of all ages—regardless of whether they are earning money. Second, how well it describes the economic situation of most people depends on how equally income is distributed; medium per capita income plus high inequality means many poor people. Third, income figures exaggerate differences between rich and poor countries because in poorer regions as a whole people produce a larger share of goods and services outside of the market; national income accounts generally undercount nonmarket goods and services.

Nevertheless, big international differences in per capita income reliably indicate large differences in overall conditions of life. Compare Switzerland, its annual income per person more than $38,000, with Sierra Leone, whose average inhabitant receives $130 per year—about 36 cents a day per person (World Bank, 2001). The differences are huge. They make it easier to understand why most people in such countries as Sierra Leone have no hope of ever acquiring goods most Western Europeans and North Americans take for granted. They have no prospect of buying automobiles, televisions, or expensive prescription drugs.

Still, we should avoid thinking that money alone makes the difference. Table 1.1 shows that national income correlates with a number of other advantages, but by no means perfectly. In the table, the highest-income countries are Norway, Japan, and the United States, in that order. The lowest-income countries are Niger and Bangladesh. In the table's two poorest countries, income per capita runs no more than $1 a day, as compared with Norway's $90 per day per person. How many people actually live above or below these national averages depends, however, on the inequality of income distribution. On the list, South Africa, Mexico, Niger, Turkey, and the United States top the other countries in their degrees of income inequality. Japan, the Czech Republic, and Norway have relatively low income inequality, which means that higher shares of their populations are sharing their countries' prosperity. The table shows that Japanese, Czech, and Norwegian citizens benefit from the greater equality of income distribution: They enjoy high school enrollments for their children and significantly lower infant mortality than rich countries such as the United States.

High average income by itself, then, does not guarantee extensive schooling or low infant mortality. Take another comparison: Australia, the Czech Republic, and France all had lower per capita incomes than the United States in 1999, but their babies more often survived their first years. Even in fairly prosperous countries with advanced medical facilities, provision of health care for poor people increased the overall population's life expectancy.

Among poorer countries, the data also show that relatively equal access to health care saves babies' lives. On vastly lower average income, China manages much lower infant mortality than South Africa or Turkey. China does so by spreading its meager health resources more evenly, and by investing heavily in public health. When poverty, inequality, and low public expenditure on health combine, nevertheless, they usually produce lower levels of schooling and much higher rates of death among the newborn. In these terms, citizens of Niger had the worst of all worlds: extremely low per capita income, high income inequality, and very small public expenditure on health. In 1998, a newborn infant in Niger was 30 times as likely to die within a year as was a newborn Japanese. Only a small minority of those who survived their first year of life in Niger were likely to complete primary school, much less to attend high school.

International inequality extended well beyond income, schooling, and life expectancy. From the perspective of people in the wealthier North American and European countries, for example, the Internet looks like a great equalizer, connecting everyone with everyone else. After all, in 2000 the United States led the world with 160 Internet-connected computers per 1,000 people; Finland followed closely with 125 connections per 1,000; and

Table 1.1. Indicators of Well-Being for Selected Countries, 1980–1999

Country	GNP per capita 1999 [1]	Income Inequality 1990s [2]	% of Age Group Enrolled in School				Infant Mortality per 1,000 births [3]		Public Expenditure on Health as % of GDP [4] 1990–1998
			Primary		Secondary				
			1980	1997	1980	1997	1980	1998	
Australia	20,050	35.2	100	100	81	96	11	5	5.5
Bangladesh	370	33.6	60	75	18	22	132	73	1.6
China	780	40.3	84	100	63	70	42	31	2.0
Czech Rep.	5,060	25.4	95	100	93	100	16	5	6.4
France	23,480	32.7	100	100	94	99	10	5	7.1
Japan	32,230	24.9	100	100	93	100	8	4	5.9
Jordan	1,500	36.4	73	68	53	41	41	27	3.7
Mexico	4,400	53.7	98	100	67	66	51	30	2.8
Niger	190	50.5	22	24	7	9	135	118	1.3
Norway	32,880	25.8	99	100	84	98	8	4	6.2
S. Africa	3,180	59.3	68	100	62	95	67	51	3.2
Turkey	2,900	41.5	81	100	42	58	109	38	2.9
U.S.A.	30,600	40.8	90	100	94	96	13	7	6.5

[1] Gross National Product/population, in U.S. dollars

[2] Gini index: 0 = perfect equality, 100 = complete inequality

[3] Deaths of children less than 1 year old in year/1,000 live births in same year

[4] GDP = Gross Domestic Product

Source: World Bank, 2001, pp. 276–287.

Iceland came next with 100. Those numbers mean that Iceland, for example, had one computer connected to the Internet for every 10 people. Over the world as a whole, the Internet had an estimated 378 million users ("Bilan du Monde," 2001, p. 33).

The total seems immense, but stop to think: It represented 6% of world population in 2000. Inverted, the figure means that 94% of humanity then lacked access to the Internet. The United States, Canada, Western Europe, Japan, and South Korea accounted for something like nine-tenths of all the world's Internet users. Less than one person in a thousand was surfing the Internet in South Asia and sub-Saharan Africa. Since connection to the Internet does, as advertised, provide rapid access to vast quantities of information and millions of people, the net effect of the Internet's impressive expansion has been to increase information inequality across the world. Most likely, computer-based communication will continue to divide the world sharply into informational rich and poor for decades to come.

Similar stories apply to other forms of globalization: Seen from centers of influence, it looks as though the entire world is globalizing. Seen from the edges, penetration of global influence is highly selective. At least in the short and medium runs, it increases inequalities. Scientific advances, for example, are having profound effects on medicine, communications, agriculture, and manufacturing. But those effects concentrate very heavily in already rich countries. To take a simple indicator, the only countries registering 10 or more patents per million population in 1997 were Japan, South Korea, Australia, Canada, the United States, the Nordic countries, and the countries of Western Europe, except for Spain and Portugal (World Bank, 2001). Their technological advantages over the rest of the world were actually increasing.

Or take the case of advances in medicine. As the HIV virus spread globally during the 1990s and the early twenty-first century, Western pharmaceutical companies started creating drugs that greatly prolonged and improved the lives of HIV victims. But the virus continued to kill in Africa. In 2000, an estimated 38.8% of Botswana's population aged 15–49 carried the virus, with rates substantially higher for women (Boyd, 2002). The hardest-hit countries—Botswana, South Africa, Zimbabwe, Zambia, and other African regions farther north—had neither the financial means nor the delivery systems to get life-saving drugs to their ailing populations.

Nevertheless, globalization was transforming the world's economic and political geography. During the period after 1945, three major shifts deserve attention: breakup or transformation of all the major socialist regimes; movement of a number of regional economies into niches of high-technology production and export; and the overall rise of Asia and the Pacific as sites of economic and political power. Socialist breakup and transformation included the disintegration of both the Soviet bloc and Yugoslavia. It also involved the cautious but quite successful movement of China toward production for world markets, notably that of North America. The new regional specialization in niches of high-tech production shows up in the countries listed by the World Bank (2001) as having at least 10% of their manufacturing exports in high-tech products as of 1998:

> Australia, Austria, Canada, China, Costa Rica, Denmark, Finland, France, Germany, Hungary, Indonesia, Ireland, Israel, Japan, South Korea, Kyrgyz Republic, Malaysia, Mexico, Netherlands, Norway, Philippines, Russia, Singapore, Sweden, Switzerland, Thailand, United Kingdom, United States. (pp. 310–311)

Alongside the old industrial countries on the list, we find ex-socialist states such as Hungary (21% of manufacturing exports high-tech), the Kyrgyz Republic (16%), and Russia (12%). We also find up-and-coming, low-wage manufacturers of Central America and the Pacific. A regional, rather than national, list would include coastal India and parts of South America's southern cone as well. In such industries as electronics, international firms based in the major industrial powers have been seeking out entrepreneurs who can supply disciplined low-wage workers for production of high-tech components. The entrepreneurs are showing up increasingly outside the traditional centers of manufacturing.

DARKER SIDES OF GLOBALIZATION

Many of the same unequal global connections that transferred wanted goods and services across the world also delivered commodities that few people desired. Global warming provides an obvious example. The world's rich countries use far more fuel for transportation, manufacturing, and heating than poor countries do. Fuel use inevitably produces atmospheric emissions of gases and particles. As a consequence of fuel consumption, carbon dioxide, methane, and other greenhouse gases are entering the earth's atmosphere, magnifying the sun's heating effect on the planet. As a result, polar ice is melting and sea levels are rising throughout the world. Low-lying settlements such as those in Bangladesh face the threat of greater and greater flooding. So far, rich industrial countries have contributed most to global warming through exhaust from their factories, houses, buildings, and motor vehicles. But because poorer industrializing countries generally consume higher-emission fuels, the balance is changing. At present rates of growth, China will pass the United States as the world's premier polluter in 2015.

Air and water pollution resulting from manufacturing, transportation, agricultural effluents, and human waste operate on smaller scales than global warming, but they likewise occur in part as results of globalization. Poor parts of the globalizing world are now urbanizing much more rapidly than rich parts of the world, with the result that people in those regions suffer increasingly from such diseases as bronchial asthma, tuberculosis, cholera, and lead poisoning. Global connections facilitated the world's influenza pandemic of 1918 and the spread of AIDS through Africa and Asia after 1990. AIDS devastates sexually active segments of populations and their children so rapidly, in fact, that it could easily obliterate economic growth in the hardest-hit African countries.

Whereas plugging local resources into world markets works all too well, the process likewise has a dark side. Once surveyors discover new deposits of oil, for example, they almost always can find international firms eager to drill and pump. But when that happens fast, it defaces the landscape, displaces the local population, attracts polluting tankers or pipelines, and rarely produces benefits for the bulk of the people in the oil-producing region. Although national treasuries and high officials have fattened on the proceeds, expanded oil production in Nigeria has left 70% of the population below the income threshold of $1 per day. Oil is not alone: Lumbering of Indonesia's lowland trees (including those officially in national parks) is proceeding so fast that one of the earth's richest forests is on its way to extinction; World Bank specialists project that the once fabulous lowland forests of Sumatra will disappear by 2005, those of Kalimantan by 2010 (Jepson, Jarvie, McKinnon, & Monk, 2001). In Indonesia, international logging firms collude with local officials to split the profits from ignoring the future, and back up their collusion with violence against anyone who tries to stop them.

Other unhappy traffics likewise result at least partly from globalization: intercontinental shipment of prostitutes, illegal arms trading, traffic in mercenary soldiers, financing of military rebels with diamonds, kidnapping for extortion and profit, forcible recruitment of child soldiers, taking of slaves, and illegal immigration. Consider the international trade in hard drugs as one of the better-documented cases in point. Westerners promoted the opium trade in China during the nineteenth century. But the twentieth/twenty-first century scale and profitability of illicit drugs outshadow earlier versions of the trade. During the late 1990s, experts in the United Nations estimated that international drug trafficking amounted to 8% of all world trade (Grimal, 2000). Let us concentrate on cocaine and heroin, which generate greater global connections than cannabis, hallucinogens, barbiturates, and amphetamines. Like most other illicit trades at the global scale, cocaine and heroin pass mainly from very poor to richer parts of the world.

They enrich criminal entrepreneurs in the richer regions and their agents in poor regions.

Consider two crucial facts about commerce in cocaine and heroin at the beginning of the twenty-first century. First, cultivators of the original crops receive no more than trivial shares of the proceeds: $1 in $2,500 of the street price for cocaine, $1 in $25,000 of the street price for heroin. (Compare the markup with oil, which at the gas pump sells for roughly 40 times its price leaving the ground.) Only very poor peasants have much to gain by producing the raw materials. Second, the markups get larger and larger as the drug approaches its distant consumers; the final wholesalers at destination make the big money. As a result, eradication of the original crops faces severe limits as an antidrug policy: Profiteers farther down the supply line have powerful incentives and means to search out new growers as the old ones give up their crops.

Three major zones produced the great bulk of commercialized opium and coca at the twentieth century's end. At that point, Afghanistan produced about 2,800 tons of opium per year. Myanmar came a close second with more than 2,500 tons. Delivered as powdered heroin to New York streets, the two regions' annual production would be worth about $1.4 trillion. Coca came largely from the highlands of Bolivia, Peru, and Colombia. Colombians also grew opium poppies, but on nothing like the Afghan scale. In the spring of 2001, Afghanistan's Muslim rulers told United Nations officials that they were eradicating the country's opium crop; if that actually had happened, we might have expected heroin production to increase in both Myanmar and Colombia, and perhaps in adjacent areas as well. Western expulsion of the Taliban from control of Afghanistan later in 2001, however, gave new freedom to the country's growers. Afghanistan soon led the world again in poppy production (Rohde, 2002).

As with other globalized products, a well-defined international division of labor has formed. Cocaine goes primarily to dealers, and then to users, in North America, with a secondary circuit through the Caribbean to Western Europe. Cali, Medellin, Miami, New York, Chicago, Los Angeles, and Trinidad all play significant parts in the cocaine network. Heroin flows from the Afghan region especially to Europe (both Eastern and Western), with Istanbul, Moscow, Palermo, Naples, and Addis Ababa significant centers of redistribution. Heroin from Myanmar and elsewhere in Southeast Asia often passes through Bangkok, Singapore, or Hong Kong on its way to Australia and the United States, while another circuit leads through Mauritius back to Italy. A shift in the major sites of production would not destroy these distribution networks, but it would alter their relative importance.

In addition to the ruined lives of many users, the trade in heroin and cocaine produces a series of deleterious side effects. It provides income for criminal networks that may invest their proceeds in legitimate businesses, but also commonly deal in prostitution, gambling, and other illicit trades. It finances civil wars as both right- and left-wing forces discover they can tax producers and distributors. It promotes money laundering on a colossal scale, which in turn supports tax-sheltered banking centers like those that dot the Caribbean map. It encourages the purchase of protection from government officials, and sometimes their direct participation in drug sales. According to the Paris-based Geopolitical Drug Observatory, the roster of states in which parts of the government or significant numbers of officials profit from the drug trade includes Albania, Azerbaijan, Cambodia, Colombia, Equatorial Guinea, Gambia, Morocco, Mexico, Myanmar, Nigeria, Pakistan, Paraguay, Peru, Poland, Russia, Suriname, Syria, Thailand, Turkey, Ukraine, and Uzbekistan. Note the division of labor: consumers and principal financial beneficiaries in wealthy countries, producers in poor countries, political profiteers mostly in between. The drug trade offers a paradigm for the darker sides of globalization.

POLITICAL FALLOUT OF GLOBALIZATION

Despite the occasional formation of an empire, through most of human history coercive means remained relatively fragmented, dispersed among communities, warlords, thugs, bandits, pirates, mercenaries, feudal retainers, religious organizations, and private armies. Over the past few centuries, humanity performed the surprising feat of placing its major concentrations of coercive means under the control of national governments. The cost was increasingly bloody international warfare. But it brought the benefit of reduction in domestic mayhem—more so in other Western countries than in the United States.

In our own time, that trend seems to be reversing. Civil war, guerrilla warfare, genocide, mass political killing, gun-running, and even mercenary activity have been rising irregularly since World War II. The U.S. Central Intelligence Agency's count of international terrorist incidents from 1968 through 2001 provides one indication (Johnson, 2001; U.S. Department of State, 2000, 2001, 2002). The *international* terrorist incidents in the count include only those in which a group based outside a given country attacked targets within that country. They therefore exclude relatively contained civil wars such as that of Sri Lanka, but emphatically include Arab and Israeli attacks on one another as well as the work of such groups as the Red Army Faction, the Red Brigade, and the Japanese Red Army. Year-to-year variation in the frequency of such events depends especially on fluctuations in bombing. Minor spurts occurred during the 1970s, which included the Munich Olympic Village attack of 1972. But the high point came in the 5 years from 1984 through 1988. After that, terrorist attacks fell off irregularly but substantially. Bombing, armed attacks, and hostage taking all became more common during the peak years. Then all—especially bombing—declined. Even the 2001 attacks on the Pentagon and the World Trade Center did not reverse the overall decline in the sheer number of terrorist incidents.

Other evidence concerning armed conflicts across the world places the post-1945 peak of interstate and civil wars around 1992 (Tilly, 2003, Chapter 3). National liberation movements played an increasingly prominent part in terrorism and civil wars as the overall frequency of incidents decreased after then. From the early 1990s onward, civil war and genocide became the world's leading sources of violent deaths on the large scale. Genocide is systematic extermination of one ethnic category's members by killers from another ethnic category. Rwanda's anti-Tutsi genocide of 1994, in which hundreds of thousands of Hutu took part, killed more people than any other single episode of the 1990s; half a million people may have died in Rwandan massacres that year. (The dead included not only Tutsis, but also Hutu who did not collaborate fully with the killing.)

The Rwandan genocide represented only the extreme and most unequal form of ethnic conflict. Coupled with muscular nationalism (the force-backed demand for a state dominated by members of a single ethnic or national category), ethnic conflict became the early twenty-first century's greatest source of political killing. The swelling of bottom-up nationalist claims during a period of globalization surprised many Western analysts. Like those who thought that simply plugging low-income economies into world markets would stimulate those economies to take off, many optimists thought that Western models of democracy and public order would spread rapidly through the globalizing world.

Some democratization did occur (Freedom House, 2002; Karatnycky, 2000). It coincided, however, with an increase in violent struggles over who would run new regimes. After World War II, decolonization brought a new wave of nationalist claims. Those claims were often even more far-fetched than those of nineteenth-century nationalists, since leaders of ethnically heterogeneous colonies whose boundaries had been formed through military conquest by colonizers regularly claimed to represent unified nations. Because great powers and the United Nations continued to honor such nationalist claims, they multiplied as the Cold War ended, socialist federations disintegrated, and the advantages of being recognized as authentic national leaders increased.

What advantages? Despite the hardships often imposed on poor countries by economic globalization and structural adjustment, those who ran states that were integrating more fully into the world economy and polity usually gained far more benefits than those who did not run those states. What Freedom House calls a "context of corruption" refers indirectly to that fact. In different parts of the world, recognition as the legitimate ruler of a state could bring foreign aid, loans, military assistance, contracts with multinational firms, bribes, and jobs for the group in power. In Europe, it could mean candidacy for membership in NATO and the European Union. In the Americas, it could mean U.S. loans, military assistance, investment, and market openings.

In addition, state power gave religious, linguistic, and ethnic groups opportunities to strike at their rivals and enemies. Where adjacent states stand to gain influence by installing rulers of similar ethnic, religious, or linguistic identity in their neighbors, the incentives to nationalism increase. Put together, the model of states as national, the rewards to recognized rulers, and the power to suppress rivals stimulated nationalist struggles for power in a large minority of the world's states. What looks at a distance like mindless hatred of one group for another, actually has a strong political rationale.

More sinister rationales for claiming state power also prevail sometimes. To run one's own state establishes a claim to collect from illegal, semilegal, or dangerous enterprises on one's own territory. In Sierra Leone, Liberia, and Zaire in the 1990s and early twenty-first century, for example, access to diamonds allowed mining entrepreneurs and aspiring rulers to turn their shared military power into great wealth. Analysts of the bloody conflict that has pitted various military forces against Russian authorities in Chechnya, on Russia's southwest border since the secession of Georgia in 1991, have plausibly but contradictorily described the struggle as:

- A claim of a unified indigenous people to independence
- A bid by nearby Muslim powers to extend their influence into a predominantly Muslim section of Russia
- A fight over control of oil drilled in or passing through Chechnya
- An attempt to create a zone where criminal enterprises could flourish

Each description contains an element of truth, but none of them alone captures the conflict's complexity. Chechnya's struggles intertwine rivalries among warlords, nationalists, Muslim activists, and criminals (Tishkov, 1997, 1999, 2001).

In Colombia, Mexico, Peru, Afghanistan, and Myanmar, the drug trade offered similar opportunities. It also provided good reasons for local rebels, whatever their announced political programs, to keep the central state and the international community at arm's length. In both Colombia and Chechnya, hostage taking for ransom has become a vicious political art form, and a major source of financial support for paramilitary forces (Ramirez, 2001; Tishkov, 2001). Not all such forces are demanding independence or state power in the names of oppressed nations. But the stakes of civil war and rebellion resemble one another across a wide range of regional conflicts. Far from being protests against globalization, furthermore, most of them feed on new opportunities offered by globalization. In that sense, globalization has promoted the rise of what outsiders call ethnic conflict, religious fanaticism, and even genocide.

Despite often being incited by outside states or by paramilitary shadows of existing states, on the whole these homicidal activities are escaping the system of state control over concentrated coercion that grew up between 1750 and 1950 or so. To the degree that international flows of drugs, arms, oil, gas, military expertise, and precious stones come under the influence of those who already dominate financial capital, information banks, or scientific knowledge, whole new forms of inequality could form, with disastrous consequences for humanity as a whole. Sound historical understanding of these complex processes, intelligently applied, can reduce the likelihood of such tragic outcomes. International transfers of knowledge and educational methods have their part to play.

REFERENCES

Bilan du monde [Balance of the world]. (2001). *Le Monde.*

Boyd, C. (2002, July 2). AIDS epidemic still spreading, UN warns. *Globe and Mail.* Retrieved July 2, 2002, from http://www.globeandmail.com.

Freedom House. (2002, March 29). Freedom in the world 2002: The democracy gap. Retrieved May 19, 2003, from www.freedomhouse.org/research/survey2002.htm.

Grimal, J.-C. (2000). *Drogue: L'autre mondialisation* [Drugs: The other globalization]. Paris: Gallimard.

Jepson, P., Jarvie, J. K., McKinnon, K., & Monk, K. A. (2001, May 4). The end for Indonesia's lowland forests? *Science, 292,* 859–861.

Johnson, L. C. (2001). The future of terrorism. *American Behavioral Scientist, 44,* 894–913.

Karatnycky, A. (Ed.). (2000). *Freedom in the world: The annual survey of political rights and civil liberties.* Piscataway, NJ: Transaction.

Ramirez, R. D. (2001). On the kidnapping industry in Colombia. In A. P. Schmid (Ed.), *Countering terrorism through international cooperation* (pp. 173–179). Milan: International Scientific and Professional Advisory Council of the United Nations Crime Prevention and Criminal Justice Programme.

Rohde, D. (2002, October 28). Afghans lead world again in poppy crop. Retrieved October, 28, 2002, from http://nytimes.com.

Tilly, C. (2003). *The politics of collective violence.* Cambridge: Cambridge University Press.

Tishkov, V. (1997). *Ethnicity, nationalism and conflict in and after the Soviet Union: The mind aflame.* London: Sage.

Tishkov, V. (1999). Ethnic conflicts in the former USSR: The use and misuse of typologies and data. *Journal of Peace Research, 36,* 571–591.

Tishkov, V. (2001). The culture of hostage taking in Chechnya. In A. P. Schmid (Ed.), *Countering terrorism through international cooperation* (pp. 341–364). Milan: International Scientific and Professional Advisory Council of the United Nations Crime Prevention and Criminal Justice Programme.

U.S. Department of State. (2000). *Patterns of global terrorism 1999.* Retrieved May 19, 2003, from www.usis.usemb.se/terror/rpt1999/index.html.

U.S. Department of State. (2001). *Patterns of global terrorism 2000.* Retrieved May 19, 2001, from www.usis.usemb.se/terror/rpt2000/index.html.

U.S. Department of State. (2002). *Patterns of global terrorism 2001.* Retrieved May 19, 2003, from www.state.gov/s/ct/rls/pgtrpt/2001.html.

World Bank. (2001). *World development report 2000/2001: Attacking poverty.* Oxford: Oxford University Press.

Chapter 2

Constructions of Internationality in Education

Jürgen Schriewer
Carlos Martinez

As noted in the Introduction to this volume, phenomena of growing global interconnectedness, conventionally phrased as "internationalization" or "globalization," have become prominent features of the contemporary world from the late twentieth century onwards. This holds true not only for economic relations, consumption, science and technology, communication media, and tourism, but also for contemporary educational systems. At any rate, indicators of an intensification in international communication and cooperation networks in the areas of educational research, educational planning, and educational policy development are as numerous as they are impressive.

CONTRASTING THEORY PERSPECTIVES

Such indicators serve as evidence in theories and empirical studies that analyze, from a social sciences perspective, the apparently all-pervasive dissemination of world-level patterns of political and cultural organization (Boli & Ramirez, 1986; Thomas, Meyer, Ramirez, & Boli, 1987). We make special reference to a phenomenological and culturalist version of world system theories, which has been developed by a group of researchers around John W. Meyer, Francisco O. Ramirez, and others at Stanford University. This approach conceives of the world system primarily in terms of an emerging world polity and a corresponding transnational cultural environment. This *neo-institutionalist approach* offers empirically well-grounded and intellectually inspiring explanations for the worldwide convergence of patterns of educational organization, of school curricula, and of patterns of expansion taking place on all levels of educational systems (see Meyer & Ramirez, 2000). Furthermore, these authors suggest the dissemination of a "world-level developmental cultural account and educational ideology" (Fiala & Lanford, 1987, p. 319) which is understood to increasingly influence and shape the conceptions of educational actors—politicians, planners, administrators, teachers, unions, as well as the broad public—and to direct educational decision making (see Fiala & Lanford, 1987). This ideology, they explain, has emerged from a combination of the key concepts that have shaped the self-interpretation of European modernity from the eighteenth and nineteenth centuries onwards. Above all, these concepts, or "institutionalized legitimating myths," include the ideas of (1) individual personality development, citizenship, and participatory competence; (2) the equalization of social and political opportunities; (3) economic development and national progress; and (4) a political order guaranteed by the nation-state (Ramirez & Boli, 1987). Following the dynamics of European expansion, this ideology has, with increasing intensity over the twentieth century, had an impact on the conceptual frames for education and development policies, and on the educational aims defined by national constitutions and basic education laws across all continents. It has, the Stanford group maintains, acquired the status of an institutionalized vision for the modern world, an account that is taken to accompany, support, and promote modernization and development processes that occur, however uncoordinated, in all parts of the world.

Not least, the neo-institutionalist model developed by the Stanford group highlights the central role that professional educational research has come to play, through its representatives (researchers, experts, and consultants), communications (publications, papers, and speeches), and communication media (journals, series, and congresses), in the international dissemination of theoretical approaches, methods, educational agendas, and organizational models. However, such an argument does not apply to the academic field of education in the heterogeneous forms it has taken in different national settings. Rather, the argument refers to a style of educational research heavily based on quantitative methods, drawing on disciplines like psychology and economics, and thus making claim to universal validity and prestige (Meyer & Ramirez, 2000). A good impression of this strand of theory, with a view to fostering its international dissemination, can be found in a series published by the International Academy of Education. In its preface, a well-known, Anglo-American specialist of psychological and educational research emphasizes in a programmatic voice: "The booklet [while based on research carried out primarily in economically advanced countries] focuses on aspects of teaching that appear to be *universal* in much formal schooling and thus seem likely to be *generally applicable throughout the world*" (Walberg, 1999–2000, p. 3f; emphases added).

Although these findings may have their value for fields such as the economics of education and educational planning, their argument hardly can be integrated with the results from the comparative history and sociology of the social sciences. Corresponding research has shown clearly that education, just as other social sciences (see Albrow & King, 1990; Genov, 1989; Ringer, 1992), inevitably is shaped by historical and cultural factors and, in this sense, can be considered an "idiosyncratic" form of theory and knowledge production (see, e.g., Keiner & Schriewer, 2000; Schriewer, 1998; Schriewer, Keiner, & Charle, 1993). A framework suited to taking this characteristic into account is offered by Niklas Luhmann's theories of self-referential social systems (from the perspective of general theory) and of the functional differentiation of society (from a historical perspective). Within this framework, educational theorizing is understood largely, although not exclusively, as self-referential system reflection. As such, it is rooted in and determined by varying contextual conditions and particular problems and issues, and by the distinct intellectual traditions and value systems characteristic of its respective system of reference and its related context of reflection. Educational theorizing, in other words, always links up with, and elaborates further, structures that work as "self-determinators for change" (Luhmann & Schorr, 1979, p. 13).

A core concept that needs to be emphasized in the context of our argument is that of "externalization." Luhmann and his educationalist co-author Schorr (1979) even consider it a "key to analyzing educational theory building" (p. 341). Limitations of space prevent us from discussing in greater detail the underlying concepts of "self-reference" and "interruptions in relations of interdependence," which would be necessary for an in-depth explanation of the externalization concept (see, however, Schriewer, 1990, 2001). Nevertheless, this concept helps analyze in a novel way two forms of reasoning characteristic of educational literature. Thus, on the one hand, "externalization to world situations" is a style of arguing typically found in bodies of knowledge conventionally called "education abroad," "comparative education," "international (development) education," or "educational policy research." On the other hand, "externalization to tradition" is the pattern of argument no less typically embedded in large parts of the literature conventionally titled "history of education" or "history of educational ideas." Both forms of argument are instances of the selective description and evaluative interpretation of international phenomena and particular theory traditions, respectively. As such they do not display the attitudes of "intellectual dissociation from one's self-centered views" (Piaget, 1970, p. 24), of "detachment" and "perspectivism" (Elias, 1983), which typically would be required from comparative analysis or historical criticism proper. In other words, externalizations to "foreign examples" or to "world situations" do not aim primarily at a social scientific analysis of cultural configurations; they instead involve the discursive interpretation of international phenomena for issues of educational policy or ideological legitimization. Similarly, externalizations to "tradition" are not directed at historicizing educational theory traditions or experiences, but rather react to the need to reinterpret and actualize these traditions' theoretical and/or normative potential in the face of urgent present-day concerns (see Oelkers, 1999; Tenorth, 1976). Therefore, both forms of externalization, irrespective of their reference to "world situations" or to "history," are "system-internal interpretative acts which don't provide reliable information on how historical processes really were or what is actually going on in the world" (Luhmann, 1981, p. 40). The floodgate metaphor Luhmann introduces in this context graphically expresses the fact that externalizations take advantage of a high degree of autonomy in the selection and interpretation of the "reference societies,"[1] development trends, or "world class models" (Chalker & Haynes, 1994; Reynolds, Teddlie, & Creemers, 2002) that they devise, even though such references and models are not fully detached from the dominant structures of the international system. Externalizations "filter" the reception and description of an international environment according to the changing problem configurations and reflection situations internal to a given system. Their potential for selection and interpretation disrupts the seemingly objective order of standing involved in an "integrated world stratification system," as it is stated by world system models, and rearranges it according to a given system's internal needs for "supplementary meaning." Moreover, the need for supplementary meaning expected to be susceptible to orientation not only varies *between* different societies or nations, but also changes over time in the course of successive political eras *within* the same society. Therefore, the combination of comparative and historical analysis not only facilitates an understanding of processes of the construction of international reference horizons, of world views and interpretations of history, exemplary reform models, or glorified figures from the educational tradition, but also shows how such constructions become subject to re-evaluation and reconstruction over time.

COMPARATIVE RESEARCH DESIGN

These contrasting theory perspectives provide the background for a comparative research project developed by the *Comparative Education Centre of Humboldt University, Berlin*.[2] This project is designed to investigate both the degree and the dimensions of the "internationalization" of educational knowledge. The units of analysis it covers are societies as distinct in terms of civilizational background and modernization paths as Spain, Russia (the USSR), and China. In the context of this project, "educational knowledge" means bodies of knowledge that, couched in sociology-of-knowledge terminology, adopt the style of argument of so-called "reformative reflection on education" (Luhmann & Schorr, 1979). The aims of these analyses are twofold. First, they are meant to describe from a sociology-of-knowledge perspective (1) the construction and reconstruction of international reference horizons and historical interpretations as embedded in the knowledge produced by representative Spanish, Russian (Soviet), and Chinese education journals; (2) the receptivity of national debates on educational reform to international models, ideas, and theory developments; and (3) the relative preference for international "model states" or "reference societies" as manifested in student exchange and migration patterns. Second, the findings so identified are then used to re-examine, by means of both cross-temporal and cross-cultural comparison, some of the assumptions linked with world-system theory that contend with the worldwide institutionalization of standardized models of education and educational development. In the light of the theories outlined above, it has become possible to formulate the hypotheses informing this project and develop a comparative research design.

One of the leading assumptions pertains to the differentiation between "internationalization" and "internationality," that is, between the level of an *evolutionary process* and that of a *semantic construction*. This differentiation is meant to elucidate the difference between the increasing intensification of global (economic, scientific, technological, and communicative) relations of interaction and exchange, on the one hand, and, on the other, the construction of world views and reference horizons out of particular sociocultural or national settings and driven by these settings' internal needs. World-system models such as the neo-institutionalist approach referred to earlier focus on the evolutionary dynamics of an intensifying transnational interconnectedness and, thus, on the growing together of just *one world*. In contrast, the externalization concept points out the "sociologic" inherent in distinct intrasocietal reflection processes. Consequently, it stresses the idiosyncrasy of meaning in specific nations, societies, or civilizations, and thereby brings into relief the persistence of *multiple worlds*.

Our analyses do not pursue a replication, let alone corroboration, of world-system analyses. Rather, these studies are framed along the classical lines of comparative inquiry, aiming at critically examining some of the hypotheses connected with world-system models. Our assumption is that processes of global dissemination and standardization, while indisputable at the macro level, are at the same time closely interrelated with recurring processes of culture-specific diversification. Such diversification processes can be developed further along the lines of a differentiation that had been introduced by Fernand Braudel but was later swallowed by the English term "world system": Braudel differentiates between a *système mondial* and several *systèmes mondes*, between the one global "world system" and varying, large-sized "system-worlds" that may be constituted on the basis of, for example, economic regions, civilizational areas, or political-*cum*-ideological systems.

The theory-critical intentions of our project have been cast into a comparative research design based on a small number of units of comparison, while representing a maximum range of sociocultural, political, and economic variation. In contrast to the designs of world-system research, which typically attempt to include as many UN member states as possible, we concentrate on analytical units that display a distinctive civilizational profile built up over long periods of time and underscored, among other things, by political power and/or demographical weight: Spain, Russia/USSR, and China. For several reasons, these countries make an array of analytical units, which is particularly instructive for comparative inquiry. First of all, they represent regions of different civilizational backgrounds: Western Europe bearing the imprint of Roman law and Latin Christendom, Eastern Europe with an Orthodox background, and East Asia molded by Confucian and Buddhist traditions. Moreover, all three countries have developed a historical self-understanding that is marked by traditions of imperial display of power and worldwide cultural prestige. Against this background, in all units of analysis, references to foreign models, model-states, or exemplary societies have enjoyed not only a distinctive tradition but also, due to intrasocietal disputes, a highly ambivalent status. Finally, from the perspective of historical process analysis, it is important to note that all three countries, after contested modernization processes from the nineteenth century onwards, went through a sequence of fundamental political and societal transformations in the twentieth century. Our research design thus makes it possible to combine cross-national with cross-temporal analysis. Thus, we have investigated not only the construction processes of international reference horizons, but also the reconstructions and transformations these reference horizons have undergone in the course of changing political regimes over time.

While world-system analyses, as a consequence of their global approach, typically are based on highly standardized source materials—constitutions, major legislation, textbooks, UN statistics, and so on—the assumptions of our project suggested the collection of much more differentiated data. Thus, as a consequence of the ideas described so far, we have applied a content analysis to the knowledge communicated in representative Spanish, Russian/Soviet, and Chinese journals on education. Our study covers a period from the early 1920s to the mid-1990s. Our data collection can be described as follows:

• Our interest first was directed at the proportions between articles whose subject matter was international in nature and articles focusing on historical topics. Obviously, these proportions vary from country to country and, within each country, from period to period. They can be seen as indicating the varying preferences given to alternative strategies of externalization, namely, "externalization to world situations" as opposed to "externalization to history." It is highly significant, indeed, from the point of view of analysis, that these alternative strategies can be interpreted as forms of generating "supplementary meaning" that do not vary haphazardly. Thus, one may contrast attempts at making sure of collective meaning and meaning-based orientation by resorting either to international structures and development trends, or to resources of legitimization flowing from the respective countries' own cultural and intellectual traditions. While the former strategy explores international situations with a view to coping with contingency, the latter scrutinizes national history with a view to making sure of one's own identity.

• Looking at the two groups of articles in greater detail, we were interested in ascertaining the frequency with which, as well as the way in which, particular countries, groups of countries, or international phenomena (in the articles on international topics), as well as particular authors and intellectual traditions (in the articles on historical topics), were dealt with. These frequencies, also subject to variation across countries and over time, are taken as indicators of the shifting degrees by which certain reference societies (in the former group) or traditions (in the latter group) are either distinguished as models worth following—as exemplary, significant, or relevant to orientation—or, on the contrary, rejected as countermodels.

• Furthermore, we investigated the reception of nonnational knowledge and its integration into each country's domestic reflection on education. We differentiated several forms of reception, namely, citations, translations, and reviews of books of authors (individual or collective) whose region of origin or professional activity was located outside the respective linguistic and national borders. The intensity of such forms of reception is seen as indicating both the extent and the relative esteem of being connected to international knowledge.

These analyses should be neither subsumed under the growing body of research on world systems nor regarded as a simple continuation of existing strands of comparative research focusing on the history of knowledge or the history of the social sciences and educational studies, respectively. Instead, they integrate elements of both research areas and, at the same time, attempt to address issues that have been raised in recent studies of comparative social and educational research. The findings of such studies, described in more detail elsewhere, suggest that processes of internationalization are by no means linear and inevitable. Rather, these processes are continually contested and challenged by antagonistic developments "of internationalization and indigenization; of supranational integration and intranational diversification; of global diffusion processes and culture-specific reception processes; [and] of an abstract universalism of trans-nationally disseminated models and of deviation-generating structural elaboration" (Schriewer, 2000, p. 327).

The complexity of social reality, addressed in these kinds of summaries, requires methods of inquiry that integrate various research perspectives. In particular, it is necessary to expand the traditional comparative approach with a macro-historical perspective, typically found in world-system studies, and to additionally include a research focus on issues of transcultural diffusion and culture-specific appropriation, respectively, which has guided research on reception processes. In the past few years, several scholars have applied such an integrative perspective in innovative ways. They have come to describe how the two tendencies, transnational globalization and culture-specific (including intranational) diversification, are intertwined and mutually enhance or weaken one another. These studies exhibit a high degree of conceptual differentiation and analytical power. To name but a few examples, they deal with the converging and diverging development tendencies in Western industrial countries (Langlois et al., 1994), investigate the "interpenetration" of socioeconomic globalization and sociocultural fragmentation (Friedman, 1994; Spybey, 1996), or examine how the comparative study of cultures and world-system analysis, both theoretically and methodologically, complement one another (Sanderson, 1995). So far, however, this theoretically and empirically fruitful approach has only rarely been applied to the analysis of knowledge, knowledge forms, and knowledge producers (e.g., Crawford, Shinn, & Sörlin, 1993). It remains a *desideratum* of social and educational research to examine in more depth the complex overlap of, and antagonistic tension between, the transnational diffusion of "modern" models and rules and the self-evolutive continuation or even revival of culture-specific semantic traditions. Considering this, the project outlined in this chapter may claim to fill a gap in this line of research.

SOURCES AND METHODS

As a consequence of the reflections and assumptions discussed in the previous section, we chose to focus on educational journals as the main source material of our analyses. The educational journals have been selected on the basis of the following criteria: They needed to be general (journals from specialized subdisciplines within education were excluded), be representative, and have a reputation as "scientific" publications within their own national contexts. In addition, each of the analyzed journals had to be acknowledged to be the leading medium of academic communication on educational research and educational policy for the time period under investigation. In most cases, official bodies, that is, state institutions or academies, published the journals. The reference horizons reconstructed from these source materials are considered to reflect a representative world view of the countries under study, in that the journals represent the knowledge of each country's educational research community. In those countries that entered a phase of political and ideological self-isolation, the journals reflect the predominant, or even the officially permitted, world view of the educational research community. According to these criteria, the journals listed in Table 2.1 were selected.

The selected journals were analyzed in roughly equivalent multiyear intervals. Key historical events in politics, economy, and society, in general, and important developments in educational policy and reform, in particular, determined which volumes were analyzed within each of the time periods. Throughout the analysis, it was essential to keep in mind that the references to "world" (i.e., references to societies and/or international developments that served as positive models) and the references to "history" (i.e., "grandeur and relevance" [Oelkers, 1999]) had to be explicit in order to qualify as externalizations. Furthermore, it was important to analyze in detail the evaluative-interpretive context in which externalizations were made and identify whether references were used as an argument for legitimization, justification, or orientation. Thus, the analytical depth of our studies rested on a minute analysis of the argumentative context in which references were made.

After operationalizing the assumptions of our research, we developed a classification system that consisted of characteristic types of argumentation.[3] These have been defined, on the one hand, with reference to the basic

Table 2.1. Examined Journals of the Spanish, Russian/USSR, and Chinese Educational Research Communities

Journal	Profile	Published	Editor
SPAIN:			
Revista de Pedagogía	General education theory discussion	1922–1936	Lorenzo Luzuriaga, acting on behalf of the state-run *Museo Pedagógico*, Madrid
Revista Española de Pedagogía	General education theory discussion	1943 to present	Instituto de Pedagogía "*San José de Calasanz*" under the umbrella of state-controlled *Consejo Superior de Investigaciones Científicas*; in 1994, taken over by the private *Instituto Europeo de Iniciativas Educativas*
RUSSIA/USSR:			
Na putyakh k novoy shkolye (Toward a New School)	Dissemination of progressive education ideas	1922–1930	Nadeshda K. Krupskaya, on behalf of the Education Department of the State Academic Council (*Gosudarstvenny Ucheny Sovyet*)
Narodnoye Prosveshchehnye (Enlightenment of the People)	Discussion of basic issues in educational theory, policy, and culture	1918–1931	*Narkompros* (People's Committee for Enlightenment)
Sovyetskaya Pedagogika; after 1991, published as *Pedagogika*	Academic educational theory discussion	1937 to present	Academy of Educational Sciences of the USSR; after 1991: Russian Academy for Education
CHINA:			
Jiaoyu Zazhi (Education Review)	General discussion of educational theory and policy; central education mouthpiece of the Chinese Republic	1901–1949 [interrupted due to war: 1932–1934, 1941–1947]	Independent intellectual group around the publishing house Shangwu Yinshuguan
Renmin Jiaoyu (People's Education)	Presentation of educational policy guidelines, methods, and pedagogical models	1950 to present	Ministry of Education (State Education Committee of the People's Republic of China)
Jiaoyu Yanjiu (Educational Research)	Educational research and theory discussions	1979 to present	China National Institute for Educational Research

operations involved in the "simple" style of comparison (Schriewer, 1990, p. 31ff), that is, the methodologically nonelaborate comparison. We focused on the reasoning or evaluative component of international references and classified these types of argumentation as characteristic of externalization to world situations. We categorized international references, for example, with regard to "superiority" (stressing unequal development), "convergence" (stressing the process of becoming increasingly similar), or "congruence" (stressing the existence of agreements) that they conveyed in their content.

On the other hand, we specified a set of argumentation types that are characteristic of externalizations to theory traditions. Relevant debates in historiography served as a foundation for developing this second set of argumentation types. Our classification system included, for example, "monumentalization" (stressing forms of transhistorical elevation or glorification), "degradation" (stressing the opposite of monumentalization), or "rehabilitation" (stressing the reversal of degradation of oblivion).

As a complement to the journals listed above, we drew on a further source material. This additional source served as the explicit "international" unit of comparison and enabled us to compare those parts of the analysis that focused on the reception of nonnational knowledge. A decided claim to "internationality" in educational knowledge was best represented by the *International Encyclopedia of Education* (IEE), edited by Torsten Husén and T. Neville Postlethwaite. There were several reasons for selecting this additional source material. First, the IEE views itself explicitly as "international" in content and conception, despite its Anglo-American bias. The editors' claim to be relevant for a large number of countries, institutions, and readers rests on the assertion that the information, the selection of entries, and the composition of literature references provided in the IEE are comprehensive. In addition, the IEE can boast a truly worldwide distribution due to the financial resources and international market position of its publishing house, Pergamon. Furthermore, this encyclopedia is "international" in the sense that its authors are from more than 90 countries. Moreover, its entries were defined in close cooperation with international organizations, notably UNESCO and the UNESCO-funded International Institute for Educational Planning, as well as the OECD, the World Bank, and the International Association for the Evaluation of Educational Achievement (Husén & Postlethwaite, 1994, p. xiii). Finally, the editors' programmatic claim to "internationality" is supported in our own findings. Our league table with the most frequently cited authors or institutions in the IEE reveals that UNESCO, the OECD, and the World Bank—in this order—are among the top-ranking references.

It is important to bear in mind that the *International Encyclopedia of Education* was published in two editions. The first edition, in 1985, comprised 10 volumes. The second edition, in 1994, contained updated material from the first edition as well as additional entries, amounting to a total of 12 volumes. We selected two comparable sets of Spanish, Russian, and Chinese journal volumes in correspondence with the time periods of these two editions. In determining the time periods for the selection of the journal volumes, we were guided by the assumption that an encyclopedia with the exceptional range of the IEE represents and accumulates the knowledge of at least 2 to 3 decades. For this reason, the first edition of the IEE was examined against the backdrop of selected journal volumes from the 1960s to the 1980s, while the second IEE edition was compared with selected journal volumes from the 1970s to the 1990s. This part of the study was meant to ascertain whether and to what extent the citation patterns of the IEE authors corresponded to the references that journal authors made in the three selected countries. The intertemporal design of the study— measuring two time periods of knowledge production in three countries and comparing them with an "international discursive space" (represented by the IEE)—enabled us to address, at least tentatively, the issue of whether there are signs of an increasing internationalization of educational knowledge or whether nation-specific traditions of thought have remained constant over the two time periods.

All data collected from these various types of sources, and according to the criteria explained above, have been analyzed using a combination of quantitative analysis and qualitative interpretation. In addition, the historical and political literature on the countries under study obviously has been taken into consideration, just as our own interpretations have been submitted for cross-checking by Spanish, Russian, and Chinese experts.

DISCOURSE PATTERNS AND SEQUENCES

The results of our analyses cannot be laid out in full detail here. We confine the presentation of our results to a summary, highlighting some of the more salient findings. They are presented in condensed form in Figures 2.1, 2.2, and 2.3. Figure 2.1 compares the proportions of journal articles with international topics with those with historical topics, as well as the variations these proportions show in each of the three countries and in each of the time periods examined in the study. Thus, the figure points to nation-specific and (historical) epoch-specific fluctuations in the choice of alternating externalization strategies. Figure 2.2 specifies the reference societies for those articles that deal with international topics. Finally,

Figure 2.1. Ratio of Articles with International Topics to Those with Historical Topics ("Other Topics" Excluded)

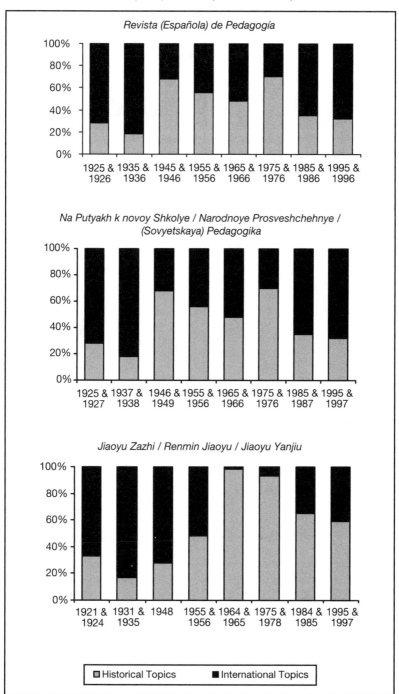

Figure 2.2. Reference Societies in International Articles

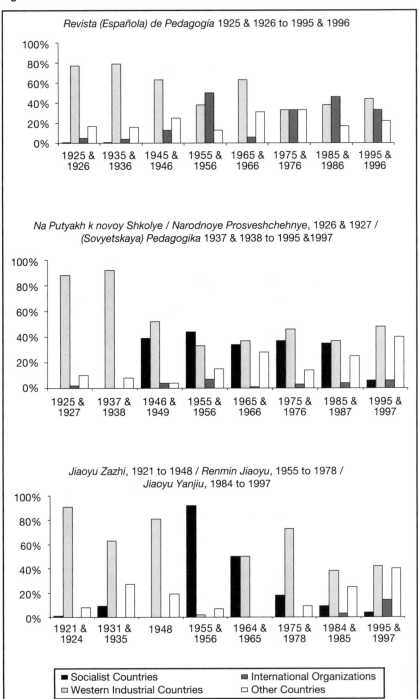

Figure 2.3. Frequency of Citations of Reference Authors (Individual and Institutional): *The International Encyclopedia of Education* (1994) Compared with Chinese, Spanish, and Russian (Soviet) Education Journals, 1970s–1990s

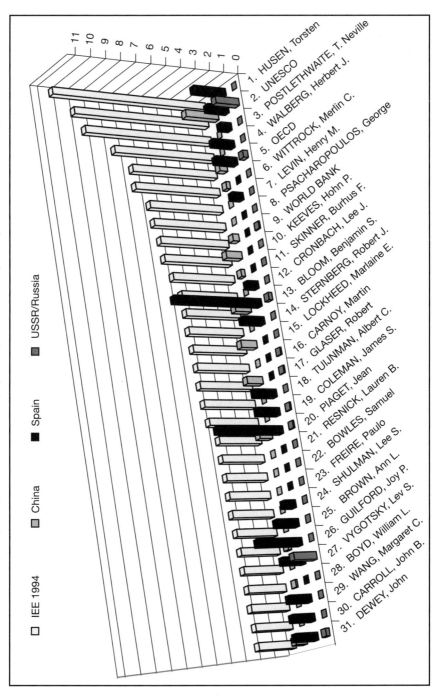

Figure 2.3 illustrates selected aspects that relate to the reception of international knowledge; to that end, the most frequently cited authors in the *International Encyclopedia of Education* are compared with the frequency of citations that these authors attained in Spanish, Russian (Soviet), and Chinese journals.[4]

At first glance, the data series documented in these figures do not reveal much of an increasing alignment of the reference societies, world views, and corresponding reform options embedded in the three societies' educational discourses with presumed world-level patterns. Rather, our data make manifest significant variations applying, for example, to the varying preferences given to either the historical or the international aspects of education; to alternative reference societies covered; to changing patterns of evaluation and interpretation; or to the kind and extent of international knowledge adopted into national reflection. These variations are not only discerned *between* the Spanish, Russian (Soviet), and Chinese discursive spaces, but also identified, in terms of considerable fluctuations over the whole period under scrutiny, *within* each of these discourse constellations. Moreover, these fluctuations—for example, from strong concerns with international issues and developments to an outlook almost exclusively centered on issues of merely national or ideological concern—by no means reflect a movement toward increasingly global convergence of educational knowledge. They obviously correspond, instead, to radical transformations in the respective countries' political systems and dominant ideologies. Along these transformations, we can discern a parallel three-phase sequence within the educational discourse of all three units of analysis. Of course, these phases cover different time periods in the cases of Spain, Russia/USSR, and China, and they also display different degrees of intensity. However, such deviations from the three-phase sequence, which by and large applied to all of the three cases, only underscore the importance of drawing attention to the different political contexts, crises, and system transformations—that is, to conditions that account for the nation-specific patterns of the three-phase sequence.

At the beginning of our period of analysis, the 1920s and early 1930s, a definitely international orientation dominated in all of the three discourse contexts. As illustrated in Figures 2.1 and 2.2, this phase of international orientation can even be regarded as the most distinct, not overlapping with the next phase. In Spain, as well as in the early Soviet Union and China, the references to "world" (references to models from elsewhere or international developments and innovations) by far exceeded retrospective considerations of nation-specific educational traditions. Politically, this phase of opening up to the international environment correlated, in all three countries, with a far-reaching transformation of the state and the social order. All three countries left the nineteenth-century history of conflict-laden modernization processes behind and—after having spent varying amounts of time to gradually dissolve the old order—witnessed revolutionary changes in the early twentieth century. It was a time when they started to distance themselves from long-standing monarchies, autocratic or semiconstitutional, and embraced a relatively open political system that heralded a profound sociopolitical transformation. In Spain, this period covered the final phase of the monarchy and the time of the Second Republic until the outbreak of the civil war in 1936. In the Soviet Union, the phase of relative openness lasted only up to the end of the 1920s, while in China, with oscillations due to warfare, it coincided with the duration of the Chinese Republic (1911–1949).

Against this background, the 1920s and early 1930s stand out as the period in history when all three countries clearly opened up their own reform reflections and displayed an enormous interest in international models, modern reference societies, and theory discussions from abroad. Certainly among the most unexpected finding so far was the large extent of internationality in educational knowledge during the interwar period. The journals, in Spain as well as in the early Soviet Union and China, focused particularly on the international progressive education movement and its major authors, and also reported and reflected on contemporary educational reform debates in Western Europe and the United States. Much in line with the externalization model, corresponding reports on and analyses of other countries were designed to contribute to ongoing reform debates at the national level, to provide orientation, and to help resolve domestic issues being debated at that time. When the authors of the three countries used this type of reasoning, they most frequently referred to developments in France, Germany, and the United States, and to a lesser extent, Great Britain and Italy. The extraordinarily high level of openness also was reflected in the various dimensions of knowledge import such as translations, book reviews, and citations, as well as a strong representation by leading authors of the international progressive education movement such as John Dewey. Based on quantitative data, therefore, our findings have come to confirm the thesis of the internationality of the progressive education reform movement (Röhrs & Lenhart, 1994), a thesis supported thus far mainly on the basis of this movement's self-interpretations developed by its followers.

Parallel to the overturn of the three countries into authoritarian or totalitarian regimes from the early or mid-1930s onwards—in China toward the end of the civil war in 1949—international references in educational journals decreased dramatically. The politically and ideologically motivated readjustments of the overall discourse on education had similar effects in all three cases: The semantics of "reform" was revamped, reference societies that previously had served as positive models were either completely dropped or depicted as negative countermodels, and an overall different rationale was introduced to substantiate the need to interpret and evaluate international issues. In contrast to the previous phase, when references to experiences from elsewhere served to emphasize similarity and highlight converging developments, the new rationale for using references aimed to demonstrate difference and create distance, and, in the case of socialist educational systems, to stress the fundamental antagonism between one's own educational structures and those of the others. Not only did these readjustments of the educational discourse lead to the reevaluation of international models and developments, but they also implied far-reaching reinterpretations of the history of educational theory by identifying different leading figures, redefining historical periods, and semantically reframing entire schools of thought. Authors who once had been glorified as outstanding models now were ideologically "degraded."

For example, the *Revista Española de Pedagogía*—founded in 1943 as a nationalist-Catholic replica of its republican predecessor review (Escolano Benito, 1992)—almost completely banned all mention of experiences and developments from elsewhere in its publications. In a similar vein, the *Sovyetskaya Pedagogika* (especially in the 1940s and 1950s) and the *Renmin Jiaoyu* (in the 1950s) reflected the post-World War II configuration of political-ideological blocs. The long-standing fascination of Russian and Chinese educationists with European—or, more generally, Western—countries abruptly gave way to articles that dealt with educational development in the so-called socialist "fraternal" countries. These countries and topics, and the argumentative patterns used to interpret them, now served to construct a specifically socialist "system-world" that, termed "internationalist," claimed internationality in turn and thereby positioned itself in a highly combative antagonism to the modernism of a "cosmopolitan-Atlantic" (i.e., Western European and North American) brand. On the other hand, from the 1960s onwards, the break with the Soviet Union and with Soviet models of development became obvious in the Chinese journals. The role of a quick-to-learn junior partner of the Soviet Union that had been imposed on China for a decade was replaced, from the late 1950s on, by considerable efforts to define a distinctively Chinese development path, drawing on the country's own educational and intellectual traditions. The resulting ideological and intellectual self-isolation of the country, intensified by the Cultural Revolution from 1966 to 1976, was clearly reflected in the fact that international articles and issues almost completely disappeared, while at the same time, especially during the 1960s and 1970s, historical topics and analyses increased dramatically. Only during the 1980s, following Deng Xiaoping's politics of modernization, did this isolation give way again to the country's cautious and gradual reopening toward the international arena.

More recent developments, starting in the 1970s in Spain, in the 1980s in Russia/USSR, and in the 1990s in China, are more differentiated in comparison with the previous phases of international openness and ideological and nationalistic seclusion. New forms of differentiation indeed are manifested both at the level of overall political and social system changes and at the level of educational system reflection and the international references embedded therein. Thus, while all three countries experienced, albeit to varying degrees and at a different pace, processes of the internal liberalization and reintegration into international economic and scientific exchange relations, the transition to a Western-type liberal-capitalist system took very different shapes. In the case of Spain, this transition took place in a long but thorough process, while in the case of Russia, this process came about abruptly and continues to be unstable to the present day. China, in contrast, still remains in a highly opaque state of economic liberalization paired with a continuing rigidity of the political regime.

At the level of educational reform reflection, the transformations in all three countries corresponded to a reopening of the discourse to international issues, references, and knowledge imports. However, this opening up remained on a much lower level compared with the decades between the two world wars, and it continued to do so well into the late 1990s—a discrepancy that is especially obvious in the Spanish and Chinese journals. Likewise, the high degree of convergence between the three country-specific discourse formations that was achieved in the 1920s and early 1930s has not been reached since. Similar results can be found when looking at the correspondence between the analyzed indicators concerning the proportion between international and historical accounts, the preference given to certain reference societies, the citations of international thinkers, and the translations of international authors. The scores found here also remain far behind the level of correspondence achieved in the interwar years. Certainly, we were able to identify a renewed interest in developments, models, and knowledge dimensions of the Western European and North American industrial countries, an interest, for example, in models of educational administration and school management, provisions for teacher education and curriculum reform, or problems with defining and measuring school quality and performance standards. However, this interest is significantly weaker and more contested by alternative concerns than in the interwar period. Indeed, the relative opening up of the journals to their international environment goes hand in hand with a considerable diversification of reference societies.

This diversification leaps to the eye in the *Revista Española de Pedagogía*. It is apparent both in terms of quantity—that is, in the increasing number of articles dealing with international organizations and countries other than those of the Western industrial world—and in terms of substance—that is, in a certain distance from American models so as to preserve Spain's own traditional values, as well as in critical reflections on the cultural costs of modernization. This new kind of diversification of regions of reference is even more obvious in the Chinese journal volumes of the past decade. Their articles increasingly refer not only to education models and programs developed by international organizations but also to non-European, notably Asian, societies. They thereby indicate the preference that, in line with Deng Xiaoping's modernization policy, is given to exploring the relations between education and development in general, and to scrutinizing the relevance of international models for restructuring competitive systems of higher education and technical training in particular. These articles also indicate the growing reluctance to prematurely borrow Western models to resolve the complex issues of educational development and societal modernization. In the most conspicuous form, however, the regional diversification of references is manifested in the case of Russia. The cautious process of the Soviet journals' reopening toward Western models that started in the 1960s, albeit accompanied by strong reservations and criticism, by no means resulted, after the disintegration of the socialist "system-world," in a substantial embrace of American and Western European educational models and programs. On the contrary, from the mid-1990s onwards, these models and programs once more became subject to criticism. The criticism is directed mostly to the moral decline that Western (American) schools supposedly promote. In stark contrast to the preceding Soviet period, this criticism is no longer fueled by political ideology, but rather by nationalistic and/or religious value systems. It also would be wrong to assume that the growing interest in non-Socialist and non-Western countries (called "other countries" in Figure 2.2), a visible trend in the articles of the *Pedagogika*, is directed to Asian or African developing countries. What we found instead is an increasing number of articles focusing on topics such as the origins and expansion of the Orthodox faith; the importance of Byzantine culture for the consolidation of Christianity in Bulgaria, Serbia, and the old Russia; the great contributions of eighteenth-century Russian scholars and missionaries in stabilizing Serbia, culturally and religiously, against Western Enlightenment and Catholic Latinity; the cultural achievements of Russian emigrants in the larger Slavonic space since the early twentieth century; the intrinsically pan-Slavonic character of Comenius's educational philosophy; or the impact of Orthodox Christianity and educational concepts rooted in Orthodoxy on contemporary

Russian culture and collective identity more generally. All these articles manifest a strong effort to replace the dissolved socialist world with an alternative, but also explicitly non-Western, "system-world" defined in terms of Slavonic Orthodoxy. The perseverance with which such antagonisms between competing "system-worlds" have been upheld, indicates how deeply ingrained traditional interpretive frameworks—which position Slavic Orthodoxy and Western Latinity, as well as Russian spirituality and European-American materialism, at two opposing poles—have been up to the recent past.

The developments described above are amply supported with empirical evidence from the citation analyses covering the period from the 1970s to the 1990s (i.e., the third of the discourse phases distinguished earlier), as shown in Figure 2.3. Even when considered in merely quantitative terms, the rankings of the most frequently cited authors manifest significant *differences* between the Spanish, Russian (Soviet), and Chinese patterns of adopting international knowledge into national discourse on education and educational reform. These rankings also testify to the enormous *distance* that the Spanish and, particularly, the Russian (Soviet) and Chinese patterns of adoption show in relation to the intellectual positions of an international reference work par excellence, namely, the *International Encyclopedia of Education*. This distance is all the more significant considering this encyclopedia's intellectual orientation, which is definitely based on quantitative research methods and on insights derived from educational psychology and the economics of education, an orientation, in other words, that exactly fits the model of a scientistic style of educational research as assumed by the "neo-institutionalist conception." It is indicative that, of the principal inter-governmental organizations, UNESCO (whose numerous publications and programs are the least embedded in an economics-of-education framework and instead advocate for universal ideals and human rights) was cited most frequently in all three discourse contexts. The World Bank, in contrast, scored the lowest with regard to citations and was entirely missing from the *Revista Española de Pedagogía*. This corresponds to another observation of our study, notably, that the internationally renowned economists of education—Psacharopoulos, Blaug, Carnoy, and Gintis—count in none of the discourse constellations under study, either in the Spanish or in the Russian or Chinese journals, among the most frequently cited authors.

The intellectual positions represented by the most frequently cited authors became the subject of a detailed qualitative analysis. This analysis revealed not only nation-specific citation profiles in each of the three discourse contexts, but also configurative patterns that vary significantly from one discourse to the other while at the same time largely displaying intranational consistency. These patterns point to the existence of a distinctive problem orientation in each of the three discursive spaces, a problem orientation that—very much in line with more general assumptions about the nature of reception processes (see Bourdieu, 1990)—functions as a "filter" for selecting, channeling, and transforming nonnational knowledge into national meaning structures.

CONCLUSIONS AND PERSPECTIVES

Even if the findings reported thus far seem too preliminary to draw strong conclusions, let alone to bear refutations, they manifest much stronger fluctuations from periods of a strong international orientation of the educational discourse to periods of sociocentric self-isolation (*within* each of the discursive spaces under study), and much bigger differences in terms of major reference societies or world views (*between* these discursive spaces) than would be compatible with the neo-institutionalist model. Contrary to assumptions about the growing institutionalization of a "world cultural environment," and regardless of diverging sociopolitical contextual conditions, the sequence, determined by our data, of radical changes in a country's social and political system and corresponding fluctuations in its decisive trends of reflection clearly underline the sustained impact of those contextual conditions. In this sense, our findings conspicuously throw into relief the interrelations, characteristic of externalizations in educational reflection theory in general, among changes in a society's social and political system, changing imperatives for educational reform, and corresponding shifts in the reflection on education and educational policy development. These findings convincingly point out how educational knowledge, reform policies, and developmental models elaborated and disseminated at a transnational level are refracted by each society's internal selection thresholds and needs for interpretation, which are the outcome of cultural traditions and collective mentality, as well as political forces and dominant ideologies. Such findings are further supported by phenomena well known by the comparative sociology of the sciences, such as the role of national language for establishing the boundaries of a particular communication space. Such boundaries, among others, account for restrictions imposed on international citations and accordingly determine the thresholds for borrowing and adopting from other communication spaces (Keiner & Schriewer, 2000). Finally, such findings also may be linked with studies in historical sociology and cultural anthropology that emphasize the contrast between a surface-Westernization in economic and institutional terms and the persistence of culture-specific patterns of meaning, and that focus on the disjuncture, characteristic of the present-day world, between "power" and "meaning" (see, e.g., Badie, 1992; Laïdi, 1992). The patterns underlying our findings are governed, in other words, much more by the *socio-logic of externalizations* than by *evolutionary forces leading to global integration and standardization.* So far, they underline the varying needs for "supplementary meaning," as determined by distinct cultural, political, or ideological settings, much more than they do the triumph of a "world-level educational ideology" substantiated by economic rationality.

NOTES

1. Using this term, we draw on Reinhard Bendix's (1978) historical-comparative analyses investigating the function of a model fulfilled by varying reference societies in the European process of modernization.

2. Members of this group are, besides the authors, João Freire, Jürgen Henze, Jörn Taubert, Aki Virtanen, Jürgen Wichmann, and Xiaoqing Xu.

3. For more details on our classification system, see Schriewer (2004).

4. For more detailed information, see the data, tables, and graphs in Schriewer, Henze, et al. (1999) as well as Schriewer (2004).

REFERENCES

Albrow, M., & King, E. (Eds.). (1990). *Globalization, knowledge, and society.* London: Sage.

Badie, B. (1992). Analyse comparative et sociologie historique [Comparative analysis and historical sociology]. *Revue Internationale des Sciences Sociales, 133,* 363–372.

Bendix, R. (1978). *Kings or people: Power and mandate to rule.* London & Berkeley: University of California Press.

Boli, J., & Ramirez, F. O. (1986). World culture and the institutional development of mass education. In J. G. Richardson (Ed.), *Handbook of theory and research for the sociology of education* (pp. 65–90). New York: Greenwood Press.

Bourdieu, P. (1990). Les conditions sociales de la circulation internationale des idées [The social conditions for the international circulation of ideas]. *Romanistische Zeitschrift für Literaturgeschichte/Cahiers d'histoire des littératures romanes, 14*(1–2), 1–10.

Chalker, D. M., & Haynes, R. M. (1994). *World class schools: New standards for education.* Lancaster, PA: Technomic.

Crawford, E., Shinn, T., & Sörlin, S. (Eds.). (1993). *Denationalizing science: The contexts of international scientific practice* (Sociology of the sciences, Vol. XVI). Dordrecht, Netherlands: Kluwer.

Elias, N. (1983). *Engagement und Distanzierung* [Problems of involvement and attachment]. Frankfurt/M, Germany: Suhrkamp.

Escolano Benito, A. (1992). Los comienzos de la modernización pedagógica durante el franquismo [The beginning of educational modernization in the Franco era]. *Revista Española de Pedagogía, 192*, 289.

Fiala, R., & Lanford, A. G. (1987). Educational ideology and the world educational revolution, 1950–1970. *Comparative Education Review, 31*, 315–332.

Friedman, J. (1994). *Cultural identity and global process.* London: Sage.

Genov, N. (Ed.). (1989). *National traditions in sociology.* London: Sage.

Husén, T., & Postlethwaite, T. N. (Eds.). (1994). *The international encyclopedia of education: Research and studies* (2nd ed.). Oxford, UK: Pergamon.

Keiner, E., & Schriewer, J. (2000). Erneuerung aus dem Geist der eigenen Tradition: Über Kontinuität und Wandel nationaler Denkstile in der Erziehungswissenschaft [Innovation along the lines of tradition: On continuity and change in national styles of educational theorizing]. *Revue Suisse des sciences de l'éducation, 22*, 27–50.

Laïdi, Z. (1992). *L'ordre mondial relâché: Sens et puissance après la guerre froide* [Disjunctured world order: Meaning and power in the post Cold War period]. Paris: Presses de la Fondation Nationale des Sciences Politiques & Berg Publishers.

Langlois, S., et al. (Eds.). (1994). *Convergence or divergence? Comparing recent social trends in industrial societies.* Frankfurt/M, Germany: Campus & McGill Queen's University Press.

Luhmann, N. (1981). *Politische Theorie im Wohlfahrtsstaat* [Political theory in the welfare state]. Munich, Germany: Olzog.

Luhmann, N., & Schorr, K.-E. (1979). *Reflexionsprobleme im Erziehungssystem* [Problems of reflection in society's system for education]. Stuttgart, Germany: Klett-Cotta.

Meyer, J. W., & Ramirez, F. O. (2000). The world institutionalization of education—origins and implications. In J. Schriewer (Ed.), *Discourse formation in comparative education* (pp. 111–132). Frankfurt/M, Germany: Lang.

Oelkers, J. (1999). Die Geschichte der Pädagogik und ihre Probleme [The history of educational thought and its predicaments]. *Zeitschrift für Pädagogik, 45*, 461–483.

Piaget, J. (1970). *Erkenntnistheorie der Wissenschaften vom Menschen* [Philosophy of the human sciences]. Frankfurt/M, Germany: Ullstein.

Ramirez, F. O., & Boli, J. (1987). The political construction of mass schooling: European origins and worldwide institutionalization. *Sociology of Education, 60*, 2–17.

Reynolds, D., Teddlie, C., & Creemers, B. (2002). *World class schools.* London: Carfax.

Ringer, F. (1992). *Fields of knowledge: French academic culture in comparative perspective, 1890–1920.* Cambridge: Cambridge University Press & Paris: Editions de la Maison des Sciences de l'Homme.

Röhrs, H., & Lenhart, V. (Eds.). (1994). *Die Reformpädagogik auf den Kontinenten. Ein Handbuch* [Progressive education across the continents: A handbook]. Frankfurt/M, Germany: Lang.

Sanderson, S. K. (Ed.). (1995). *Civilizations and world systems: Studying world-historical change*. Walnut Creek, CA & London: Altamira & Sage.

Schriewer, J. (1990). The method of comparison and the need for externalization: Methodological criteria and sociological concepts. In J. Schriewer (Ed.) in cooperation with B. Holmes, *Theories and methods in comparative education* (3rd ed.; pp. 25–83). Frankfurt/M, Germany: Lang.

Schriewer, J. (1998). Etudes pluridisciplinaires et réflexions philosophico-herméneutiques: La structuration du discours pédagogique en France et en Allemagne [Interdisciplinary research and philosophical-hermeneutical theorizing: The structuration of educational discourse in France and Germany]. In P. Drewek, C. Lüth, et al. (Eds.), *History of educational studies—Geschichte der Erziehungswissenschaft—Histoire des sciences de l'education* (pp. 57–84). Paedagogica Historica, Supplementary Series, Vol. III. Gent, Belgium: C.S.H.P.

Schriewer, J. (2000). World system and interrelationship networks: The internationalization of education and the role of comparative inquiry. In T. S. Popkewitz (Ed.), *Educational knowledge: Changing relationships between the state, civil society, and the educational community* (pp. 305–343). Albany: State University of New York Press.

Schriewer, J. (2001). *Formas de externalização no conhecimento educacional* [Forms of externalization in educational knowledge]. Series Cadernos Prestige, Vol. 5. Lisbon, Portugal: Educa.

Schriewer, J. (2004). Multiple internationalities. In C. Charle, J. Schriewer, & P. Wagner (Eds.), *Transnational intellectual networks*. Frankfurt/M, Germany: Campus.

Schriewer, J., Henze, J., et al. (1999). Konstruktion von Internationalität: Referenzhorizonte pädagogischen Wissens im Wandel gesellschaftlicher Systeme (Spanien, Sowjetunion/Russland, China) [Constructions of internationality: Reference horizons of educational knowledge in societies undergoing change (Spain, Soviet Union/Russia, China)]. In H. Kaelble & J. Schriewer (Eds.), *Gesellschaften im Vergleich: Forschungen aus Sozial- und Geschichtswissenschaften* (2nd rev. ed.; pp. 151–258). Frankfurt/M, Germany: Lang.

Schriewer, J., Keiner, E., & Charle, C. (Eds.). (1993). *Sozialer Raum und akademische Kulturen/A la recherche de l'espace universitaire Européen* [Social space and academic cultures: European universities and disciplines]. Frankfurt/M, Germany: Lang.

Spybey, T. (1996). *Globalization and world society*. Cambridge: Polity Press.

Tenorth, H.-E. (1976). Geschichte und Traditionalisierung [Historiography and traditionalization]. *Bildung und Erziehung, 29*, 494–508.

Thomas, G. M., Meyer, J. W., Ramirez, F. O., & Boli, J. (1987). *Institutional structure: Constituting state, society, and the individual*. Newbury Park, CA: Sage.

Walberg, H. J. (Ed.). (1999–2000). Series preface. *Educational practices series*, Nos. 1–3 (pp. 3–4). Brussels, Belgium & Geneva, Switzerland: International Academy of Education & International Bureau of Education.

Chapter 3

Toward a Theory of Policy Attraction in Education

David Phillips

Difficulties with the term "borrowing" in educational policy often have been reiterated. "Copying" and "reproduction" are among alternatives that sometimes have been preferred to describe the transfer of policy from one national context to another. Finegold, McFarland, and Richardson (1992, 1993) speak of "appropriation," and Matthew Arnold wrote—in a letter of 1868—of "importing" (Murray, 1997, p. 240). But if we leave aside all terminological quibbles about the meaning of "borrowing" and its precise use to describe the processes involved when policy makers in one country seek to employ ideas taken from the experience of another country, we can try to make sense of those processes in terms of analysis and explanation.

In various previous work (Phillips, 2000a, 2000b, 2002) I have used the example of British interest in education in Germany (which can be traced at least over a 200-year period) to exemplify aspects of policy borrowing, and—most recently together with Kimberly Ochs (2003)—have proposed typologies and models that endeavor to describe the processes involved. This chapter will attempt to synthesize our recent work and to contribute to the development of a possible theory of policy attraction in education.

THEORETICAL CONSTRUCTS

There is typically some kind of stimulus or catalyst that sparks off the "cross-national attraction" that eventually might result in policy borrowing. Such stimuli might have their origin, among other things, in

- Political change
- Systemic collapse to varying degrees (evident inadequacy of present provision)
- Internal dissatisfaction (manifested by parents, teachers, students, inspectors; often encouraged by the media)
- Negative external evaluation (through, for example, IIE studies, PISA, OECD country reports, etc.), often resulting in what Gita Steiner-Khamsi (2003) calls "scandalization" of the home system
- New configurations and alliances, whether planned (European Union policy, for example) or not (globalizing forces)
- Knowledge and skills innovation (new technologies)
- The aftermath of extreme upheaval (war, natural disaster) (Phillips & Ochs, 2003)

Particular examples of the catalysts within these categories, which can provide the initial stimulus for the processes of cross-national attraction, would include

- Urgent endeavors on the part of policy makers in England both before and after the 1870 Education Act to explore the experiences of other countries in introducing compulsory elementary education and in particular to discover solutions to the religious question (see the section on Germany later).
- The Sputnik shock of the 1950s, when there was concern that the Soviet Union was making advances in science and technology that could not be matched in the United States because educational provision had fallen behind. The very title of Trace's (1961) book, *What Ivan Knows That Johnny Doesn't*, is revealing of the anxiety created by Soviet achievement. Trace began with mathematics and science: "The concern of most of the recent comparative studies of American and Soviet schools has been to show that American schools are lagging woefully behind Soviet schools in the teaching of mathematics and the sciences" (p. 3); but he proceeded to argue too that "the humanities are . . . shamefully neglected in American schools" (p. 4).
- The sudden impact of various types of political events, ranging from a major government publication or statement (such as British Prime Minister James Callaghan's famous Ruskin College speech of 1976) to a significant change of education minister, or new political alliances, or a change of government. In recent years among the most significant instances have been the abrupt changes in Eastern Europe following the events of 1989–1990 and in post-Apartheid South Africa.

- The "shock" results of the OECD's PISA study (2001) for those concerned with educational policy in Germany. In this widely reported and hotly debated survey, Germany was reported as performing far less well than had been expected, and this sparked off a widespread debate about how to remedy the situation, with talk of the "PISA-Schock" (Fahrholz, Sigmar, & Müller, 2002).
- Developments in European Union education and training policy, including such agreements as the Bologna Protocol; while often not binding on Member States, EU policies have a tendency to encourage and facilitate harmonization (Phillips & Ertl, 2003).

Whatever the catalyst for change, it will create conditions that make possible the search for examples of successful approaches elsewhere. We have attempted (Ochs & Phillips, 2002b) to identify six "foci of attraction," as illustrated in Figure 3.1.

Figure 3.1. Structural Typology of "Cross-National Attraction"

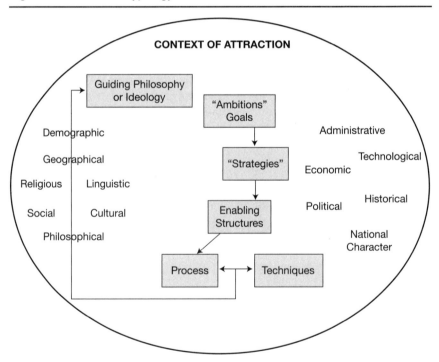

These foci of attraction represent what we have called "externalizing potential"—that is, elements of the foreign system that are theoretically "borrowable," their "internalizing" potential then depending on the contextual receptability of the "borrower" country. They have been situated in a field of contextual factors that will have influenced those aspects of the educational approach attracting attention from elsewhere and that should be taken into account as the appropriateness of borrowing is considered. They are incorporated in a series of conditions of borrowing described in Ochs and Phillips (2002a).

- The circumstances in the "home" country that create the need to examine experience elsewhere that might be "borrowed," that is, the preconditions for attraction
- The nature of the inquiries that identify those features in a "target" country that might inform policy in the "home" situation
- The contexts in the "target" country that have created those features of its educational system that have attracted attention
- The compatibility of the contexts in the "target" and "home" countries
- The means by which "external" aspects of educational provision can be "internalized"
- The efficacy of such "internalized aspects"

These foci of attraction form part of the first stage of the processes involved in policy borrowing from "impulse" to implementation and evaluation. We postulate four stages:

- Cross-national attraction (impulses and externalizing potential)
- Decision
- Implementation
- Internalization/indigenization

These four stages are represented diagrammatically in Figure 3.2. They constitute a continuous circular progression: impulse for change → policy attraction → decision → implementation → internalization → further impulse for change.

The second stage here encompasses various types of decisions. These might be *theoretical* in nature, with particular ideas taken from the foreign example constituting a guiding principle for change. Or they might be essentially *phony*, where political expediency results in lip-service being paid to the attractiveness of features of education elsewhere, with little will— or insufficient time within the period of office of a government—for

Figure 3.2. Policy Borrowing in Education: Composite Processes

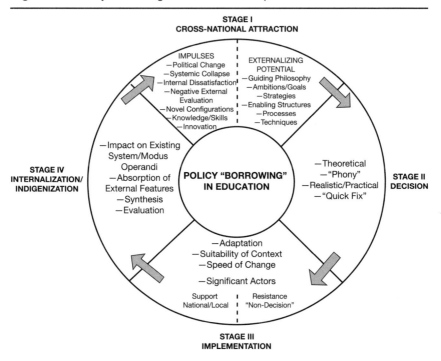

implementation to be feasible. They also might, however, be what we term "realistic" or "practical" in nature, where implementation has been carefully anticipated and judged to be both possible and desirable. Or they might constitute what can be described as "quick fix" solutions, where an idea is adopted that would appear to satisfy internal criticism, while actually being inappropriate to the home context.

The third stage, implementation, involves the adaptation that any foreign model will undergo in the context of the borrower system. Change will occur at different degrees of speed, depending on the accommodating potential of the new context. Successful implementation also will depend on the extent of promotion of, or resistance to, the new measures. "Significant actors" at various positions in the administrative structures on which implementation depends might, if they have the power or opportunity to do so, either facilitate or block new initiatives, using a variety of tactics such as inaction, delay, or what has been termed "non-decision" (Theocharis, 2002).

The final stage, that of "internalization" or what Steiner-Khamsi (2000, p. 162) and others have called "indigenization," covers the processes by which a new policy becomes part of the borrower system. The result, in Hegelian terms, is a new "synthesis," which might be subject to a future "antithesis" in the form of further "impulses" or "catalysts" for change of the kind described above. Thus, the whole process might begin afresh, with the foreign example being used as a potential remedy for any newly perceived deficiencies.

Let us now look at aspects of British interest in education in Germany.

THE CASE OF GERMANY

Education in Germany has been a consistent source of fascination and attraction for foreign observers since at least the early years of the nineteenth century (see, for example, Armytage, 1969). The Germans, however, had made advances in educational provision long before the systematic interest of outside observers began. Even in the enlightened despotism of the eighteenth century, the state's obligation to provide for the education of its people had been recognized and acted upon, so that Prussia, through Frederick the Great's decrees of as early as 1763 (the *General-Land-Schul-Reglement*) and 1765, had sought to introduce compulsory elementary education for children aged 5 to 13–14, something that England did not achieve until the Forster Act of 1870 (Melton, 1988; Paulsen, 1908).

We can trace the specific case of British interest in Germany through a variety of sources:

- Official documents (archival records, legislation, Cabinet papers, ministerial publications, parliamentary debates)
- Scholarly analyses (academic books, pamphlets, belles-lettres)
- Accounts of travelers and others (popular books, diaries, memoirs)
- Journalism (newspapers, periodicals)

In previous studies (Ochs & Phillips, 2002b; Phillips, 2002) accounts have been provided of the detailed efforts made by officialdom to collect evidence on educational provision in the states that constituted "Germany" at various points in the nineteenth century. Such efforts were, it has been argued, commendably pragmatic in nature, with a focus principally on what we have identified in Figure 3.1 as the "enabling structures" and "processes" in educational provision that might lend themselves to successful borrowing, rather than on an idealistic guiding philosophy or ideology (see previous section).

We have examined the background to various significant legislative and other governmental developments in England from the 1830s to the 1980s and have found much consistent interest in education in Germany in the discussions and investigations that led up to the promulgation of a new Education Act or a significant official report. Two examples may serve to illustrate the degree of attention devoted to the German experience.

The first is the work of the Royal Commission on the Elementary Education Acts, published in 1888 and known as the Cross Report. After long years of debate and controversy, the Elementary Education Act of 1870 brought compulsory elementary education to England for the first time. The Forster Act (named after W. E. Forster who introduced it and who was the son-in-law of Thomas Arnold, and Matthew Arnold's brother-in-law) established "School Boards," which would "fill the gap" left by the provision made by the voluntary bodies. Section 74 of the Act outlines the requirements for compulsory attendance (Glen, 1887). But by the mid-1880s it was clear that there were problems concerning the voluntary schools that had come under the Act, and both the Catholic Church and the Church of England authorities had expressed some disquiet. As a result, the Royal Commission was established to report on the workings of the existing legislation.

In preparation for the Royal Commission's deliberations, a circular was sent in March 1887 to various foreign governments, requesting detailed information on primary education. The circular was in the form of a schedule of 57 questions, many of which had several subsections. The main purpose of the questions was to collect basic statistical information, together with details about the compulsory nature of the educational system and school attendance, the public management of schools and financial matters, curricular provision (especially regarding religious education), teachers and their qualifications and terms of employment, school inspection, and the provisions for secondary education. For Germany, information was requested from Bavaria, Frankfurt am Main, Hamburg, Prussia, Saxony, and Württemberg. Despite the difficulties involved in supplying such detailed information, substantial returns were received (although not from some of the countries approached), and these were published in 1888 as a special 335-page volume (*Foreign Returns*) of the Cross Report. As an example of one country's "official" attempts to gather systematic information on provision elsewhere, the Royal Commission's efforts were outstandingly thorough.

The final part of the schedule of questions put to foreign governments in March 1887 will serve to illustrate the thoroughness of the investigation:

47. Is Elementary Education maintained from Public Funds or from Voluntary Contributions, or from both sources combined? State the proportion of each.

48. Under what circumstances, and on what conditions, are Grants made to a Locality or School from National or from Local Sources?

49. Is any extra assistance given to Poor Districts?

50. What is the Cost of School Maintenance per scholar in attendance, in (i) elementary and (ii) higher elementary schools, excluding the cost of administration?

51. Is Elementary Instruction Gratuitous? If paid for by the Parents, what are the fees? How are Arrears of Fees collected?

52. What is the usual Rate of Wages for (a) Skilled or (b) Unskilled labour?

53. Is there any Public Aid for Feeding or Clothing Indigent Children who attend the elementary schools? Is there any provision for admitting such children free?

54. What is the Total Number of the children under Instruction in the Elementary Schools of the State, and what is the Cost per Child—
   a. To the Parents?
   b. To the Locality[?]
   c. To the State?

55. Is there a Public System of Secondary Education in the Country?

56. Is it Gratuitous? If not, what does each scholar pay?

57. Is there any system by which poor and deserving scholars are enabled to rise from Elementary Schools into the Higher Schools? (*Source:* Public Record Office, FO83/978. Initial capitalization of individual words as in original)

The Commission (which—not unexpectedly—was divided in its recommendations) benefited from a wide range of information from Germany that had to do with the practical workings of provision of education in the German states. Unlike previous investigations, that set in motion by the Commissioners was not so much concerned with the philosophy of education in Germany and with pedagogy, as it was with the technical means by which effective compulsory schooling could be realized. In terms of our checklist of processes, therefore, the Royal Commission focused on *strategies*, *enabling structures*, and *processes*.

Some 100 years later, in the discussions that led up to the 1988 Education Reform Act in England—the most wide-ranging legislation for education since the famous 1944 Education Act—the German example also loomed large. There had been much discussion of an influential article by Prais and Wagner (1985) that had argued—not uncontroversially—that pupils in England of average and below-average ability lagged behind their German counterparts by the equivalent of 2 years of schooling. In 1986 a report by Her Majesty's Inspectors of Schools on aspects of curriculum and assessment in German schools was published. This report, the first in what was to be a substantial series of studies of aspects of education in other countries, focused on a number of issues that were germane to the measures eventually included in the Act. The Inspectors clearly identified considerable attractions in the German system, although, as they conceded, "some aspects of the system of assessment . . . appeared likely to lead to serious problems if translated into an English context" (Department of Education and Science, 1986, p. 37). The attractions included continuous assessment, oral testing as part of the formal examination process, a national grading system (the *Notenskala*), the higher status of teachers, and higher salaries compared with those in England.

In terms of our typology, the Inspectors focused principally on examining the *processes* of the German system. Although lessons were learned from the investigation, the underlying *enabling structures* in England and a number of contextual factors challenged the potential for "borrowing," although it was clear that the regular testing and the long-established, agreed-upon curriculum in each German *Land* provided evidence to support ideas that were to find expression in the 1988 Education Reform Act.

Here I have used only two historical examples of the interest of "officialdom" in education in Germany at points when important decisions were being made about educational provision in England. Table 3.1 presents eight examples of British educational reform in which the German example was used, and identifies the factors that account for this national attraction.

According to our analysis here of the main focus of attraction in each selected "snapshot" of legislation and official reporting, the emphasis seems to be on ways to plan for change and to adjust the structures and processes that control educational provision. There seems to be a lack of specific intent to take on board the underlying principles (philosophy, ideology, political aims/ambitions) of the foreign system, but rather an intention to concentrate on the practical lessons that might be learned and the pragmatic practices that might be adopted and adapted from the German example.

The work of nineteenth-century scholars and popular writers who reported, sometimes in great detail, on education in Germany also is revealing in terms of the use made of the German example. Prominent writers like the Quaker polymath William Howitt (1792–1879) and the leading exponent of "philanthropic journalism" and writer on the poor of London, Henry Mayhew (1812–1887), examined the educational scene in Germany at first hand and, although they found much to admire, were inclined to quote experience in Germany to warn against what a late-twentieth-century British education minister (Kenneth Baker, the author of the 1988 Act) was to describe as "[going] down the completely regimented German way."

Table 3.1. Categorization of Legislation, etc., in Terms of Use of the German Example, 1834–1986

Legislation, Reports, etc.	Factors in Cross-National Attraction	Results
Select Committee Report on the State of Education, 1834	*strategies, enabling structures, processes, techniques*	Accumulation of considerable evidence to inform future discussion
Newcastle Report on the State of Popular Education, 1858	*enabling structures*	Preparing the ground for the introduction of compulsory elementary education
Cross Report on the Elementary Education Acts, 1888	*strategies, enabling structures, processes*	Potential models for the solution of problems resulting from legislation
1902 Education Act (the Balfour Act)	*strategies, enabling structures, processes*	Introduction of local education authorities
1918 Education Act (the Fisher Act)	*strategies, enabling structures, processes*	Principled support for notion of continuation schools
1944 Education Act (the Butler Act)	*guiding philosophy, ambitions, enabling structures, processes, techniques*	Selective secondary education, based on a tripartite system
Robbins Report on Higher Education, 1963	*strategies, enabling structures*	Expansion of higher education
HMI Report on Education in the Federal Republic, 1986	*enabling structures, processes*	Introduction of national curriculum; national testing

Source: Ochs & Phillips (2002b).

Howitt (1844) used Germany to argue against state intervention in educational provision in England; Mayhew (1864), who tended to emphasize the exotic in what he observed (particularly in the German universities), remained convinced of the general superiority of the British approach to education.

A very influential figure with a profound interest in and knowledge of education in Germany—and in quite a different intellectual league from Howitt and Mayhew—was the distinguished poet and inspector of schools, Matthew Arnold (1822–1888), who undertook several official visits to Germany to report on educational matters. Arnold spent considerable time on the Continent in 1859 and 1865. The first visit resulted in the report published as *The Popular Education of France* (1861), which also had sections on Holland and Switzerland; in 1864 he returned to education in France in *A French Eton, or Middle-Class Education and the State*. Following his visits in 1865, when he reported on higher schools and universities in France, Germany, and Italy, he produced *Schools and Universities on the Continent* (1868); the German parts of this study were reissued in 1874 as *Higher Schools and Universities in Germany*.

For a visit to Germany in 1886, he was given a meticulously detailed brief that required him to report on free education; the quality of education; the status, training, and pensioning of teachers; and compulsory attendance at and release from school (Arnold, 1886; Phillips, 2002). Like all of Arnold's work, his report of 1886 is meticulous and elegant in its preparation and argument. In his conclusions he supports the retention of school fees and argues passionately for the development of secondary education. And in terms of general comparisons of popular education, he finds England wanting.

> The things on which we pride ourselves are mere machinery; and what we should do well to lay to heart is that foreign schools with larger classes, longer holidays, and a school-day often cut in two ... nevertheless, on the whole, give, from the better training of the teachers, and the better planning of their school course, a superior popular instruction to ours. (p. 25)

Arnold's report provided additional evidence for the Royal [Cross] Commission, as had his previous undertakings for other official bodies. He is a supreme example of the informed academic researcher feeding ideas and judgments into the policy-making process.

Alongside the work of popular and scholarly authors of books dealing with education in Germany, there has been a large corpus of reporting of all kinds that has brought the German example to the attention of the British reading public over the past 200 years and more. Much of the material published in the nineteenth century was of a serious, if at times opinionated, kind. This work, too, helped to keep interest in the German educational scene alive.

The German example serves as a prominent instance of sustained interest on the part of policy makers in one country in what might be learned from experience in another. The features of educational provision in Germany isolated as being worthy of particular investigation at various times over the past 200 years or so have served a multiplicity of purposes—often to warn against certain courses of action, sometimes to encourage and stimulate policy debate, and always to provide an alternative and essentially informative view.

IMPLICATIONS

This contribution has attempted to summarize some recent work in Oxford on policy borrowing and to suggest explanatory and analytical models to assist our understanding of the processes involved in such borrowing. Our analysis of the origins and outcomes of British interest in education in Germany has resulted in the devices described above. In a recent paper Waldow (2002), writing in a different context, has reminded us that "further differentiation and modification is probably the fate of all 'grand theories' when they come into contact with the actual empirical evidence" (p. 123). And in terms of our aim to contribute to the development of a theory of cross-national attraction in education, the testing of our models against the evidence of further examples of one country's interest in education in another country will be illuminating.

There is much potential here. Analysis of the attraction of aspects of educational provision in Japan to American observers over a long period, for example, would be of considerable interest. So too would detailed examination of the foreign models used in the policy discussions in the countries of Eastern Europe following the dramatic changes of 1989, or of the influence of child-centered primary education in Britain on policy and practice in other parts of Europe and elsewhere since the mid-1960s.

The devices described above are intended to promote processes of analysis, explanation, and understanding. Like all such devices they are open to criticism and amendment, and the principal purpose of describing them here, and relating them specifically to British interest in education in Germany, is to encourage reaction that will result in their further development.

Acknowledgment. I am, as ever, grateful to Kimberly Ochs for her helpful comments on an earlier version of this contribution.

REFERENCES

Armytage, W. H. G. (1969). *The German influence on English education*. London: Routledge & Kegan Paul.

Arnold, M. (1861). *The popular education of France*. London: Longman, Green, Longman & Roberts.

Arnold, M. (1864). *A French Eton*. London: Macmillan.

Arnold, M. (1868). *Schools and universities on the continent*. London: Macmillan.

Arnold, M. (1874). *Higher schools and universities in Germany*. London: Macmillan.

Arnold, M. (1886). *Special report on certain points connected with elementary education in Germany, Switzerland and France*. London: Eyre & Spottiswoode.

Department of Education and Science. (1986). *Education in the Federal Republic of Germany: Aspects of curriculum and assessment.* London: HMSO.

Fahrholz, B., Sigmar, G., & Müller, P. (Eds.). (2002). *Nach dem Pisa-Schock. Plädoyer für eine Bildungsreform* [After the PISA shock: A plea for school reform]. Hamburg, Germany: Hoffmann und Campe.

Finegold, D., McFarland, L., & Richardson, W. (1992, 1993). Something borrowed, something blue? A study of the Thatcher government's appropriation of American education and training policy. *Oxford Studies in Comparative Education, 2*(2), *3*(1). Wallingford, UK: Triangle.

Glen, W. C. (1887). *The Elementary Education Acts, 1870–1876* (5th ed.). London: Shaw & Sons.

Howitt, W. (1844). *German experiences.* London: Longman, Brown, Longman & Roberts.

Mayhew, H. (1864). *German life and manners* (Vols. 1–2). London: Allen.

Melton, J. V. (1988). *Absolutism and the eighteenth-century origins of compulsory schooling in Prussia and Austria.* Cambridge: Cambridge University Press.

Murray, N. (1997). *A life of Matthew Arnold.* London: Sceptre.

Ochs, K., & Phillips, D. (2002a). *Towards a structural typology of cross-national attraction in education.* Lisbon, Portugal: Educa.

Ochs, K., & Phillips, D. (2002b). Comparative studies and "cross-national attraction" in Education: A typology for the analysis of English interest in educational policy and provision in Germany. *Educational Studies, 28*(4), 325–339.

OECD. (2001). *Knowledge and skills for life: First results from PISA 2000.* Paris: Author.

Paulsen, F. (1908). *German education, past and present.* London: Unwin.

Phillips, D. (2000a). Beyond travellers' tales: Some nineteenth-century British commentators on education in Germany. *Oxford Review of Education, 26,* 49–62.

Phillips, D. (2000b). Learning from elsewhere in education: Some perennial problems revisited with reference to British interest in Germany. *Comparative Education, 36,* 297–307.

Phillips, D. (2002). *Reflections on British interest in education in Germany in the nineteenth century: A progress report.* Lisbon, Portugal: Educa.

Phillips, D., & Ertl, H. (Eds.). (2003). *Implementing European Union education and training policy: A comparative study of issues in four member states.* Dordrecht, Netherlands: Kluwer.

Phillips, D., & Ochs, K. (2003). Processes of policy borrowing in education: Some analytical and explanatory devices. *Comparative Education, 39*(4), 451–461.

Prais, S. J., & Wagner, K. (1985, May). Schooling standards in England and Germany: Some summary comparisons bearing on economic performance. *National Institute Economic Review, 112,* 53–76.

Steiner-Khamsi, G. (2000). Transferring education, displacing reforms. In J. Schriewer (Ed.), *Discourse formation in comparative education* (pp. 155–187). Frankfurt/M, Germany: Lang.

Steiner-Khamsi, G. (2003). The politics of league tables. *SOWI, 1* (on-line journal).

Theocharis, D. (2002, July). *"Non-decision" in educational politics.* Paper presented at the 20th CESE conference, London.

Trace, A. S. (1961). *What Ivan knows that Johnny doesn't*. New York: Random House.
Waldow, F. (2002). The neo-institutionalist account of the emergence of mass schooling: Some remarks on the Swedish case. In M. Caruso & H.-E. Tenorth (Eds.), *Internationalisation—Internationalisierung* (pp. 109–124). Frankfurt/M, Germany: Lang.

PART II

The Politics of
Educational Borrowing

Several observations inform our research on the politics of policy borrowing. First, references to other educational systems ("externalization") tend to occur more frequently for those domestic reforms that are highly politically contested, such as privatization of education, standardized student assessment, outcomes-based educational reform, or the deunionization of teachers (Jester, 2001). Second, at the local (implementation) level, borrowed models barely resemble their original sources, either because they have been locally adapted or because the references to lessons from elsewhere served exclusively to justify a domestic policy (Kissane, 2001). We also found cases where references to educational reforms from elsewhere, having originally served as a model, become eradicated once domestic reforms have been implemented. Third, decision makers and policy makers sometimes make international references and borrow successfully implemented educational reforms from other countries, even though similar educational reform models already exist in their own backyard (Steiner-Khamsi & Quist, 2000).

There is a curious phenomenon that is actually quite common in policy practice: "phony policy borrowing" (Phillips, this volume, Chapter 3). Why would politicians and decision makers in education bother borrowing from other countries only the policy talk, but not concrete models and practices? In Chapter 4, Iveta Silova tackles this fascinating phenomenon of discursive policy borrowing whereby policy makers and decision makers borrow only the rhetoric from elsewhere without the intention of ever implementing the practices that accompany the particular policy talk (Cuban, 1998). Her study of Latvian language policy is a salient illustration of how local decision makers in education creatively deal with external policy pressure. Accordingly, she documents the push by Latvian politicians to ratify a series of international human rights agreements that would ensure a fair treatment of linguistic minorities in Latvian institutions, including schools, as separate schools for Latvian and Russian speakers came under global attack.

In Chapter 5 Tali Yariv-Mashal investigates the case of the "Israeli Black Panthers," a grassroots political movement of Mizrahim activists started in 1971. Borrowing the name and the strategy of political resistance from the U.S. Black Panthers, the Israeli Black Panthers ("Panterim Shchorim") successfully introduced integration reform in Israel by using external references to the desegregation movement in the United States. Yariv-Mashal examines the tremendous pressure that the Israeli Black Panther movement placed on Israeli politicians to acknowledge, at least rhetorically, the need to pursue a policy of integration in education.

One of the most fascinating questions in our research area is why political change drastically increases policy import from elsewhere. Chapter 6 by Carol Anne Spreen is a case study of policy import in post-apartheid South Africa. Spreen examines how various models of outcomes-based education (OBE) circulated across Australia and New Zealand, and throughout the United States and Canada, and then, with funding from bilateral donor organizations, were imported to South Africa by domestic experts in the period immediately following the end of apartheid in 1994. Drawing upon Margaret Archer's (1996) work on external transactions, Spreen presents the different phases of borrowing in the South African educational context. She draws our attention to the last phase (1996–1998), which tends to be neglected in policy borrowing research: the phase that is characterized by a vanishing of international references whereby references to OBE experiences elsewhere are purposefully erased. It is in this final stage of borrowing that the imported policy is fully "indigenized" and redefined as "home-spun."

In Chapter 7, Bernhard Streitwieser addresses a long-standing debate in German education thought that distinguishes between two concepts for education: *Erziehung* (education with an emphasis on personal, social, and political development) and *Bildung* (education with an emphasis on literacy). In Imperial Germany (pre-World War I), *Bildung* was "a privilege of the upper social classes" (Drewek, 2000, p. 298) and was offered in academically oriented schools, whereas the masses were placed in nonacademically oriented schools that predominantly targeted *Erziehung*, that is, the teaching of skills (rather than knowledge) that were considered relevant for their future lives as farmers or workers. During the Weimar era in the 1920s, these two concepts of education merged, and elementary school teachers in Germany from then on were considered to be "Bildners," charged with the task of teaching pure literacy. As a corollary, other educative institutions (e.g., family, church, etc.) were envisaged as alternative sites to develop personal, social, and political skills.

Sociologically speaking, the expulsion of education for life (*Erziehung*) from formal schooling and its delegation to other educative sites reflects a process of functional differentiation in German society. From the 1920s on, several subsystems of society (e.g., schools, family, church, etc.) inherited the task of covering different aspects of education. Undoubtedly, the distinction remained contested and tensions ensued, among other reasons because teachers were trained to think that they did a more professional job of educating children (in the sense of *Erziehung*) than did parents and priests.

Streitwieser's analysis, however, sheds light on a different historical period: the postunification period of the 1990s. After World War II, the two Germanies chose different paths with regard to *Bildung* and *Erziehung*. The Federal Republic of Germany (FRG) continued with the tradition from the Weimar reform and restricted formal education to teaching literacy; the German Democratic Republic (GDR), on the other hand, revitalized the German concept of *Erziehung*, filling it with socialist content. For more than 40 years, the two German educational systems pursued culturally opposing conceptions of "good education." What happened when they became unified into one: the West German conception?

Streitwieser's study explores an interesting case of imposed cultural transfer and, more specifically, a case of imposed educational borrowing. Using four schools in eastern Berlin as case studies, Streitwieser interviewed principals and teachers to ascertain how they handled the pressure to adopt West German educational concepts in their teaching. In so doing, he developed a complex account of teaching under conditions of imposed educational borrowing and documented the experiences of former GDR teachers and principals who either fully adopted, selectively borrowed, or outright rejected the imposed reform on the schools in eastern Berlin. In his encounters with the teachers, he found legacies of their socialist past in that they continued to struggle to integrate the two conceptions of education, *Bildung* and *Erziehung*, in their daily work.

In Chapter 8, William deJong-Lambert illustrates the responses of the Polish academic community to the prohibition of genetic research that emerged in several states of the former Soviet Union from the late 1940s through the early 1960s. Genetics was described as a "reactionary," "imperialist" science that sought to justify the inequalities of capitalism and promote a bourgeois, capitalist agenda. Darwin and his theory of genetics were regarded as the class enemy as they emphasized competition and the survival of the fittest, rather than the communist ideas of solidarity and the victory of the collective good.

deJong-Lambert focuses on Trofim D. Lysenko, the Soviet protagonist of Marxist genetics in Poland. The case of Lysenkoism, or Michurinism, often is cited in historical research as an example of how Stalin's totalitarianism controlled every aspect of life, including scientific development. deJong-Lambert's study shows that newly emerging theories in Soviet science were instrumental in providing Leninism and Stalinism with "scientific rationality." His study further illuminates the tensions that emerged during the transition from one ideological framework to another and demonstrates how the increasingly marginalized and oppressed reference system (genetics) struggled for survival in the scientific underground of the Polish academic community.

In Chapter 9, Frances Vavrus examines the re-contextualization of the World Bank's privatization philosophy by Tanzanian government policy makers. She illustrates how the economic principles that undergird World Bank policies about the privatization of water get translated, both literally and figuratively, in Tanzanian environmental policies (written in Swahili) that are designed to conserve water in different regions of the country. The discursive analysis at the beginning of the chapter is followed by an analysis of qualitative and quantitative data from fieldwork in the Kilimanjaro region of northern Tanzania—a region facing an imminent water shortage due to the melting of the ice cap on the mountain. By placing her focus on how these local agents are reproducing global ideas about "good" development policy, she adds an important perspective to research on policy borrowing.

Drawing from borrowing and lending research and refining it with Bourdieu's conception of "field" enables her to dismiss erroneous dichotomies such as frequently made distinctions between external and internal, global and local, as well as changes "from above" and changes "from below." Among others, these dichotomies suffer from the assumption that there is "a single vision of development emanating from Washington, DC or Dar es Salaam." She finds that some of the World Bank reform policies are similar to those requested by Tanzanian groups in the 1980s, notably by groups of urban dwellers, agricultural producers, and cross-border traders. The pressure on the government was, therefore, exerted both by Tanzanian groups ("from below") and by the World Bank ("from above"). Vavrus's line of argumentation goes right to the core of a theory of attraction (Phillips, this volume, Chapter 3) and provides empirical evidence that global agendas can be transferred only if they resonate with local constituents that, incidentally or not, pursue similar agendas.

In Chapter 10, Thomas Luschei focuses on the theory of externalization in times of political change by exploring the Brazilian policy context under the presidency of Fernando Henrique Cardoso (1994–2002). In 1998, the Brazilian government began the implementation of the first of a series of education reform projects entitled "Fundescola I, II, III," projected to last until 2010. Luschei draws special attention to "Fundescola I" (1998–2001), a $62.5 million World Bank loan that included a reform component ("Escola Ativa") borrowed from school reform experiences in Colombia ("Escuela Nueva"). In announcing the Fundescola I loan, the government insisted that the Escola Ativa program target fundamental school reform in a manner quite different from the goals and objectives of any previous reform project funded by the World Bank. In effect, it signaled a complete reorientation in Brazilian education reform. These statements are not commonsensical, given the long list of loans that the Brazilian government has signed for the education sector since 1980. Why would a government discredit previous reform efforts, especially given that these efforts resulted in major investments that left huge debts behind? Luschei's study seeks to solve this puzzle, exploring the political reasons for announcing a reform as fundamentally new.

REFERENCES

Archer, M. S. (1996). *Culture and agency. The place of culture in social theory* (rev. ed.). Cambridge: Cambridge University Press.

Cuban, L. (1998). How schools change reform. *Teachers College Record, 99*(3), 453–477.

Drewek, P. (2000). The educational system, social reproduction, and educational
    theory in imperial Germany. In T. S. Popkewitz (Ed.), *Educational knowledge:
    Changing relationships between the state, civil society, and the educational commu-
    nity* (pp. 285–302). Albany: State University of New York Press.
Jester, T. (2001). *Standards-based educational reform in an Alaskan school district: Im-
    plications for implementation.* Unpublished doctoral dissertation, Teachers
    College, Columbia University, New York.
Kissane, C. (2001). *Schools and history "in transition": The case of Kazakhstan.* Un-
    published doctoral dissertation, Columbia University, New York.
Steiner-Khamsi, G., & Quist, H. O. (2000). The politics of educational borrowing:
    Reopening the case of Achimota in British Ghana. *Comparative Education Re-
    view, 44*(3), 272–299.

Chapter 4

Adopting the Language
of the New Allies

Iveta Silova

With the resurgence of democracy in Eastern Europe and the former Soviet Union, educational borrowing has become one of the key strategies in postsocialist education reform processes. In addition to adjusting the inherited educational systems to the needs of the market economy, the newly established democracies have been "required" to reform their educational systems as a precondition for integration into the European Union (EU). Driven by a strong desire to join the Western alliance, policy makers have made extensive references to Western educational concepts such as "democracy," "pluralism," and "multiculturalism." At the same time, however, adopting the language of the new allies has triggered major conceptual disputes about how these newly "borrowed" ideas should be understood, internalized, and implemented locally.

In order to explain the role of educational borrowing in postsocialist education transformation, it is important to recognize the dynamic interaction between international pressures for Westernization and the constraints imposed by Soviet legacies (Silova, 2002a). Focusing on the *process* of educational borrowing, this chapter refines theoretical insights from several subfields of comparative education, political sociology, and history, including: (1) the culturalist perspective on educational borrowing in the context of globalization; (2) the effects of Soviet institutional and cultural legacies; and (3) discursive power. Combined, these different research strands provide a better possibility of capturing a complex interaction between the global and the local, thus rendering more complete explanations of education reform processes in Eastern Europe and the former Soviet Union.

First, the culturalist approach to educational borrowing challenges the assumption that globalization leads to homogenization and results in the international convergence of educational systems. Recognizing the complexity of current global networks and the dynamic nature of the interaction between global pressures and local practices, the culturalist approach places the local agency in the center of education transformation, thus emphasizing "borrowing" as a self-regulated reflection on educational reform. Building on Luhmann's (1990) theory of self-referential systems and Schriewer's (1990) work on externalization, Steiner-Khamsi (2000) suggests that referring to existing models outside the educational system, and appropriating the language that goes along with these borrowed models, allow policy makers to make the case for new educational reforms at home that otherwise would be contested. Within this context, educational borrowing is not necessarily imposed, but can be used by the local agency as a mechanism for meeting its own needs, such as legitimizing contested educational reforms domestically, objectifying value-based decisions, or "signaling" certain reform movements internationally (Halpin & Troyna, 1995; Lynch, 1998; Steiner-Khamsi & Quist, 2000). Consequently, the local agency is not perceived as a "helpless victim" that is ruthlessly manipulated and controlled by global forces. Rather, the local agency is capable of pursuing its own interests by manipulating global forces (Silova, 2002b).

Second, this chapter suggests that social actors do not operate in a contextual vacuum. While pursuing their specific goals, local actors may be constrained or enabled by institutional and structural legacies, depending on particular social locations, times, and events (Silova, 2002a). Historical contexts play a particularly important role in the transformation processes in the former socialist bloc. As Barkey and von Hagen (1997) explain, the collapse of empires often leaves a legacy of political, cultural, and educational institutions, as well as cultural norms and behaviors that continue to exist long after their demise, thus influencing postsocialist transformation processes. Whereas comparative education research traditionally has argued that educational borrowing is used to replace "old" educational institutions, norms, and practices with "new" ones during a period of political transformation, this chapter suggests that borrowing in fact may be used to legitimize the maintenance of "old" institutional structures to be used for "new" purposes in a postsocialist context.

Finally, most comparative research examining the politics of educational borrowing focuses on mapping the transfer process by tracing what aspects of "borrowed" educational models have been modified, omitted, or accepted as a result of the transfer process (Halpin & Troyna, 1995;

Phillips, 1993; Spreen, 2000). In other words, the emphasis is on examining the implementation of specific educational *practices* in different historical, political, and economic settings. However, it is important to recognize that transfer can involve not only practices, but also *discourses*. As Steiner-Khamsi (2000) points out, the fact that the borrowed program was not implemented does not mean that the transfer did not occur. Instead, what was transferred was not a particular aspect of educational reform, but rather a political discourse associated with it. By acknowledging the significance of cultural and political discourses in shaping complex event sequences, this chapter synthesizes not only structural but also cultural and discursive factors that entail a more complete explanation of social action and local agency during the transition period.

Conceptualized within the culturalist framework and drawing from the studies of discourse formation advanced by Foucault (1977, 1991), this chapter focuses on Latvian minority education reform during the 1990s and examines how "new" ideas borrowed from the West interacted with the constraints imposed by the "old" education structures inherited from the Soviet Union. In particular, it traces a discursive shift whereby Russian schools in post-Soviet Latvia moved from being associated with sites of occupation in the beginning of the 1990s to symbols of multiculturalism by the end of the decade. Based on the examination of historical legacies and a rapidly changing political context, this chapter suggests that change of discourse has not necessarily meant that the "ethnic issue" has been resolved. Instead, it has been reformulated or "re-framed" in an attempt to reconcile international pressures for *multiculturalization* with domestic politics of *Latvianization* (Silova, 2002b). In this context, adopting the language of new allies has been used primarily to signal the new loyalties of postsocialist politicians.

FROM SITES OF OCCUPATION TO SYMBOLS OF MULTICULTURALISM: THE LATVIAN CONTEXT

One of the Soviet legacies, which continuously demonstrates ethnic tensions and fragmentation in post-Soviet Latvia, is the existence of two parallel school structures—one using Russian language instruction and the other using Latvian. Established during the Soviet period, separate schools for different ethnolinguistic groups served to ensure ethnic enclosure, partitioning, and ranking, and enable an effective surveillance of ethno-nationalistic sentiments in the titular republics. Thus, students attending Latvian schools primarily associated themselves with Latvia and were mostly bilingual, whereas students attending Russian schools typically had a "strong Russian orientation" and spoke Latvian relatively poorly (Karklins, 1998). Furthermore, Soviet separation of the educational system along ethnolinguistic lines put ethnic Latvians at a certain political, economic, and social disadvantage. At the same time, however, the existence of a parallel set of educational institutions for Latvian speakers and Russian speakers—with limited communication across the language divide— served as a useful mechanism for resistance, strengthening Latvian nationalism and ethnic survival.

After the restoration of Latvian independence in 1991, the purpose, relevance, and need for separate educational structures became seriously questioned in light of Latvia's reorientation from Soviet to Western European educational space (Silova, 2002b). In the early 1990s, a wide range of policy options was publicly discussed, including the closing of Russian language schools, merging them with Latvian language schools, and other varieties of reform. By the end of the 1990s, however, the decision was made to leave separate school structures for different ethnolinguistic groups intact, with the justification that this institutional arrangement provided a better possibility to take into consideration and develop the unique cultural characteristics of different ethnolinguistic groups. Whereas the structure of the school system did not substantially change after the collapse of the Soviet Union, educational reform discourse about separate schools for Russian and Latvian students underwent a great transformation. Russian language schools moved from being associated with "Soviet/Russian state instruments" and "nests of Soviet occupants" in the early 1990s to "symbols of multiculturalism and pluralism" by the end of the decade. Importantly, separate schools for Latvian- and Russian-speaking students are now supported by both sides—the "nationalizing" Latvian majority and the "nationalized" Russian-speaking minorities—as necessary elements of democratic development in Latvia.

SEPARATE SCHOOLS AS DISCIPLINARY TECHNOLOGIES

Before tracing the change of discourse in Latvian minority education in the 1990s, it is important to explore the emergence and institutionalization of separate school structures for Russian and indigenous nationalities in the context of the following Soviet ethnic policies: (1) indigenization or *korenizatsia*, and (2) assimilation or *Russifikatsia*. Although the early Soviet policy of *korenizatsia* was implemented before Latvia was annexed by the Soviet Union, it had a lasting impact on Soviet education policies and therefore warrants special consideration.

Korenizatsia

The ultimate goal of the early Soviet nationality policy was to order multitudes of Soviet nationalities into specific categories and territories. According to Foucault (1977), the first of the great operations of discipline is "the constitution of 'tableaux vivants,' which transforms the confused, useless or dangerous multitudes into ordered multiplicities" (p. 148). To achieve this goal, the period of indigenization was accompanied by a rapid spread of mass education, as well as development of languages and cultures for all nationalities and ethnicities in the territory of the Soviet Union. All non-Russians were "nationals" entitled to their own territorial units and their own schools. Thus, by 1927, 93.7% of Ukrainian and 90.2% of Belarussian elementary school students were taught in their "native languages," that is, languages implied by their nationality. Theoretically, a Jew in Ukraine was to be educated in Yiddish even if his parents preferred Ukrainian (Slezkine, 1994, p. 432). Further, native language was seen as "a means of social discipline, as a social unifier of nations and as a necessary and most important condition of successful economic and cultural development" (Davydov as quoted in Slezkine, 1994, p. 430).

As Brubaker (1994) pointed out, implementation of the indigenization policy allowed the Soviet government to achieve two things: first, "to harness, contain, channel, and control the potentially disruptive political expression of nationality by creating national-territorial administrative structures"; and second, "to drain nationality of its content even while legitimizing it as a form" (p. 49). In this way, the indigenization policy gave Soviet nationalities symbolic autonomy by granting cultural and linguistic rights to ethnic groups, while preserving political and economic status for Russians.

Russifikatsia

By the end of the 1930s, indigenization shifted toward a policy of *Russifikatsia* aimed at "social and cultural unification of all ethnic groups on the basis of Soviet Russian culture" (Khazanov, 1993, p. 183). Implemented under the slogan of "merging the nations," the Russification policy led to a drastic decrease in the number of national units and the promotion of Russians as a nationality in their own right (Slezkine, 1994). For example, the number of languages of instruction in schools of the Soviet republics decreased from 102 in 1932 to 40 in 1988 (Zhdanova, 1989, p. 91). In this way, Russification was to be achieved by means of convergence and acculturation of different ethnicities in order to allow for more effective management and control of Soviet nationalities.

Immediately following the incorporation of Latvia into the Soviet Union in 1944, Russian language departments were established in institutions of higher education. By the end of 1945, Russian language schools were founded alongside Latvian language schools. As a result of the Russification policies, the percentage of students attending Russian language schools rapidly increased, while the percentage of students attending Latvian schools began to decrease (see Table 4.1). By 1989, 71% of the Latvians in cities and 57% in the countryside spoke Russian as a second language, whereas only 22% of Russian nationals and 18% of other non-Latvians spoke Latvian, resulting in "asymmetric bilingualism" between the Latvian- and Russian-speaking groups (Vebers, 1994).

Based on a Foucauldian framework of disciplinary power, the establishment of separate schools for different ethnic groups in Latvia and other Soviet republics can be viewed as deployment of "disciplinary techniques" necessary to produce subjective and practiced or, as Foucault (1977) puts it, "docile" bodies. These disciplinary techniques aimed to "establish absences and presences, to know where and how to locate individuals, to set up useful communications, to interrupt others, to be able each moment to supervise the conduct of each individual, to assess it, to judge it, to calculate its qualities or merits" (p. 143). In the case of the Soviet Union, establishment of separate schools for Russian and indigenous populations ensured strict control not only over the content of education, but also over student and teacher behavior. Thus, separate schools for Latvian students allowed for rigid control of any unwanted nationalistic sentiments. Similarly, separate schools for Russian students ensured that all students attending these schools were loyal to their "external" motherland, that is, Russia, rather than the republic they resided in.

Furthermore, Soviet schools were controlled through the projection of power onto educational time. Foucault (1977) describes how the "seriation" of successive activities in schooling provides the possibility of "a detailed control and a regular intervention (of differentiation, correction, punishment, elimination) in each moment of time" (p. 160). This "discipline of the

Table 4.1. Number of Students Studying in Latvian and Russian Language Schools (1955–1989)

Language of Instruction	1955–56	1980–81	1986–87	1988–89
Latvian	67%	55.9%	53.1%	52.4%
Russian	33%	44.1%	46.9%	47.6%

Source: Central Statistical Board of the USSR, 1958, p. 193; Zhdanova, 1989, p. 90.

minute" can be identified easily in the centralized administration of Soviet schools. As Hamot (1996) vividly describes, during the Soviet times all schools of a particular type (ranging from elementary schools to universities) and of a particular grade level were required "to teach the same lessons from the same books with the same methods at the same time" (p. 11). This orchestrated administration of school time turned Soviet schools into ultimate learning machines for supervising, controlling, and hierarchizing the Soviet child and teacher.

THE "METAMORPHOSIS" OF SEPARATE SCHOOLS DURING THE TRANSITION PERIOD

The campaign for democratization during the Perestroika period (1985–1991) brought the "ethnic question" to the forefront of a new political agenda. According to the United Nations Development Programme (UNDP) (1996), however, the first several years after the restoration of independence were devoted primarily to reform in Latvian language schools, as government officials "were not prepared to develop a unified national school system" (p. 72). During 1991–1996, for example, educational reform focused on Latvian language schools aiming to *Latvianize* the existing curriculum, raise the quality of instruction, and increase their prestige. In addition, special attention was paid to the restoration of schools for historical minorities in Latvia, including Polish, Jewish, Ukrainian, Estonian, and Lithuanian national minority schools, as well as Roma and Belarussian classes.

Importantly, Russian schools were not included in the category of "minority" schools until the end of the 1990s because of their close association with the Soviet imperialistic practices, strong connections to Russia, large student populations, and highly multiethnic character. According to the UNDP report (1996), a total of 39.1% of all students in Latvia were enrolled in Russian schools in 1995. Compared with other minority schools, Russian schools enrolled a large percentage of non-Russian minorities, including 91.9% of Belarussian students, 90% of Ukrainian students, 78.6% of Polish students, and 59% of Estonian students (UNDP, 1996). Since the Russian schools did not fit the traditional criteria of "minority schools," which typically were perceived as mono-ethnic and mono-cultural, Latvian policy makers created a special category of "Russian language schools," which existed along with minority schools and Latvian language schools until the end of the 1990s.

Although different options were discussed with regard to the future of Russian schools in Latvia—including the creation of a unified educational system, transformation of Russian schools into minority schools, and even the closure of Russian schools—it was decided by the end of the 1990s to leave separate educational structures for Latvian- and Russian-speaking students intact. The official argument was that it was important to recognize "the uniqueness and specific development" of Russian schools and that separate structures provided a better possibility "to take into account the psychology and mentality of the children and to avoid threatening their identity" (UNDP, 1997, p. 62). In 1998, Russian schools were included in the category of minority schools and began to be referred to by some government officials and most of the Latvian media as "signs of multiculturalism and pluralism." Furthermore, this continuing separation of schools along ethnic lines was justified by some scholars (Karklins, 1998) as "the linchpin guaranteeing ethnic peace" (p. 283), safeguarding Latvians and non-Latvians alike.

GLOBAL PRESSURES, LOCAL POLITICS, AND NEW WAYS OF REASONING

The new discourse on multiculturalism and ethnic integration emerged in the context of wider educational, political, and social transformations. Having expressed an interest in joining the Western alliance, the Baltic states in general and Latvia in particular have come under pressure to meet the requirements put forth by such international agencies as the EU, the Organisation for Security and Co-operation in Europe, the North Atlantic Treaty Organization (NATO), and others. Specifically, the linguistic rights of minorities became the subject of a variety of international instruments, including the *1996 International Covenant on Civil and Political Rights*, the *1996 International Covenant on Economic, Social, and Cultural Rights*, the *1995 Framework Convention for the Protection of National Minorities*, the *1996 Hague Recommendations Regarding the Education Rights of National Minorities*, and the *1998 Oslo Recommendations Regarding the Linguistic Rights of National Minorities*. By September 2000, Latvia had already acceded to most of the major international human rights instruments necessary for its accession to the EU. Of 18 international human rights conventions and protocols, Latvia had ratified 13. As of the beginning of 2004, the *Framework Convention for the Protection of National Minorities* and the *European Social Charter* remain among those international human rights instruments that Latvia still has not ratified.

Ratification of the international human rights instruments became one of the main prerequisites for Latvia's possible affiliation with Europe. As Hyde-Price (1996) summarized, "the new nationalist myth" of belonging to Europe triggered the definition of contemporary national identities in Eastern and central European countries in terms of European values such as respect for human rights, pluralism, and tolerance. Therefore, countries aspiring to EU and NATO membership had "a powerful incentive to treat ethnic minorities well, respect international borders and international norms, and conduct their internal and external affairs peacefully" (Brown, 1995, p. 37). Emphasizing the symbolic importance of Latvia's affiliation with the West, one of Latvia's politicians, Janis Urbanovics (interviewed by Fridrihsone, 1999), stated:

> We need to be prepared to take into consideration the recommendations of the European experts, even though they seem unacceptable at times. It is not profitable for Latvia to wait tens of years to be integrated into European Union structures. There are still wars going on in the world. *If we are not together with Europe, then with whom will we be?* (p. 3; emphasis added)

While setting broad guidelines for minority education development, international standards did not provide any specific policy recommendations. Facing increasing international pressures but unable to find "the European model" of minority education, Latvian- and Russian-speaking politicians adopted fairly broad language of the new Western allies regarding minority education. In the 1998 election, for example, different political parties used similarly broad declarations regarding their commitment to minority education, including such language as, "education content should correspond to European Union criteria" (Latvian Way, 1995), "equivalent to European Union education" (Latvian Way, 1998), "movement towards European state structures" (For Freedom and Fatherland/ Latvian National Independence Movement, 1998), "the integration of ethnic groups to create a multicultural society" (People's Harmony Party, 1998), "state integration of ethnic groups . . . guarantee ethnic and other human rights based on widely accepted international human rights documents" (Latvian Social Democratic Alliance, 1998), and "guaranteeing everyone internationally accepted human rights" (Latvian Democratic Party "Saimnieks," 1998). In other words, there emerged a seemingly unanimous consensus among different local groups regarding the role, purpose, and nature of minority education (Silova, 2002a).

However, a closer examination of the newly emerging ideas of multiculturalism and ethnic integration reveals the existence of a "hybridity" of discourses, which have been transferred selectively and used inconsistently by different ethnolinguistic groups. While borrowing the same Western lexicon of "integration" and "the right to preserve minority language and culture," both Latvian and Russian speakers gave different meanings to the integration concept and its constituent components, thus modifying the broad notion of integration and multiculturalism. For example, Latvian language speakers argued for maintaining separate schooling structures primarily as a mechanism to protect Latvian schools from the increasing number of Russian-speaking students. Continuing to perceive themselves as a national minority, many Latvians feared that incorporation, integration, or even assimilation would hinder the process of healing ethnic Latvian identity, which was silenced during the Soviet period (Silova, 2002a). On the other hand, some Russian-speaking groups argued for maintaining Russian language schools as separate educational institutions to ensure their autonomy, which, in some cases, would allow for the continuing Russification of some Russian-speaking minorities, or for promoting the idea of a superior, "great Russian culture" (Silova, 2002a). In both cases, the borrowed concept of integration underwent major conceptual modifications and, in its extreme interpretations, led to equating integration with ethnic separation.

These different interpretations of discourses also are reflected in statements and publications issued by the Ministry of Education and some leading Latvian academics. While claiming that separate schools illustrated the multicultural character of Latvian society, the Ministry of Education made an attempt to clarify that "multicultural" schools meant "separate," not "mixed" schools. As some Russian parents began to send their children to Latvian schools, it was stated officially that the creation of ethnically and linguistically "mixed" schools and classes was "not advisable." As leading Latvian sociolinguist Ina Druviete (1998) explained, creation of ethnolinguistically mixed classrooms would not produce "the expected results in Latvia," because "children arrive at the education establishment without any knowledge of Latvian, and progress is very slow. . . . The language barrier becomes an obstacle to knowledge, the teachers have to switch to Russian quite often, and usually Latvian children learn Russian before non-Latvians learn Latvian" (p. 178).

Consequently, the borrowing of international discourse on integration was accompanied by the emergence of a "manipulated consensus" among Latvian and Russian language speakers about its application in the minority education area (Silova, 2002a). On the one hand, there was a "consensus" about the external usefulness of the new discourse, which was necessary to signal Latvia's departure from Soviet to European space. On the other hand, there was an internal "manipulation" of this consensus, allowing both Latvian- and Russian-speaking groups to pursue their own political agendas, while maintaining an internationally acceptable discursive facade.

This conscious attempt to keep strict separation of schools for Latvian and Russian students can be viewed as a reformulation of "disciplinary" technologies needed to keep control over the diverse ethnic and linguistic groups in post-Soviet Latvia. This time, however, the principles of control have been re-inscribed as "help" provided for Russian students integrating into the Latvian society, while at the same time keeping their cultural heritage. This help, also referred to as "pastoral care" by Popkewitz (1998), has included various school inspections, national examinations, specially developed bilingual education programs for students, as well as language tests and special courses for teachers. For example, Russian schools have been visited frequently by inspectors from the Ministry of Education to examine whether the appropriate textbooks are used in classrooms and displayed in libraries, and whether the appropriate languages are used during lessons. Following a theoretical framework of discourse and power developed by Popkewitz (1998, 2000), I suggest that the borrowed pedagogical discourses were used to normalize the child in a space that is different from that of the "reasonable" person. As clearly stated in the UNDP's *Latvia Human Development Report* (1999), ethnic, economic, gender, educational, and other differences, which recently have become more pronounced, "should be perceived as a natural developmental process of society, as these differences must be recognized before socially acceptable mechanisms can be developed for reducing these differences" (p. 110). Meanwhile, "disciplinary technologies" created during the Soviet period continue to maintain complex spaces that are at once architectural, functional, and divisive.

To summarize, it is important to recognize the dynamic nature of the national question as well as to examine the political conditions and institutional legacies inherited from the Soviet Union, in order to explain the reasons underlying a shift of public discourse in the context of democratization. Using the suggested interpretive frameworks of globalization, borrowing, Soviet legacies, and discursive power, this chapter suggests that the shift of discourse whereby Russian schools moved from being associated with sites of occupation to signs of multiculturalism in post-Soviet Latvia does not necessarily mean that the ethnic question has been solved. Instead, the issue has been "re-framed" to legitimize the use of "old" educational structures for "new" purposes (Silova, 2002b). First, borrowing of global discourse on multiculturalism has become useful both for "nationalizing" Latvian elites and "nationalized" Russian minorities in the context of Latvian integration into the European Union, which seeks to encourage international investment, attract aid, and ensure Latvia's national security. Second, borrowing of new discourse on multiculturalism has provided an opportunity for "nationalized" Russian minorities to externalize the autonomy issue in order to gain international support for their local demands. Finally, application of the newly borrowed discourse to the "old" educational structures—separate schools for different ethnic groups—has contributed to a "re-ethnification" of various ethnic groups and thus has allowed for more effective management of the national question by the "nationalizing" elites in post-Soviet Latvia. In this case, the transfer of global discourse on multiculturalism has not led to "internationalization," "Westernization," or "Europeanization," as traditionally has been argued by consensus and conflict theorists. Instead, adopting the language of new allies has been used skillfully by the local agency to reach other ends, including a reconciliation of international pressures for multiculturalization with the local politics of Latvianization.

REFERENCES

Barkey, K., & von Hagen, M. (Eds.). (1997). After empire: Multiethnic societies and nation-building: The Soviet Union and the Russian, Ottoman, and Habsburg empires. Boulder, CO: Westview Press.

Brown, M. (1995). The flawed logic of NATO expansion. *Survival, 37*(1), 34–52.

Brubaker, R. (1994). Nationhood and national question in the Soviet Union and post-Soviet Eurasia: An institutionalist account. *Theory and Society, 23,* 47–78.

Central Statistical Board of the USSR. (1958). *Cultural progress in the USSR.* Moscow: Foreign Languages Publishing House.

Druviete, I. (1998). Republic of Latvia. In B. Paulston & D. Peckham (Eds.), *Linguistic minorities in central and Eastern Europe* (pp. 160–183). Clevedon, UK: Multilingual Matters.

Foucault, M. (1977). *Discipline and punish: The birth of the prison.* New York: Pantheon Books.

Foucault, M. (1991). Governmentality. In G. Burchell, C. Gordon, & P. Miller (Eds.), *The Foucault effect: Studies in governmentality* (pp. 87–104). Chicago: University of Chicago Press.

Fridrihsone, M. (1999, December 9). Valodas likuma jauno redakciju vērtē četru Saeimas frakciju pārstāvji [Four Saeima deputies evaluate the new draft of the Language Law]. *Jauna Avize,* p. 3.

Halpin, D., & Troyna, B. (1995). The politics of education policy borrowing. *Comparative Education, 31*(3), 303–310.

Hamot, G. E. (1996, Fall). The case of teacher education in Poland's transitional democracy: "The school in a democratic society." *International Education,* pp. 5–21.

Hyde-Price, A. (1996). *The international politics of east central Europe.* Manchester, UK: Manchester University Press.

Karklins, R. (1998). Ethnic integration and school policies in Latvia. *Nationalities Papers, 26,* 283–302.

Khazanov, A. M. (1993). Interethnic relations in the Soviet Union during the first years of "restructuring." In H. G. De Soto & D. G. Anderson (Eds.), *The curtain rises: Rethinking culture, ideology, and the state in Eastern Europe* (pp. 182–206). Atlantic Highlands, NJ: Humanities Press.

Luhmann, N. (1990). *Essays on self-reference.* New York: Columbia University Press.
Lynch, J. (1998). The international transfer of dysfunctional paradigms. In D. Johnson, B. Smith, & M. Crossley (Eds.), *Learning and teaching in an international context: Research, theory, and practice* (pp. 7–33). Bristol, UK: University of Bristol, Centre for International Studies in Education.
Phillips, D. (1993). Borrowing education policy. In D. Finegold, L. McFarland, & W. Richardson (Eds.), *Something borrowed, something learned? The transatlantic market in education and training reform* (pp. 13–20). Washington, DC: Brookings.
Popkewitz, T. S. (1998). *Struggling for the soul: The politics of schooling and the construction of the teacher.* New York: Teachers College Press.
Popkewitz, T. S. (2000). Globalization/regionalization, knowledge, and the educational practices: Some notes on comparative strategies for educational research. In T. S. Popkewitz (Ed.), *Educational knowledge: Changing relationships between the state, civil society, and the educational community* (pp. 3–30). Albany: State University of New York Press.
Schriewer, J. (1990). The method of comparison and the need for externalization: Methodological criteria and sociological concepts. In J. Schriewer (Ed.) in cooperation with B. Holmes, *Theories and methods in comparative education* (3rd ed., pp. 25–83). Frankfurt/M, Germany: Lang.
Silova, I. (2002a). Manipulated consensus: Globalization, local agency, and cultural legacies in post-Soviet education reform. *European Educational Research Journal, 1,* 306–327.
Silova, I. (2002b). Returning to Europe: Facts, fiction, and fantasies of post-Soviet education reform. In A. Nóvoa & M. Lawn (Eds.), *Fabricating Europe: The formation of an educational space* (pp. 87–109). Dordrecht, Netherlands: Kluwer.
Slezkine, Y. (1994). The USSR as communal apartment, or how a socialist state promoted ethnic particularism. *Slavic Review, 53,* 414–452.
Spreen, C. A. (2000). *Globalization and educational policy borrowing: Mapping outcomes-based education in South Africa.* Unpublished doctoral dissertation, Columbia University, New York.
Steiner-Khamsi, G. (2000). Transferring education, displacing reforms. In J. Schriewer (Ed.), *Discourse formation in comparative education* (pp. 155–187). Frankfurt/M, Germany: Lang.
Steiner-Khamsi, G., & Quist, H. O. (2000). The politics of educational borrowing: Reopening the case of Achimota in British Ghana. *Comparative Education Review, 44*(3), 272–299.
United Nations Development Programme. (1996). *Latvia human development report.* Riga, Latvia: Author.
United Nations Development Programme. (1997). *Latvia human development report.* Riga, Latvia: Author.
United Nations Development Programme. (1999). *Latvia human development report.* Riga, Latvia: Author.
Vebers, E. (1994). *The ethnic situation in Latvia: Facts and commentary.* Riga, Latvia: Ethnic Study Center, Institute of Philosophy and Sociology.
Zhdanova, M. P. (Ed.). (1989). *Narodnoye obrazovaniie i kultura v SSSR* [State education and culture in the USSR]. Moscow: Finances and Statistics.

Chapter 5

Helping to Make the Case
for Integration:
The Israeli Black Panthers

Tali Yariv-Mashal

After the Vadi Salib riots, the new trend was to send social workers to the slum neighborhoods. . . . So there we were—a group of 18 year olds . . . , many of us, looking for something to do, frustrated and angry. Avner, the social worker, who was the kind of person that would rather give us the fishing pole than let us have the fish, told us about the Black Panthers in America, about Che Guevara and Bader Meinhof . . . , and we wanted to be all those combined and to create a social revolution. Anger we had plenty of already . . . ; all we needed was for someone or something to translate the anger into action. The name "The Black Panthers" did that first step for us.

> —Former Israeli Black Panther in an interview
> by Levi-Barzilai, 2002 (translation of author)

In 1971, a group of young Mizrahi[1] Jews between the ages of 18 and 20 from the slum neighborhood of Musrara in Jerusalem proclaimed themselves as "Panterim Shchorim"—the "Black Panthers." The Israeli Black Panthers demanded greater concern for the plight of the Mizrahi Jews in Israeli society, more equality among the ethnic groups, more social participation of the Mizrahi community, and "national integration." The name of the group—Black Panthers—began as a reference to the American group: "We will be like the 'Black Panthers' in the sense of being militant and frightening the establishment" (Bernstein, 1984, p. 130). This reference was picked up by a journalist, who used it in the first article published about the group in the media, and immediately was adopted by the group leaders and their opponents. The reference to the American Black Panthers was reinforced throughout the Panthers' actions and rhetoric, although there was never any contact between the Israeli and the American groups. In numerous interviews, members of the Israeli Black Panthers claimed that they did not really know what the American group stood for, but were fascinated by the strength and influence that the group had in the United States, and chose the name as a populist move more than anything else: "We chose the name the Black Panthers because nobody had ever heard of an organization—which exists—called Katamon Residents for Katamon.[2] We had to have a way to publicize our cause" (Saadia Marciano, interviewed in 1971; see Bernstein, 1976).

Due to the Israeli Panthers' problematic political position, their tactics, rhetoric, and ways of protest were usually very bold and dramatic. The initial members of the group were all people from the Musrara community and neighborhood who had no influence within the government and no interest group in the Knesset (the Israeli parliament). These circumstances dictated that the Panthers, in order to achieve any success, had to act in a dramatic fashion. They relied heavily on demonstrations in large cities; placards and chants emphasized poverty, discrimination, and a demand for equality in educational opportunities and housing conditions of the Mizrahi community. They emphasized the use of the term "Blacks" when referring to the Mizrahi community. Often the language chosen in referring to the government was characterized by mocking taunts, and violence with the police occurred occasionally in demonstrations (Shama & Iris, 1977).

The creation of the group, its rhetoric, and explicit frustration with the Israeli establishment shocked most of the Israeli public. A society preoccupied for many years with external tensions, war, and relations with Arabs in the occupied territories was made rudely aware of the existence of serious racial and ethnic unrest in its midst. The rhetoric and references used by the Panthers created a discourse that was considered, at least among the leading political and social groups, foreign to the Israeli scene, indirectly linking the Mizrahi minority in Israel, the Black minority in the United States, and the social and educational mission of equality and equity. One has only to look at the 1971 "mission statement" of the Israeli Black Panthers (as quoted in Iris & Shama, 1972, p. 43). This statement, published on posters and placards used in demonstrations, included a specific reference to the American Black Panthers, as well as highlighted statements that referred to what were—at times American, at times Western European—concepts of equality, democracy, and democratic means of participation and influence. It also called for educational reform and "integration" of Mizrahi children into the educational system. This was not a demand for equality before the law, as the American Black Panthers had demanded; legal equality in Israel already existed and had never been questioned. The Mizrahi students were never *officially* segregated from the system (in contrast to the Black minority in the United States to which the reference was made). The Israeli Panthers sought equalization not of governmental outputs, but of governmental outcomes; they sought an awareness of the problem by both governmental officials and Israeli society. Although the ways of influence and political participation were blurred, the goal was clear: The Panthers wanted to become "Israeli," or, for that matter, "Israeli-Mizrahim"—referring to the goal that their culture and history be included in the Israeli social scene and considered as an integral part of the Israeli state and culture. They wished to develop, with the help of the educational system and the political establishment, what was perceived by this establishment as the "backward" Mizrahi community, and to turn this community into an equal participant in the modernized, Western European Israeli identity that the Israeli state defined as its goal.

MIZRAHI CULTURE IN ISRAEL

The Israeli nation-state is one in which the process of ethnic diversity and stratification among the Jewish population, resulting from successive waves of immigration, has had a profound effect on the social structure, organization of society, and cultural characteristics of the state. Mass immigration following the establishment of the state in 1948 created a diverse Jewish population: After 1948 the Ashkenazi group comprised 48.4% immigrants, and the Mizrahi group 51.6% (Bernstein, 1976). Although the Zionist idea stressed the importance of creating a Jewish homeland for all Jewish communities in the diasporas, it also implied a denial of the "East," defining the Middle East as Arab-Muslim in character, and the land of Israel as the Jewish homeland—based on the European idea of the modern nation-state—and making no reference at all to the Arab majority in Palestine. In this "blocking" of Arab self-definition within the Israeli vision, there was also a crucial cultural blocking of that which was considered part of the Arab existence and heritage. In Israel (and on the stage of world opinion), the hegemonic voice of Israel historically and almost invariably has been that of the European Jews (Shohat, 1997).

Middle Eastern cultures were perceived by the Zionist movement as "backward cultures," and hence Mizrahi immigrants were asked to shed their way of life, language, and heritage as quickly as possible. They were to learn and adopt existing norms, values, and customs through state education and adult guidance, and to become affiliated with one of the existing secular or religious political parties. The absorption of Mizrahi immigrants into Israeli society entailed the acceptance of the established consensus of the "host" society and the abandonment of what were, by the Zionist consensus, "backward traditions." Cultural differences were posited as the cause of maladjustment (Hever, Shenhav, & Motzafi-Haller, 2002, p. 10; Shohat, 1997, p. 57).

Until the 1960s (and with only few changes to this day), one of the main goals of the educational system was to work toward socialization and acculturation, attempting to have not only the children but also their families "learn" and fit into the "Israeli culture" (which is predominantly Western) as soon as possible. Practically, the schooling system formulated suitable curricula, imparting basic principles of Western culture to the educational system, setting specific concepts of modernization and Westernization as its educational and social goals, and creating two different high school tracks, each implicitly intended to channel students into either an academic (mainly for the Ashkenazi students) or vocational (mainly for Mizrahi students) educational process (Yona & Saporta, 2002).

Not surprisingly, the educational system ran into difficulties, many of them pronounced, especially from the 1960s onwards. Some had to do with economic difficulties, others with the immediate social and cultural context of Jewish society. One of the most prominent of these difficulties was the issue of housing and geographical isolation of the new immigrants from Asia and Africa who were dispersed among various border settlements or housed in transit camps ("Ma'abarot"). The practical result was a lower standard of housing in outlying areas, where Ashkenazim, both new immigrants and veterans, either refused to go or were quicker to leave. The fact that the Mizrahi communities were isolated made their acculturation process much more difficult. The geographical isolation had immense influence on the educational system, as it meant that teachers had to be sent considerable distances. In practice, the teachers who were sent to these new settlements were the least experienced (Peled, 1979). Because the "development" areas (a term used to this day in Israel when discussing immigrant border settlements) were generally poverty-stricken, the children often worked to supplement the family income. As a result, some 40% of the children in the transit camps, and at the beginning of the 1950s in the public housing projects, never completed elementary school (Swirski, 1999). The difficult situation of the Mizrahi population caused much frustration and anger, which eventually developed into various forms of social, cultural, and political resistance.

By the end of the 1960s, as economic difficulties and disparities between the Ashkenazi and Mizrahi communities grew worse, as the educational system failed to answer the calls for change and equity, and as new social and political forces slowly emerged on the Israeli political scene, a new wave of civic movements emerged, placing ethnic relations at the center of political discourse in Israel.

THE ISRAELI BLACK PANTHERS: 1971–1972

In June 1967, Israel was engaged in the Six-Day War. During the years following this war, problems of security were exacerbated, and authorities tended to neglect internal social problems even more. But after a cease-fire was achieved in 1970, the frontiers were quiet. Many Israelis then turned their attention from grave national problems to personal, day-to-day grievances and became more aware of internal political and social issues. In this situation, one particular set of circumstances sparked the fire of the Black Panthers' protest: changes in the nature of immigration to Israel and in the "absorption policies" of the authorities. The immigrants who came after 1967 were mostly Eastern European Jews, or people from Western countries, and, relative to the standards of immigration policies in previous years, the authorities treated them exceptionally favorably (Cohen, 1997). The correlation between immigrant status and low socioeconomic status, so common in Israel since the creation of the state, disappeared. The recent European immigrants had been accustomed to a relatively high standard of living, and the authorities were anxious to give them any possible assistance. Their arrival was heralded as the realization of the Zionist dream. All of this contrasted sharply with the welcome given to the Mizrahi immigrants when they first immigrated, as well as with the treatment accorded them during their many years in the country.

The Black Panther movement in Jerusalem started as a community-based group in one of Jerusalem's community centers. As mentioned previously, no contact was ever made between the Israeli and the American Black Panthers, but the Israeli Panthers repeated their aspirations to create "a real change like the American Panthers did," to "be a real social movement," and to "fight the establishment" (Bernstein, 1976, p. 14; see also Levi-Barzilai, 2002). This rhetoric was a new phenomenon on the Israeli political scene and signaled the creation of a new discourse and political rationalization in Israel. It was no longer enforced as only an internal, local argument, but one that touched the Western-Democratic regime, and had to do with international goals and aspirations as much as with the internal political scene (Schriewer, 2000).

Beyond the Panthers' immediate argument against material discrimination, there was a larger issue of symbolic neglect. The Panthers' protest was intended largely to vent feelings of exclusion: "Golda, teach us Yiddish" was one of the slogans in the Jerusalem Panther demonstration of May 18, 1971 (the biggest demonstration the Panthers organized), asserting the feeling that only those who know the European-Jewish language of Yiddish could become a part of the Israeli society. The main thrust of the Black Panthers was against the government. They held the authorities responsible for the demoralizing effects of the slum conditions on Mizrahi youth; they wanted this youth to be taken within the fold and rehabilitated, for example, by admitting them to elite army positions, or to elite high schools (Cohen, 1997). The various demands and claims of the Panthers boiled down to one general assertion: The system blocked their avenues of advance and acceptance to the wider Israeli-Jewish society. The dominant theme of the Black Panthers was a demand for a full share in society—socially, economically, politically, and culturally (Bernstein, 1984). For the first time in many years, the Israeli establishment had to face a radical force that enjoyed considerable popular support from underprivileged groups. The Black Panthers held a view that was to eventually reinforce the notions of nationality and statehood in Israel by integrating all Israeli citizens. It was a call for recognition of an "other" and, at the same time, acceptance of that other into the Israeli-Western-Zionist discourse.

As support for the group grew wider and touched people of various social, educational, and economic strata, the Black Panthers, more than any other social protest group, succeeded in gaining access to the top national leadership (Cohen, 1997). The reaction of the political leadership was two-fold: On the one hand, the government took some practical steps to deal with the Panthers' threat and to prevent the spread of the unrest. Some of the demands were fully accepted, and considerable sums of money for rehabilitation, youth programs, and education were appropriated to deal with the pressing problems in the urban slums. At the same time, the political leadership attempted to neutralize the Panthers through the co-optation of their leaders, while the police applied a "stick and carrot" policy, intended both to intimidate and to mollify.

It was not only the establishment that was touched by the political change that the Panthers brought. The Panthers also succeeded in capturing the attention of the Israeli public to an unprecedented degree. Among both the Ashkenazi and the Mizrahi communities, the general attitude was that the Black Panthers, what they represented, and their means of protest were all important issues that needed to be addressed and resolved (Sprinzak, 1973).

After a period of demonstrations and political activity, by 1972 the Panthers who remained from the core group were largely inactive. The group's inability to change from a community-based civil protest group into a political force was widely related to problems in the administration and organization of the group, due to the inexperience of the leadership and lack of professional support (Bernstein, 1984; Cohen, 1997; Dahan-Calb, 1991). Most of the group's periphery of active supporters had dispersed, and only a few hundred people attended their demonstrations. In 1973 a small group of the Panthers' leaders joined a former parliament member to create a joint party. However, in October 1973 the Yom-Kippur war broke out, forcing attention back to questions of defense and foreign policy. The Panthers did not get a candidate into the Knesset or any of the 26 local councils for which they ran.

But regardless of the electoral failure, the actual transformation into a political party had important implications: The ethnic theme entered the established political arena and created the Mizrahi community's first channel for political influence. From this point on the issue of ethnic discrimination and inequality entered the main political discourse, forcing the largest political parties to discuss the problems publicly and to give voice to Mizrahi leadership within their campaigns. The most radical change on the Israeli political scene—the "Mahapach" (turnaround) of 1978, in which for the first time the labor party lost its majority to the "Likud" party led by Menahem Begin—was attributed largely to this change in political discourse. With this discourse came a change in the educational sphere, which at the same time signaled, signified, and modified the political atmosphere. The terms "integration" and "multiculturalism" entered as a dominant theme in what emerged as the new educational policy, intended to solve some of the problems raised by the Mizrahi political leadership. But, as I will show, the meaning and definitions of these terms remained blurred and simply were never defined, either within the educational system or in political and parliamentary discussions that dealt with educational policy. When an attempt was made to give some definitions to the terms, an interesting process of "indigenization" (Steiner-Khamsi & Quist, 2000, p. 290) occurred, in which a "local" meaning and context were given to the terms "integration" and "multiculturalism," refining them as part of an educational discourse. Let me, then, describe the educational reforms of the 1970s and discuss the aspects of international flows and transfers of educational and political discourse within this reform.

PARLIAMENTARY COMMITTEES AND
SCHOOL REFORMS, 1968–1972

In 1962, when Zalman Aran, the Minister of Education, announced the "biggest and most significant processes of educational reform in Israel yet," he did not mention the term "integration" as the title of this reform. In fact, he did not think this was, or should have been, the major part of his plan (Aran, 1972). The most significant change Aran and his committee had in mind when announcing the beginning of the implementation of the school reform in 1966 was structural: changing from a system that provided 8 years of elementary school and 4 years of postelementary school, to a 6 (elementary), 3 (middle school), 3 (high school) system. This change in structure was very much influenced by the American 6-3-3 educational system and, in fact, was one of the requirements of the American aid agencies that were funding much of the Israeli educational system at the time (Swirski, 1999). The proclaimed goal of this change was to allow more students 3 years of postelementary education. One of the consequences of this change was that the "placement test"—an exam that every student had to pass after elementary school to be fitted into one of two tracking systems, vocational or academic—was cancelled, and students were tracked into different high schools at the end of ninth grade according to their academic achievements. But when Aran and his professional committee announced the initial reform plan, a political storm broke out, with opponents calling for a more significant social change, one that finally would solve the gaps and inequality between the different schools and students in Israel. In 1968 the Knesset formed a new committee that would be responsible for reassessing the reform and finalizing the change. In this committee, all 19 political parties in the parliament were represented. It was, obviously, a political committee, aimed at solving a delicate political issue. The goals of the committee underwent political turbulence, and apart from achieving political calmness regarding the issues of educational inequality through minor changes in the educational system and a political rhetoric of reassurance and promises, it was hard to ascribe any actual significance to the committee's work.

As social discomfort grew larger and louder, much was expected from this committee and from the school reform that eventually would grow out of it. Various civic groups as well as educational leaders expected the committee report to be the social and political solution that would, hopefully, settle much of the emerging discomfort. Aran, an experienced and sharp politician, was very much aware of the social discomfort growing within the slum neighborhoods and development towns, and he knew that a different angle should be highlighted so that the reform would be politically and professionally accepted. In the midst of discussions in the parliament, Aran chose, once again, to state the educational goals of the school reform. Here, for the first time, he stated:

> The first goal of this reform is to see how we can better use the intellectual and human potential of our young generation; the second goal is to speed the process that would eventually eliminate the ethnic gap in education, especially among those children who are second generation to Mizrahi parents. (Knesset, 1968, p. 121, translation of author)

This was a statement that clearly placed a political responsibility on the committee and on the expected educational reform. By May 1968, when the committee published its recommendations, three final goals were stated.

> The three main goals for which the change in the educational system is required are: Improvement of the standards of teaching in all stages of the educational process; reduction of the existing gap between the children of our nation in educational standards as well as in the chances to be part of social and the economic spheres, and finally, integrating children from various backgrounds in regional educational frameworks. (Knesset, 1968, p. 236, translation of author)

For scholars and practitioners of education, these goals seemed abstruse. How were these three different (and some claimed contradicting) goals to be achieved? Can and should the educational system be responsible for such wide and problematic social problems? What is the actual meaning and purpose of "regional educational frameworks"? All these were left vague enough for the political as well as the educational authorities to mold and change, as social and political circumstances developed. The main actual changes within the educational system were left as they were stated by the committee of 1963—primarily structural changes, as well as a change in teacher education programs.

It was only in 1970 that the term "integration" actually arose, first in the parliament, and slowly within the educational scene, bringing a *rhetorical resolution* to the problem. The initial hope, especially among educators and within the educational administration, was that this rhetoric would be a first step toward a change in the system. Yet, the term was never translated into educational means or plans of action. It was merely a change in discourse, one that would dominate the educational scene for many years, but was never transformed into clear educational reform acts (see Peled, 1979; Swirski, 1999). Within the emerging discourse of "integration" in 1969–1970, the only significant change that was pointed out by politicians as well as educators sponsoring the reform, was a change in "school zones." Middle schools were built as "integrative" schools: They were placed outside of specific neighborhoods, and students were taken by bus to schools outside their geographical communities. This, it was claimed, was to create a heterogeneous student body in the middle schools, one that consisted of students from different neighborhoods and social backgrounds. The change in school zones and the creation of integrative middle schools were announced only in 1971 (although they were described to the public as an integral part of the 1968 reform). This announcement took place after the 1971 Black Panther demonstrations and was considered by many a consequence of them. David Elazar (1994), an educational historian, claims, for example, that there was no intention to proceed with this change before the Black Panther protests, but it was the "politically correct" announcement to make at the time, as it was hoped it would answer some of the most pressing demands of the Panthers for a better chance for equal opportunities within the schooling system, as well as inclusion of the Mizrahi culture and history on the Israeli cultural scene. Bringing students together, the political leadership claimed, would give them a chance to learn and know more about one another, and to accept the various community and family cultures around them. Cultural pluralism was addressed as something that could be dealt with through creating a multicultural, heterogeneous group of students, rather than an idea or ideology to be accomplished within these communities (Lam, 1997).

The political discourse that was highlighted (if not initiated) by the Black Panthers forced not only the attention of the political regime but the restructuring and maneuvering of the educational one, placing an immense political and social responsibility on the educational system. Any political or social resolution had to start with an educational change; education was the future, the promise for a better chance for the younger Mizrahi generation. The educational system and the reform that by 1970 had started taking place, had to reassess its goals, practices, and most of all its discourse in order to be able to relate to the social and political unrest. The deliberate decision of Aran to adopt the term "integration" as the core of the committee report and the reform that came after it were consequences of this reassessment and reflected the political responsibility that was placed on the educational system.

The process of highlighting the rhetoric of "integration" as part of the educational change had two goals: It was intended to create a sense of professionalism, one that touched the global (mostly American at the time) discourses regarding education and gave a sense of political as well as professional "security" (Schriewer, 2000; Steiner-Khamsi, 2000). Yet, at the same time, the term was left sufficiently vague and undefined throughout the reform plan to leave a political space in which to operate and to be able to locally adjust or "indigenize" the term in the specific context, according to timely uprisings and political changes (Steiner-Khamsi, 2000). The lack of a definition for the term "integration" within the Israeli context, is, I believe, crucial to understanding the significance and influence that the 1970s school reform has had on both educational and political developments in Israel since.

THE CREATION OF DISCOURSE AS THE BASIS
FOR THE CREATION OF EDUCATIONAL REFORM

It was through the changing political definitions of the term "integration" that the school reform of the 1970s was not only created, but also legitimized. The self-legitimization of the discourse of ethnicity and integration rested on nothing outside itself, using a rhetoric that ensured its political and social acceptance, and applying a set of changing and vague definitions that enabled a sense of flexibility and responsiveness among educators. Since 1968, the discourse has been reproposed ceaselessly, developing each time its own languages of self-validation to fit within its specific social and political context. This same discourse, one must add, is still dominant in the schooling system in Israel today.

A complex process of discourse formation is exposed by using a comparative framework that emphasizes the interaction between the global and the local (Schriewer, 2000; Steiner-Khamsi, 2000) to analyze the changes in the Israeli educational context of 1970–1973. At no point during the years analyzed was there a specific reference to a "borrowing agency," or a defined comparison between global forms of educational power and the Israeli one. Such references would, I believe, undermine the complex processes of discourse formation that were part of the ongoing change in Israel at the time. It is exactly this point that I find important and fascinating within the case of the Israeli Black Panthers and the preceding school reform. The discourse of "integration" was a consequence of the complex realities of the global political changes and powers at the time, and the local desire to create a new social reality. The reference to the American Black Panthers, implying issues of ethnic construction of the Mizrahi citizens, was part of a production of ethnic power. In order to establish such power, a reference to "Black" power was made, and a discourse was created that would validate and strengthen the local context, establishing a "truth" that was at the same time local and global. For the educational system, the discourse of "integration" that came along with this political power provided a rope to hold onto when the system was drowning in the sea of political demands and expectations, again linking citizenship, multiculturalism, equity, and education; validating its rightfulness and establishing its place within the discourse; and always keeping any actions or practices vague enough to be changed and modified over time.

By presenting this case I have attempted to deepen the concepts of transfer of ideas by highlighting the importance of recognizing that transfer and reform can involve not only actual practices, but also discourses within a complex system of flows of power and truths. As Steiner-Khamsi (2000) points out, the fact that a specific program is or is not implemented does not mean that the transfer of ideas did or did not occur. Instead, what is being implemented is not a particular aspect of educational reform, but rather the political discourse associated with it, part of a much larger flow of ideas within and between the local and the global.

NOTES

1. I use the terms "Mizrahim" (Easterners) and "Ashkenazim" to distinguish between non-European-born Jews and European-born Jews, respectively. Although both communities span various continents and regions, the terms have been used and generalized in Israel and abroad to make a basic distinction between them.

2. Katamon is a slum neighborhood in Jerusalem.

REFERENCES

Aran, Z. (1972). *Written and oral speeches*. Tel-Aviv: Am Oved.

Bernstein, D. (1976). *The Black Panthers of Israel, 1971–1973: Contradictions and protest in the process of nation-building*. Unpublished doctoral thesis, University of Sussex, Sussex, UK.

Bernstein, D. (1984). Conflict and protest in Israeli society. *Youth and Society, 16*, 129–152.

Cohen, E. (1997). The Black Panthers and Israeli society. In T. Herman (Ed.), *Social parties and political protest in Israel* (pp. 43–65). Jerusalem: Hebrew University Press.

Dahan-Calb, H. (1991). *Vadi Salib and the Black Panthers: Implications on Israeli society*. Unpublished doctoral thesis, Hebrew University, Jerusalem.

Elazar, D. (1994). *Education in a society at a crossroad: Implications for the study of Israel educational system*. Jerusalem: Institute for the Study of Educational Systems.

Hever, H., Shenhav, Y., & Motzafi-Haller, P. (Eds.). (2002). *Mizrahim in Israel: A critical observation into Israel's ethnicity*. Jerusalem: Hakibbutz Hameuchad Publishing House.

Iris, M., & Shama, A. (1972). Black panthers of Israel: The movement. *Society, 9*(7), 42–43.

Knesset. (1968). *Knesset committee for disparities in education: 1st report*. Jerusalem: Knesset of Israel Archive.

Lam, Z. (1997). Pluralism as an idea and its implementation in the Israeli educational system. In I. Gur-Zeev (Ed.), *Education and the postmodern discourse* (pp. 143–164). Jerusalem: Magnes.

Levi-Barzilai, V. (2002, July 5). Black Panther returns. *Haaretz*, (daily newspaper, Tel Aviv), p. 5.

Peled, E. (1979). *The hidden agenda of educational policy in Israel: The interrelationship between the political system and the educational system*. Unpublished doctoral dissertation, Columbia University, New York.

Schriewer, J. (2000). Comparative education methodology in transition: Towards a science of complexity? In J. Schriewer (Ed.), *Discourse formations in comparative education* (pp. 3–52). Frankfurt/M, Germany: Lang.

Shama, A., & Iris, M. (1977). *Immigration without integration: Third world Jews in Israel*. Cambridge, MA: Schenkman.

Shohat, E. (1997). Sepharadim in Israel: Zionism from the standpoint of its Jewish victims. In A. McClintock, A. Mufti, & E. Shohat (Eds.), *Dangerous liaisons: Gender, nation and postcolonial perspectives* (pp. 39–68). Minneapolis: University of Minnesota Press.

Sprinzak, E. (1973). *Beginning of politics of delegitimation in Israel, 1967–1972*. Jerusalem: Hebrew University Press.

Steiner-Khamsi, G. (2000). Transferring education, displacing reforms. In J. Schriewer (Ed.), *Discourse formation in comparative education* (pp. 155–187). Frankfurt/M, Germany: Lang.

Steiner-Khamsi, G., & Quist, H. O. (2000). The politics of educational borrowing: Reopening the case of Achimota in British Ghana. *Comparative Education Review*, *44*(3), 272–299.

Swirski, S. (1999). *Politics and education in Israel*. New York: Falmer.

Yona, Y., & Saporta, Y. (2002). Vocational education and the beginning of an Israeli working class. In H. Hever, Y. Shenhav, & P. Motzafi-Haller (Eds.), *Mizrahim in Israel: A critical observation into Israel's ethnicity* (pp. 68–104). Jerusalem: Hakibbutz Hameuchad Publishing House.

Chapter 6

Appropriating Borrowed Policies: Outcomes-Based Education in South Africa

Carol Anne Spreen

Educational borrowing has had a significant impact on shaping the new curriculum in post-apartheid South Africa. In response to the country's changing needs, policy makers have actively looked overseas to select, borrow, or learn from reforms that will transform education into an equitable, world-class system. As one might expect, much of the understanding and perceptions about the international influences on educational reform are viewed with considerable skepticism and resistance in South Africa. Yet, as there has been a range of actors in educational policy making, there has been a range of local meanings and constructions of borrowed ideas, lending themselves to a hybrid homegrown version of educational reform. In this chapter I will look at the ways in which key decision makers linked to the transition process have used policy borrowing as a strategy to leverage educational change in South Africa.

In many ways, examining borrowing is instructive because it lodges the analysis of educational policy making within an international context by mapping out the complex ways in which international social and cultural ties, political and economic relationships, democratic imperatives, and shifting roles of global and local participation all influence policy decisions. Taking a closer look at what it means to borrow or adopt imported concepts outside their place of origin, this case study focuses not on what works with borrowing, but on how reforms get defined and appropriated in a different national context. This historical analysis of borrowing shows that while initially international lessons learned were important levers for policy making and legitimizing contested approaches, as different features of reforms are institutionalized and become mainstream concepts, they are politically viable only if their international origins are concealed.

In our current era of globalization, educational policy makers increasingly look to international trends, ideas, and standards to underscore the urgency for dramatic school change. Through worldwide diffusion of ideas, concepts, and educational blueprints, references to international reforms serve to reify the notion of international relatedness and legitimate the use of international standards. Elsewhere in this volume, scholars have described the ways in which *das internationale Argument* is used to fuel social change as well as support contested policy developments at home (also see Schriewer, 2000).

Previous chapters in this volume have illustrated and discussed the ways in which different borrowing strategies have been used by policy makers in a variety of national contexts. Yet the idea that there is worldwide diffusion of educational policy making floating around to be scooped up whole by policy makers bears closer attention. We must be reminded of the cultural imperatives and local nuances that contribute to educational approaches and understandings. Underscoring the clear need to examine the transnational and cultural environments of international educational policy borrowing, it is also helpful to study how policies unfold in one place over time. Most studies view borrowing as a snapshot in time, yet the ways in which borrowing strategies and tactics change over time bear equal attention. Little has been said about when and how the international origins of reforms actually become a political liability.

THE PERIODIZATION OF BORROWING

Policies are not merely the products of rational, analytical decision making; instead they are part of an inherently political process affected by interests, events, local priorities and understandings, and a host of financial and other constraints. Most important, policies should not be viewed as static and unchanging; they are the product of agency and resistance, negotiation, bargaining, and accommodation, constantly evolving over time.

While there is an enormous literature on policy making and the policy process, relatively little has been directly applied toward understanding policy formulation in the context of a transitional society that is politically polarized and is rapidly changing due to globalization. Hence, given the contested nature of global influences—particularly those lodged within distinct historical first/third world relations—one must query whether and when international references are useful, and at what point policy makers and governments attempt to obscure traces of international borrowing to indicate local ownership and/or ensure relevance in their particular national contexts.

This case study of educational policy making in South Africa provides a powerful example to illustrate when in the policy process, borrowing is and is no longer useful as a key element of educational change. It demonstrates that at certain points in policy making it becomes more important for governments to appropriate reforms, establish ownership, and conceal their international origins, so they will not be rejected outright.

Elaborating on the phases of borrowing by tracing the origins and evolution of educational reform in South Africa, I will show that international features are used deliberately and quite selectively as a means of educational theorizing and/or policy making across various stages of the policy process, only to vanish when the reform comes under greatest scrutiny. Using Archer's (1984) framework to describe policy formulation (external transactions, political manipulation, and internal initiative), the case of the origins and trajectory of outcomes-based education (OBE) in South Africa brings a sense of the complexity of power relations that shape and pattern educational planning across time and events.

SOUTH AFRICAN CONTEXT FOR OUTCOMES-BASED EDUCATION REFORM

In most countries the introduction of OBE has brought with it much controversy and resistance. Upon its formal introduction in South African schools, OBE received considerable scrutiny and was increasingly at the center of a heated national policy debate. The OBE controversy was not only about changes in teaching and learning, but also about its origins and its relevance to South African schools. OBE in South Africa can be mapped to the early competency debates in Australia, New Zealand, Scotland, and Canada, and also to William Spady's work in the United States (see Jansen, 1999; Spreen, 2000).

The 1998 implementation of OBE in South African schools marked a dramatic departure from the former educational system, bringing on a major paradigm shift from content-based to outcomes-based teaching and learning. Under OBE training, educators develop curriculum plans and objectives from agreed-upon outcomes within a particular context or learning area. Not surprisingly, as different versions of OBE and competency-based learning resonated with different policy actors—even within the educational community—different linkages and approaches to borrowing were established. As a result, several competing definitions of OBE currently operate in South Africa and often occur within the same policy document. These ideas eventually were met with myriad existing beliefs and understandings about teaching and learning from across the South African social and cultural landscape. Yet, even as a shared rhetoric around OBE was established, different interest groups were able to point to vague definitions, loosely constructed learning outcomes, and global buzzwords to support their existing programs, instead of having to challenge and/or define specific ideas about teaching and learning.

DEFINING THE STAGES OF POLICY BORROWING
IN SOUTH AFRICA

In describing the policy process, Archer (1984) supplies three helpful sets of arrangements to describe how new educational policies emerge: through external transactions, political manipulation, and internal initiative. Each of these phases are used to describe the way in which South Africans have leveraged international trends and policy borrowing as a strategy to influence educational reform.[1] Table 6.1 provides a brief overview of the three periods of policy making, the reasons for borrowing during each period, borrowing strategies used, the educational context or aims, and what was borrowed during each period. The following sections describe in more detail the borrowing strategies and outcomes in South African educational policy.

Phase I: Period of External Transactions (1976–1993)

During the stage of *external transactions*, groups outside the dominant system who are dissatisfied with the current policy directions engage external references to negotiate with the government of the day. To expand this argument within an international context, interest groups use *das internationale Argument*, whereby foreign models and ideas are circulated and reviewed for their relevance and applicability; often, their international status alone lends them credibility and authority.

Steiner-Khamsi (2000) draws our attention to transferred discourses and to the global language of education. External or international references to model innovations, to examples abroad, or to important aspects of "internationality" represent a form of reformative reflection on education that, as Schriewer and Martinez (see Chapter 2, this volume) suggest, resorts to the external environment. Many scholars suggest that rather than reforming or borrowing actual ideas or models from outside, policy makers point to international rhetoric and the vague global discourse that surrounds educational reform, where they can identify examples of models similar to their own in other foreign systems (Steiner-Khamsi, 2000, 2002a). Schriewer (1992) points out that policy makers often borrow the language of reform programs as a self-referential discursive act to build support for their own systems without actually borrowing anything. Similarly, Lynch (1998) uses the phrase "flags of convenience" to show how policy makers use particular buzzwords to attract attention and/or international funding, regardless of their true relationship to the initiative. In this way the mere mention of borrowed concepts helps contested ideas gain credibility even before they are ever implemented. Thus, external references or flags of convenience serve to buttress the credibility of contested initiatives.

We find this to be particularly true in transitional societies (such as South Africa) that are trying to reposition themselves in the global order. In such cases, policy makers commonly use international reforms and concepts to signal modernity and denote participation in the world society (also see Chisholm & Fuller, 1996; Steiner-Khamsi, 2000).

The early phase of the policy process in South Africa is characterized by the period of resistance against the apartheid state (from the 1970s through 1990s), wherein external references provided important levers and international relationships offered important allies for the anti-apartheid activists. During this first period of education policy formulation, borrowing and seeking the advice of international consultants in order to legitimate a controversial or weak policy position such as OBE, and/or linking education and training through outcomes- or competency-based approaches, were components of a widespread policy strategy.

In these early days of policy formulation, the government-in-exile and anti-apartheid activists associated with the African National Congress used multiple references to international trends, models, and programs in their education policy documents. Policy advocates participated in numerous study tours of other countries' educational and training systems. Numerous white papers, consultation and discussion documents, and expert-based technical reports made widespread references to particular countries. Leveraging new policy initiatives by touting them as "proven elsewhere" was one way to ensure their acceptance. In this way, "lessons learned from elsewhere" provided an argument for what might have been (and indeed became) a controversial and contested education and training initiative. It is worth noting that this style of international reporting was done not solely to present a distorted view of "other ways of doing" in a new South Africa; it also helped to clarify and define an emerging set of values, world views, and orientations that already had a long history in South Africa.

Table 6.1. Three Stages of Policymaking

Period	Reasons for Borrowing	Borrowing Strategies	Educational Context and Aims	What Was Borrowed?
Period I (1976–1993) Borrowing as external transactions or external referencing Policy actors are outside of the political establishment	Problem solving Conscious selection Lessons learned from elsewhere Leverage for contested policy initiatives Looking for a solution to a stalled program for workers Unavailability of internal references	Media reports Study tours Adapted training modules from Australia, New Zealand, and Scotland Numerous references to international models in public debates, proposals, and policy documents	Education for liberation or people's education Literacy training and organizing for collective bargaining, emphasizing "civic and democratic" participation	A competency-based model for workplace training and a framework for recognition of competencies
Period II (1994–1998) Borrowing as a form of political manipulation Legitimating a contested reform	Characterized by emerging power of the liberation movement, particularly the trade unions Power was consolidated with a tripartite alliance among government, business, and labor Legitimacy required political expediency—need to provide a quick fix solution; "rhetorical reforms" to signal change	International technical assistance Long-term international consultants (worked with unions) Study tours Numerous international references in all policy documents Assistance from international consultants Strong reliance on expertise from repatriated South Africans	Transfer of credit systems, flexibility, mobility, and structures of accreditation Competing discourses on integration of education and training Introduction of broader education community into policymaking; some resistance to competency or outcomes-based education emerging, especially from education community	NQF structures (NZ) SAQA and quality assurance indicators from UK, specifically Scotland and Young with NQVs "Competency-based learning" (influenced by the Finn and Mayer Reports in Australia) The introduction of international trends, comparative models, and "world-class" standards

Table 6.1. (cont'd)

Period	Reasons for Borrowing	Borrowing Strategies	Educational Context and Aims	What Was Borrowed?
Period III (1998–present) Internal initiative or establishing ownership	Political symbolism—need to demonstrate that government is driving change Emphasis on ownership and a South African product Established structures for adaptation through stakeholder negotiating forums Vanishing of international references in policy documents	Long-term consultancies Study tours Literature and materials Conferences and workshops sponsored by aid organizations International participation in the Curriculum Coordinating Committees, Reference Groups, and Learning Area Committees Dropping of international references in policy documents	Learning areas—based on the organization and language of "Common Curriculum" in Canada Introduction of the term "OBE" by Spady in the U.S. Division emerging between education and training Materials and curriculum contents reflect an amalgam of ideas about OBE, particularly Australia and the United States Workshops presented by INGOs and by locals	Curriculum 2005, an amalgam of international and local reform ideas Indisputable outcomes—vague enough to have wide appeal Competing models and confusing definitions of OBE

Phase II: Period of Political Manipulation (1994–1998)

In the second stage, *political manipulation*, groups that are in the process of gaining political power are able to conceive and push through policies that generally have not been produced by "local policy experts" previously working in the area. There is considerable negotiation and often the "displacement" of existing reforms by ideas, concepts, or models that reflect more "modern," efficient, and accountability-based changes in education. More often than not, mere association by local initiatives with more broad international reform efforts helps to signal that these changes will cause educational institutions to move in a modern, effective, and internationally competitive direction.

I describe the second stage of policy making in South Africa as a period of "political manipulation," underscoring the fact that South Africa's governance structures were in a transitional stage as the country began to shed the isolation and oppression of the apartheid era and participate in the global arena. The building of new power structures in this emerging democracy required consolidation of power and leverage from borrowed policies to help legitimate the new and controversial ideas of a fragile emerging state.

The political manipulation phase (1994–1998) characterizes a period of internal political struggle and competition to secure the prevailing educational ideology. During this time many actors and ideas competed to fill the same narrow policy space. Many believe that the political system's loss of legitimacy and the conflictual state of educational policy were the driving forces behind educational decision making.

Placing South Africa on the global stage was also increasingly important at this time. The attention from the international community both excited and bolstered the trajectory of educational reform. Money from international aid flowed during this period, as did the visibility of the newly elected government (Jansen, 2000). During these early years—the honeymoon period—emerging leaders described an "international menu a la carte" to pick and choose programs and policies that would drive the new administration.

Here in the political manipulation phase, borrowing strategies are characterized by two concurrent motivations: (1) the emerging government's need to legitimate itself (hence the emphasis on a policy rhetoric and broadly constructed policy frameworks that had wide appeal) and provide ready-made policy solutions to myriad social problems; and (2) the need to stake out a place and position that would indicate South Africa's emergence into the global arena. On one level, OBE initiatives also had to be locally legitimated (emphasizing a redistributional framework and addressing the concerns of equity and redress; reflecting a dramatic departure from the former apartheid system; and promising a change for the better). On another level, new government leaders had to signal that they were constructing policy reforms that were recognized as fair, equitable, and in line with "world-class standards." These sometimes competing demands required democratic consultative forums to validate the content and direction of OBE. Hence, the OBE language at the national policy level tended to be driven by economic concerns, but when it reached the more concrete classroom level, it was about equity, access, and redress.

Phase III: Internal Initiative or Ownership (1998 to present)

Finally, in a stage of *ownership* or *internal initiative*, people within the institutional framework of the policy process begin to identify deficiencies in the current policy directions and try to indigenize or recontextualize reforms in order to implement the necessary corrections. Schriewer (2000) describes actors in this process as engaging in "reflective theory" (vs. scientific theory), explaining that educational reforms do not develop first and foremost based on scientific truths, but instead evolve as theories to foster self-understanding and self-steering.

Yet while Schriewer (2000) describes reflective theorizing in the early stages of policy borrowing, this does not explain the ongoing processes of meaning making and local understandings that are created out of international reformative reflection. Therefore, because external references do not make use of cross-cultural analysis, and instead rely on individual national descriptions, policy makers often fail to foresee their applicability and use locally, or the contested nature of borrowed forms of information.

During the implementation phase of internalizations and ownership, global skills and international competitiveness—rather than proven practice as determined by implementation elsewhere—are touted as features of reform. In terms of establishing local meanings and understandings, ownership, rather than imported ideas, brings legitimacy to a policy initiative.

This stage is described as an "internalization" or appropriation phase because it is characterized by a vanishing of the international origins or external references to OBE. During this phase, government structures are established, policies drawn up by consultation to reflect the internal or local demands, and comments and/or criticisms aired through a series of discussion documents and negotiating forums. During this time, debates provoked by OBE illustrate how difficult it becomes to distinguish purely "imported ideas" from true appropriation of the concepts. Appropriation of OBE was part of the government's need to demonstrate leadership and accountability and its ability to establish a coherent plan to dramatically change education. Yet, throughout implementation, many South Africans became increasingly skeptical about the nature and direction of OBE and began questioning whether leaders had really thought through the pedagogical implications of an outcomes-based system and the integration of education and training in a country plagued by educational inequality and ill-prepared teachers.

Here, the relevance and applicability of international aspects of reforms came under greater scrutiny (e.g., there were increased concerns expressing, "If it didn't work there, why should it work here?" or "We are not like these other countries, why should it work here?"). As OBE became a mainstream concept in South Africa, more "borrowing critics" emerged. Some of the most vocal critics came from the education community. Many of these policy actors began to emerge, using borrowing to displace the labor movement's plan for reform.

The result was an amalgam of international ideas and a truly hybrid version of a homegrown South African OBE. At this stage, borrowing was not used to introduce a new reform or concept, but instead to alter the direction and displace the labor emphasis on vocational aspects of OBE. This illustrates how borrowing is often a contradictory, contested, and faltering process, even when it is done consciously and for a particular purpose.

Interestingly and probably most significantly, it is also during the internalization or appropriation phase that references to international influences vanish completely from policy documents, curriculum guides, and even the public discourse. Only vague recollections of the origins of OBE can be found anywhere.

THE VANISHING ORIGINS OF OBE

This analysis of borrowing underscores what many others (including Chisholm & Fuller, 1996; Christie, 1996, 1997; Steiner-Khamsi, 2002b; Unterhalter & Samson, 1998) have argued, that an understanding of borrowing requires an examination of the complex relationships between global trends and local contexts in understanding educational policy and reform. What is clear from this brief overview is that the purposes and strategies around borrowing OBE reflect an amalgam of interests and initiatives and the hybridization of rationales drawn primarily from international contexts. In this era of global circulation of ideas, movements, and people, it is difficult to pinpoint precisely when and how a concept arrives. Moreover, what might be the same on paper is understood and implemented very differently at the classroom level.

By outlining and detailing the various phases of policy development, we can point to the significance of periodization in studying borrowing. Historical analysis of borrowing strategies illustrates when and how borrowing is useful, and when it is a liability. In the first phase, borrowing was for the narrow and specific purpose of solving a particular problem. There was careful consideration of different options and scrutiny of many models. In many ways this application of competency-based or outcomes-based education was not designed to be an all-inclusive educational reform initiative or the central mechanism for transformation.

During the transition years, borrowing was done for leverage, legitimation, and recognition, both nationally and internationally. Significantly, the devastating history of apartheid made immediate change a political imperative, and as a result many of the more thoughtful earlier contributions around the CBE/OBE reform were pushed to the background. In order to escape apartheid, ideas had to originally appear to be brought in from outside. In the ownership or appropriation phase, as the policy agenda widened, the discourse around OBE had to become broad enough so that anyone could tack on their own interpretation and meaning to it. The result was competing models of OBE operating (with the support and assistance of international consultants) within and across South Africa. As the policy gained momentum and expanded during its implementation, the purpose of borrowing and uses for OBE changed considerably, most notably in the disappearance of international reference points. Outcomes-based education had to be its own South African concept.

The periodization of borrowing and appropriation of OBE shows that as international policies are introduced and begin to be implemented, there is a shift from specific national features or attributes to a more general reference to global reforms or international norms and standards. Eventually, as policies unfold into practice, emphasis is placed on domestic and/or regional experiences and understandings. In many ways, the shift from particular international references (e.g., "In Scotland, OBE is practiced as such . . .") toward general references to "globalization" helps to conceal the origins of educational reforms imported from elsewhere. Hence, while a large body of research on borrowing clearly has documented the uses and abuses of borrowing and transfer, it is important to know at what point and in what context borrowing is no longer a viable way to legitimate reform.

In addition, these stages illustrate that while initially, internationally developed reforms were used by reformers to craft solutions to problems and then to legitimate a controversial policy agenda, as the policy became more concrete and as proposals came under greater scrutiny, external references were dropped because they were seen as not viable in a South

African context. Hence, while "international contemplation" often is used in the early stages of policy planning without any cross-cultural examination, once concepts and approaches hit the ground and come into conflict with local nuances and cultural understandings, its international applicability is called into question. This specifically speaks to why early on external references (such as national frameworks, curriculum models, or reform ideas like decentralization) are powerful and legitimate policy tools, and why later on the same international references are widely scrutinized and often concealed. It is precisely when ideas begin to take hold and become national policies that they must confront cultural beliefs, practices, and local understandings; then the international argument loses weight.

Lastly, one might question whether borrowing worked in South Africa. While it is too early to determine the impact of OBE on learners, teachers, and school organization, OBE has brought new ideas and stimulated a detailed and lengthy discussion around the principles of teaching and learning and directions for educational change that still continue today in South Africa.

NOTE

1. Methodological note: This framework evolved from fieldwork that was conducted while I was a Visiting Scholar at the University of Witwatersrand in Johannesburg, South Africa, from December 1997 through January 1999. My understanding of the points of view of South African policy makers and educators came from several months of interviews, focus groups, and informal conversations, as well as from extensive review of policy documents from the early 1980s through the present. Although the findings in this chapter focus mainly on the viewpoints of policy makers, they also are informed by interviews and focus groups with teachers, activists, and government critics. For a more detailed overview of this research, see Spreen (2000).

REFERENCES

Archer, M. (1984). *The social origins of education systems*. London: Sage.

Chisholm, L., & Fuller, B. (1996). Remembering people's education? Shifting alliances, state building and South Africa's narrowing policy agenda. *Journal of Education Policy, 11*, 693–716.

Christie, P. (1996). Globalization and the curriculum: Proposals for the integration of education and training in South Africa. *International Journal of Educational Development, 16*, 407–416.

Christie, P. (1997). Global trends in local contexts: A South African perspective on competence debates. *Discourse, 18*, 55–69.

Jansen, J. D. (1999). Globalization, curriculum and the third world state: In dialogue with Michael Apple. *Current Issues in Comparative Education, 1/2.* Retrieved May 14, 2002, from http://www.tc.columbia.edu/cice/articles/jj112.htm.

Jansen, J. D. (2000). Education after apartheid. Intersections of politics and policy in the South African transition 1990–2000. Unpublished manuscript.

Lynch, J. (1998). The international transfer of dysfunctional paradigms. In D. Johnson, B. Smith, & M. Crossley (Eds.), *Learning and teaching in an international context: Research, theory, and practice* (pp. 7–33). Bristol, UK: University of Bristol, Centre for International Studies in Education.

Schriewer, J. (1990). The method of comparison and the need for externalization: Methodological criteria and sociological concepts. In J. Schriewer (Ed.) in cooperation with B. Holmes, *Theories and methods in comparative education* (3rd ed.; pp. 25–83). Frankfurt/M, Germany: Lang.

Schriewer, J. (2000). Comparative education methodology in transition: Towards a science of complexity? In J. Schriewer (Ed.), *Discourse formation in comparative education* (pp. 3–52). Frankfurt/M, Germany: Lang.

Spreen, C. A. (2000). *Globalization and educational policy borrowing: Mapping outcomes-based education in South Africa.* Unpublished doctoral dissertation, Columbia University, New York.

Steiner-Khamsi, G. (2000). Transferring education, displacing reforms. In J. Schriewer (Ed.), *Discourse formation in comparative education* (pp. 155–187). Frankfurt/M, Germany: Lang.

Steiner-Khamsi, G. (2002a). Re-framing educational borrowing as a policy strategy. In M. Caruso & H.-E. Tenorth (Eds.), *Internationalisierung—Internationalisation* (pp. 57–89). Frankfurt/M, Germany: Lang.

Steiner-Khamsi, G. (2002b). Re-territorializing educational import: Explorations into the politics of educational borrowing. In A. Nóvoa & M. Lawn (Eds.), *Fabricating Europe: The formation of an education space* (pp. 69–86). Dordrecht, Netherlands: Kluwer.

Unterhalter, E., & Samson, M. (1998, April). *Unpacking the gender of global curriculum in South Africa.* Paper presented at the annual meeting of the American Educational Research Association, San Diego.

Chapter 7

Local Reactions to Imposed Transfer: The Case of Eastern Berlin Secondary School Teachers

Bernhard T. Streitwieser

The fall of the Berlin Wall in November 1989 brought many changes to the former East Germany (German Democratic Republic, GDR), not the least of which was felt in the realm of education. As part of the country's reunification process, the new government directly transferred the West German (Federal Republic of Germany, FRG) educational system into former East German schools, dramatically changing the way that teachers in those schools went about their jobs.

Over the first postunification decade (1989–1999), education researchers often characterized the change process quite differently. Some saw what was happening in the five new eastern German states as a "laboratory of large-scale educational and social change" (Weiler, Mintrop, & Fuhrmann, 1996, p. 1), or "a (great) transformation experiment" (Döbert, 1998, p. 4). Others regarded the educational change process less positively, describing what they saw as a "culture of dominance" (Händle, 1997, p. 391, citing Rommelspacher, 1995) and even a new kind of colonization (Dümcke & Vilmar, 1994). Toward the end of the decade, however, some researchers began to question the colonization hypothesis, arguing that some educational changes in the New Federal States were consistent with pre-reunification reform ideas and, thus, had not been forced from outside after all (Pritchard, 2002).

Although the effects of the educational transfer raise many questions for researchers and historians, perhaps the most central concern for the East German teachers was how they would or would not continue in their role as "social" educators. This difference for GDR teachers between what the Germans call *Bildung* (emphasis on literacy and academic education) and *Erziehung* (personal and social development) became a prominent theme in a study conducted in four secondary schools in eastern Berlin, and it will be the basis for this chapter.

THE STUDY

The fieldwork and collection of qualitative data took place between March 1998 and October 1999. During this time, I interviewed principals, administrators, and 50 teachers in four different school types in an eastern Berlin inner-city district. Concurrently, the school data were triangulated with education policy-maker interviews at the federal, state, and district levels; with analysis of relevant literature on education in the divided Germanys; and with analysis of the educational discussions among politicians and the media in the post-reunification period. (For more detailed information on the four case studies, see Streitwieser, 2000b.) At the conclusion of the field research, a survey was administered to further probe issues specific to the new educational requirements for secondary school teachers.

The general aim of the research was to study a sample of teachers in mid-career at the time of the reunification and learn how they managed over the following decade to come to terms with unplanned and in some cases undesired professional shift. More narrowly, the case studies considered how the teachers dealt with the West German education system at the local level and how they adapted their GDR training and experiences to work within that new system.

The West German system represented not only a change in educational philosophy from Marxist-Leninist-inspired education in the East, but also a radical change in the setup and structure of schooling. Primary and secondary education in the GDR included 10 years of a mandatory comprehensive "polytechnic" school (*Polytechnische Oberschule*), followed by either the highly selective 2-year, college-preparatory extended secondary school (*Erweiterte Oberschule*) or one of several vocational schooling options. The West German system, dating back to before World War II, on the other hand, consisted of a tripartite school structure: college-preparatory *Gymnasium*; intermediate-level *Realschule*; and lower-level *Hauptschule*. In the late 1960s, a comprehensive school, the *Gesamtschule*, also was introduced in the West German system.

THE END OF THE GDR AND THE INTRODUCTION
OF WEST GERMAN SCHOOLING

In the early postunification period, most schoolteachers in East Berlin were fortunate to be spared the large-scale layoffs that quickly began to downsize the remaining professional landscape of eastern Germany. What for many segments of the population came to be regarded as a sudden institutional takeover by West Germany, for the majority of teachers was at first little more than a welcome salary increase and the chance to start over in new schools with new colleagues. These benefits, and the relative comfort that teachers received as newly minted civil servants, came, however, with a wrenching condition: disavowal of their pedagogical training and the belief system that had provided meaning to their cumulative professional experiences as educators thus far.

Immediately following the collapse of the GDR's government and prior to official reunification, the excitement for educational reform and the willingness, especially on the East German side, for change and improvement—rather than complete abandonment of educational ideas and structures—were clearly articulated. The call was loud for critical reflection and a "readiness to change or to conserve as necessary" (Behrendt, Knoop, Mannschatz, Protz, & Sladek, 1991, p. 38). Calls from East to West for an "exchange of methodological experience" and a search for "what is common to both" (Hinke, 1991, p. 92) were unmistakable. However, when the 1991–92 school year began, the West German structure and educational philosophy quickly overran what had existed in the East. The opportunity to collaborate with a reform-minded community of intellectuals in East Germany was missed. A stubborn reliance on an entrenched yet proud educational tradition in the West—despite years of heated reform debate—overrode the possibility that positive elements of GDR education would be recognized in a discredited and politically tainted East. For West German education policy makers, the belief in their own system overrode any positive aspects of GDR education, where the larger societal symbols of political repression and a backward infrastructure were enough to dismiss the education system out of hand.

Following this development, the earliest predictions at the beginning of the decade were that with the help of re-education courses over the ensuing years, teachers who so far had been "loyal executors of the hitherto official doctrines" (Mitter, 1992, p. 51) gradually would adjust to West German schooling. At the same time, some early research on teachers right after the implementation of the new school system anticipated a difficult transformation and one that would require time (Rust & Rust, 1995).

For many teachers, however, when the hope was dashed of working together with West German educators to create a different and perhaps stronger school system in the new Germany, the initial excitement gave way to disappointment and resignation (Tillman, 1996). By mid-decade, research found teachers still uncomfortable about discussing their past roles in the East German schooling apparatus and continuing to reinforce the old authority patterns (Mintrop, 1996). Although teachers clearly were making efforts to adjust to the new demands, many were found still to "stress continuity over change with regard to their values and teaching styles" (Weiler, Mintrop, & Fuhrmann, 1996, p. 110). By decade's end, the research continued to detect this continuity of educational "notions and behavior" as GDR schooling and teachers were seen still falling back on the "familiar and accustomed" (Döbert, 1998, p. 14).

With the East's quickly unraveling social fabric and demands on teachers to change so profoundly over the course of the decade, this reliance on past experiences should not have been so surprising. However, not all of these coping behaviors simply occurred subconsciously or as a natural reaction. The research discussed in this chapter found that, to subvert their losses and preserve some of their identity as educators, some teachers in the change process also chose deliberately to continue practicing what they regarded as sound and effective pedagogy from the former system. Although officially few aspects of GDR education were adopted by the West, some teachers carried on—or, to be more exact, transferred over—aspects of the old pedagogy and methodology that they felt addressed the deficiencies they saw in the new system.

Over the post-*Wende* decade (1989–1999), conforming to a radically different and formerly ideologically opposed system left many East Germans feeling nostalgic for the past and sometimes resistant to change (Berdahl, 1999). For many teachers, the massive and sudden changes in the educational landscape were tantamount to a devastating professional, and in some cases even personal, betrayal. Some who looked back critically at the former education system began to feel duped by its inconsistencies and falsities. Had they really just been pawns of the state? Had they as teachers really exercised excessive control over their students' private lives? At the same time, they also began to realize how their association with a rigid and conformist education system might jeopardize any chances to serve as positive agents for reform in the new system.

Despite an outwardly chilly reception to their ideas and experiences (Streitwieser, 2000a), when asked, some of the positive attributes about the school system that former GDR teachers pointed out included:

- Untracked, comprehensive schooling in grades 1–10 that provided a general education for children of all ability levels in the same schools and class groups (although mathematics and sciences were heavily emphasized over arts and the humanities).
- Relatively generous state funding for education that allowed more schools to be built, greater numbers of teachers to be trained and hired, and class sizes to remain comparatively small. Funding also provided for more extracurricular activities and class outings aimed at bringing about closer student–teacher relations and making school feel like a community.
- A national, centralized curriculum with standardized examinations and textbooks systematically structured to each year of instruction from one grade level to the next. The centralized system facilitated school and teacher accountability and provided a standard upon which to comparatively assess achievement throughout the country. (It must be noted, however, that the highly prescriptive teacher guides also created a notoriously rigid curriculum that left virtually no room for the instructor's own creativity and innovation.)
- Finally, in the GDR particular emphasis was placed on socially training young people to the norms of behavior that were expected in East German public and private life. To that end, teachers were charged with the responsibility to mold the "socialist personality" and to help guide students into finding their proper place as productive members of society. This charge gave teachers wide powers to visit students in their homes or even to inform parents' employers if there were problems with their child at school. By the same token, it also gave teachers time and the resources to come to know their students on not only an academic but also a deeper personal level. (This level of teacher power sometimes has been heavily criticized since 1989 by some former East Germans and Western critics alike.) While the role of *Bildung* was given top priority on paper, the emphasis on *Erziehung* also played an inordinately important role (Händle & Streitwieser, 2002).

INDICATORS IN THE GERMAN EDUCATIONAL TRANSITION: *BILDUNG* AND *ERZIEHUNG*

In an atmosphere of often open hostility by some Germans toward the GDR and its legacy in the aftermath of the collapse of the GDR, this study found that teachers quickly were given the impression that their training and experiences were negligible in the new system. However, most teachers were struggling to meet their new challenges and responsibilities head on. In the interviews conducted in this study, teachers continually noted how *Bildung* and *Erziehung* were two particularly salient notions that were directly challenged by the change process and required some re-evaluation.

Bildung and *Erziehung* are two concepts that have different and important meanings in German. *Bildung* is educational training in the formal, academic sense as defined by the school curriculum, while *Erziehung* is the inculcation of societal rules, norms, and expectations passed on to students by teachers, parents, and the community. Most definitions of the terms, when translated into English, amorphously use the word *education* to evoke both academic education and the teaching of social values interchangeably. In fact, there are important differences in meaning between the terms.

Recognizing the importance these two educational concepts played in the transition process, it becomes easier to understand some of the difficulties that East German teachers experienced throughout the decade. In the changeover from one system to the other, GDR teachers came to realize that the new system forced them to re-evaluate their understanding of what each of these educational notions meant to them, and how each idea was intended to function under the changed political and social system. The very different interpretations that the GDR and FRG attributed to each concept required a definite break between how each side interpreted education. More important even than this break between the old and the new, was the more likely possibility that no matter how subtle, former GDR teachers eventually might blend, or hybridize, a way of thinking about pedagogy and methodology that eventually could combine aspects of both experiences. If this is a possibility, then how has one set of former GDR teachers, out of habit but also consciously, tried to meld their *Bildung* and *Erziehung* ideals from the old system into the new one?

HYBRIDIZING *BILDUNG UND ERZIEHUNG*

Officially, GDR education was completely dismissed. However, unofficially and as manifested in the training and experiences of East German teachers, it remained very much present. Only with time could the "new" slate in the eastern states possibly take on a West German hue. Even more likely, however, was that the new slate would come to represent an amalgam of both educational ideals as embodied in the thousands of teachers rapidly gaining experience in another system. Linda Darling-Hammond (1994) argues that teachers need to make judgments not following "standardized instructional packages," but based on their knowledge about pedagogical theory and how to develop the learning capacities of children.

Teachers, she argues, constantly need to formulate curriculum and assessment according to the learning abilities and backgrounds that their students bring with them to school.

In *Tinkering Toward Utopia* (1995), David Tyack and Larry Cuban argue for teachers to take the reforms introduced into their schools and "create hybrids suited to their context" (p. 83), rather than just blindly adapting mandates from outside without working to fit them into their local situations. Teachers cannot help but adapt what comes in from the outside to fit their schools in a way that makes sense to them at the ground level. In this way, the process that former East German educators went through in struggling with change from the West and using what Tyack and Cuban call their "wisdom of practice" (p. 83) should be regarded not only as a positive and appropriate coping behavior, but also as a natural, understandable, and in most cases unavoidable reaction. What critics of GDR teachers decried as dangerous would have been more rationally viewed as understandable and transitory behavior in the ongoing assimilation process.

In the East German socialist education system, the process of *Bildung* and *Erziehung* was not as subtle as the dictionary definitions above imply. For the East German educator, the inseparability of these two concepts was a key factor in the formation of the "socialist personality." Many former East German teachers interviewed in this study explained that their training to become loyal to and believe in the virtues of socialism was deliberately overt. The impression made on many teachers was that formal academics came second to teaching their students how to become active and political citizens. For example, in recommending a student for higher-level study at the *Erweiterte Oberschule*, academic achievement and intellectual promise were not always enough; the political loyalties of the candidate and his or her relatives also could matter.

In the West German system, on the other hand, the deliberate separation of these ideas was always an important assurance that schooling would serve a pluralistic purpose. Therefore, while in the East teachers linked academic preparation with social formation in school and through satellite political organizations like the Free German Youth (the youth organization of the GDR's ruling party, the Socialist Unity Party),[1] in the West teachers were required to carry out their educational duties while leaving social and political training as a parental responsibility. In this way, each system starkly defined itself by how it interpreted the meaning, scope, and practice of *Bildung* and *Erziehung*.

After the *Wende* of 1989, the great differences between how former GDR teachers regarded their duties and obligations in the East versus what was expected of them in the West did not disappear overnight. Contrary to what many dismayed observers expected early on, mentality differences and work habits of GDR educators were slow to change. To understand how difficult this required change must have been, it is necessary to understand exactly how *Bildung* and *Erziehung* were understood in the GDR.

To explain how some teachers felt they should continue *Bildung* and *Erziehung* as they understood the concepts before, and what influence this had on their work after the Wall fell, it is instructive to re-examine the introductory section of the East German Council of Ministers' *Law on the Unitary Socialist Education System of the German Democratic Republic*. The 1971 publication date of this document was deliberately selected to reflect the school laws as they existed at the time when most of the teachers interviewed in this study received their teacher training.

> (5.4) Secondary school students, apprentices and university students are to be taught a thorough understanding of the teachings of Marxism-Leninism. They are to recognize the laws of nature, of society and of human thought and to utilize them properly in becoming convinced Socialists. In this way they are to be given the tools to understand the purpose of life in our time and to think, feel and act as Socialists.
> (5.5) The process of educating and socially training, as well as structuring the lives of secondary school students, apprentices and university students is to function in and through the collective, such that they are taught to act as moral and aware citizens of the state. They are to be made to understand that a willingness to help others, friendliness, politeness and an obliging stance toward others, respect of their parents and elders as well as honest and clean relations between the sexes are all characteristics of the Socialist Personality. (Council of Ministers of the GDR, 1971, pp. 13, 32ff, translation of author)

Most important in points 5.4 and 5.5 is the clear statement of the *legally bound uniformity* of education and social training as a single concept beholden to the state.

In unified Berlin's school law, the section on the *Duties of the Teacher* discusses education and social training as a striking counterstatement to the earlier GDR publication.

> Social training implies that while the teacher may address questions that fall outside the curriculum, it is the curriculum that is always to be given top priority. The right of parents to socially train their children is to be respected. The duty of socially training students is only to occur within the realm of school. [Teachers should] restrain themselves from addressing political questions. Any one-sided influence by the teacher toward his students on matters that fall outside of the stated educational goals is discouraged, according to paragraph 2. The goal is the development of students' individual abilities to think for themselves, not the missionary instruction of the teacher's opinions.

While the teacher retains the right to express his own opinions in the classroom, paragraph 2 binds him to the plurality of the curriculum. (Berlin House of Parliament, 1992, p. 21ff, translation of author)

The contrasting version of education and social training in the "new" Berlin clearly states the *legally bound separation* of education and social training.

In the West German education system that East German teachers joined, quick adjustments were necessary for very different conceptions of what academic training and social training required. Too often since 1989, the function of the GDR educator as not only an "academic worker" but also a "social worker" has been simplified to that of only "indoctrinator." In many cases, former GDR teachers made commitments to closer and more meaningful relations with students, which since have been discredited as leftover, politically motivated bad habits. Large differences in understanding developed over the 1990s between how East teachers were regarded and what more factually explains some of their work habits and supporting belief systems.

IN THEIR OWN WORDS

At the end of the field study (Spring 1999) I administered a survey to 50 teachers (from four schools in one district of eastern Berlin). The results of the survey, discussed below, illustrate that former GDR teachers' understandings of *Bildung* and *Erziehung* resonate with some important conceptions of education they held in socialist times.

The survey asked teachers to define and explain the concepts of *Bildung* and *Erziehung* as they were in the GDR and as they are now. The purposes of the survey were to (1) see how teachers would define each concept, (2) give them the opportunity to explain each concept as they learned it in the GDR, and (3) find out if their experiences in the post-reunification decade had altered these definitions. Most important, the survey aimed to learn the extent to which teachers would argue for a transfer of each GDR-inspired definition into the new system and if these definitions had changed as a direct result of working in the new system.

The survey had a response rate of 62%, and the open-ended items yielded detailed written comments. The responses indicated how important teachers felt it was to explain their views on each concept and to discuss their interpretations as influenced by the *Wende*.

While the ways in which respondents worded their definitions of *Bildung* and *Erziehung* varied slightly, in the aggregate they explained each concept as follows:

- *Bildung*: Providing for and developing in young people all-round general education and knowledge in as many subject areas of the general curriculum as possible.
- *Erziehung*: Teaching young people basic humanistic, moral, and ethical norms of behavior and developing in them a sense of responsibility and a positive attitude toward work and life in a democratic society.

Respondents' written comments in the open-ended items argued strongly that *Bildung* and *Erziehung* should remain inseparable under the West German education system. Importantly, the definitions left out political references for social training, although a number of respondents wrote passionately about the stark political differences between the GDR and the FRG and their impact on education. Respondents were nearly unanimous in arguing for the importance of teachers to be both education workers (*Bildungsarbeiter*) dedicated to academic training, and social workers (*Erziehungsarbeiter*) dedicated to teaching social values. As one teacher explained, "There is no such thing as education without social training; social training without education is like animal training."

In the survey, 85% of the respondents recalled that during the GDR they agreed with the school laws that explained *Bildung* and *Erziehung* as one concept. Ninety-six percent of the respondents indicated that they still regarded both concepts as one and did not, in fact, believe that the new system could de-emphasize *Erziehung* over *Bildung*. They felt, however, that the new system made practicing both ideas in equal measure difficult. As one teacher explained:

> *Bildung* and *Erziehung* are only in official terms separate concepts. In actual teaching they are impossible to separate. Officially the state emphasizes social training but in reality it prevents it in that it makes the teaching of norms more difficult.

Slightly over half the respondents, 51.5%, did not feel that the West German school system necessarily forced the separation of social and educational work. Rather, they felt that in a capitalist system—where they argued money is the primary determinant of how decisions are made—*Erziehung* had become an empty concept devoid of its former meaning. Eighty-two percent of the respondents argued that both concepts still must be given equal weight under today's school system, despite the fact that Berlin's school law clearly states that "the curriculum is always to be given top priority." The sentiments expressed by many of those in the study who supported a combination of *Bildung* and *Erziehung* are perhaps best explained by the following comment:

Educational training *and* social training is necessary in order to bring the best potential of children and young people to fruition. Educational training—the acquisition of knowledge and ability—is necessary for a proper social training, and social training is necessary so that the acquisition of knowledge and ability can be used in a humane, responsible way.

The majority of teachers lamented that the demands and requirements of the new selective school system undervalued and made social work exceedingly difficult when it was urgently needed now more than ever. With greater social problems among students and heavier demands on teachers' time, many respondents argued that school was becoming increasingly limited in what it realistically could achieve. In this process, students were ending up as the ultimate victims. This fact left many teachers feeling unsatisfied and frustrated.

Today teachers are increasingly overloaded with bureaucratic responsibilities so that the actual goal of schooling—social training and educational training—comes up short. . . . By constantly cutting back on the number of teachers while requiring more work from those already employed and allowing politicians to create a negative perception of teachers, our ability to work successfully in a social sense is reduced. It is in this kind of atmosphere that parents have also begun to question the competence of teachers more than they used to. . . . The current political situation in Germany— characterized by selfishness, corruption, and the unequal distribution of tax money in favor of the rich—has had a negative impact on the social training of young people and adults. In such a context it is difficult to instill positive and lasting moral influences.

Teachers in the aggregate were left with the realization that how they decided to work as educators now was very much an individual and personal decision and no longer largely determined by, or of great interest to, the state. As one teacher explained:

I do not believe that that the FRG has any developed conceptions about *Bildung* and *Erziehung*. At best there is a general consensus in society about the importance of certain aspects of *Bildung* and *Erziehung*. But here, too, there are considerable differences between what the business sector expects and what the educational sector can provide. Selections made in terms of academic materials and decisions influencing social training lie mostly in the hands and judgments of each individual teacher.

The field-study data show teachers' intentions of continuing in the post-reunification decade the practice of two positive educational notions they valued in the GDR and, as a result, decided to transfer into the new system. However, on a more general level, there is a chasm today between teachers who uphold the GDR's educational philosophy of educating *and* also socially training their students, and those who regard social education now as more of a parental responsibility. Those who favor a combined approach believe that both concepts practiced together positively defined their own educational experiences. As such, they feel an obligation to carry on this form of teaching, regardless of the political system in which they find themselves. On the other hand, those who argue for separation certainly may still be committed to engaged teaching, but also want to confine their work to the classroom and not interfere in what they now consider to be personal and no longer the state's domain.

One important limitation of this study is the issue of the selective memory of the respondents. Asking someone to not only reach back a decade into their memories, but also to recall their feelings on intangible notions like *Bildung* and *Erziehung*, and to do so in a vastly different political and social situation, invites any number of potential biases that must be acknowledged.

CONCLUSION

A poster on several kiosks around Berlin in the early days after the fall of the Wall symbolized the inevitable: Below a caption reading, "Thy will be done" [German: *Dein Wille Geschehe*], juxtaposed images from each country's flag showed the large West German eagle swooping down to clutch the small leafy East German wreath in its mighty claws. Many teachers who began the 1990s anticipating a new Germany and an educational landscape changed for the better were left at the end of the decade with a sense of loss and disappointment. Most of the teachers in this study felt that, in retrospect, the period between 1989 and 1991 represented lost opportunities for reform and squandered chances for creating better secondary education in a unified Germany. This realization not only made the first post-*Wende* decade less pedagogically enriching for them than it could have been, but also diminished the potentially positive contributions many teachers initially hoped to make in the new system.

Although many teachers in this study expressed the wish that things would have turned out differently, how they dealt with their feelings of disappointment differed: Some became bitter and resigned; some were hopeful but cautious; and still others were ambitious and proactive. The changed responsibility of schooling in the West German system brought into sharp focus questions that now lay at the heart of every teacher's adjustment and outlook: What is my responsibility in terms of the job, what is my responsibility as an educator, and how should I balance them?

Through retaining what teachers regard as important educational ideals about *Bildung* and *Erziehung* from the GDR and hybridizing these with the *Lehr- und Lernfreiheit* (pedagogical freedoms) they now have in the new system, a subtle reform process is taking place in certain pockets of German education. However, because this reform is unofficial and occurring only through the work of certain teachers in certain schools—rather than as an official program launched by policy makers—it represents the possibility for change as shaped by the visions and ideas of the former East German teachers themselves, even if in modest numbers, in their own classroom practices, and on a small scale. Having by now gained training and experience in both of the German education systems of the past half century, these educators have taken their own initiative to formulate, combine, and remake education as they see it best suited for the future of German education as a whole.

Whereas West German teachers had stability and security over the entire post-World War II period and were only minimally affected by reunification, East German teachers spent the 1990s learning to cope within an entirely new system. As I have argued in previous research (Streitwieser, 2000b), with their dual perspective from experience in two systems, the change process fresh in their minds, and a willingness to act as agents of change in a role denied to them in 1989–1991, a case can be made that East German teachers are likely to be more reform-minded than their western German colleagues. If more of the positive educational traditions practiced by former GDR teachers become overt and accepted by education policy makers over time, it is possible that some aspects of the GDR educational experience initially shunned after the *Wende* eventually will be accepted as originating from the East after all.

While tensions over interpretations of *Bildung* and *Erziehung* are not new in German educational philosophy and their discussion is not in its own right unique to the post-reunification period, the views and experiences brought by East German teachers into the West German school system have triggered a debate about the purpose of education that has revitalized the *Bildung und Erziehung* discussion in an exciting and interesting way.

NOTE

1. As the socialist youth organization of the GDR's ruling party, the Socialist Unity Party (Sozialistische Einheitspartei), the Free German Youth (Freie Deutsche Jugend) by the mid-1980s had membership numbers totaling 75% of the youth population (ages 14–25). Broadly, the goals of the organization were to influence the political and ideological behavior of young people in the GDR through the teachings of Marxism-Leninism.

REFERENCES

Behrendt, W., Knoop, J., Mannschatz, E., Protz, S., & Sladek, H. (1991). Discussion of school and educational reform: Secondary education in renascent GDR society. *European Education, 23*, 37–50.

Berdahl, D. (1999). "(N)ostalgie" for the present: Memory, longing, and East German things. *Ethnos, 64*, 192–211.

Berlin House of Parliament. (1992). Law on the educational constitution for schools in Berlin. Reprinted in *My rights in schools: A guide for students, parents and teachers. The law on the educational constitution with recommendations, explanations and addresses* (pp. 21ff). Berlin: House of Parliament.

Council of Ministers. (1971). *Law on the unitary socialist education system of the German Democratic Republic* (pp. 13–17, 32ff). Berlin: Council of Ministers.

Darling-Hammond, L. (1994). Reframing the school reform agenda: Developing capacity for school transformation. In L. Darling-Hammond, A. Lieberman, D. Wood, & B. Falk (Eds.), *Transforming school reform: Policies and practices for democratic schools* (pp. 3–18). New York: NCREST.

Döbert, H. (1998, June). *Schools in change: Outcomes of transformation research in Germany*. Paper presented at the meeting of the World Council of Comparative Education Societies, Cape Town, South Africa.

Dümcke, W., & Vilmar, F. (1994). *Kolonialisierung der DDR* [Colonization of the GDR]. Münster, Germany: Agenda.

Händle, C. (1997). Teachers in the transformation of the school system in German unification. In B. J. Biddle, T. L. Good, & I. F. Goodson (Eds.), *International handbook of teachers and teaching* (pp. 353–410). Dordrecht, Netherlands: Kluwer.

Händle, C., & Streitwieser, B. (2002). *Integrative Traditionen in der Sekundarstufe? Porträts von vier Ostberliner Schulen* [Integrative traditions at the secondary school level? Portraits of four schools in East Berlin]. Hamburg, Germany: Verlag Dr. Kova.

Hinke, B. (1991). A challenge: Confrontation or encounter between the educational systems of East and West? *European Education, 23*, 74–96.

Mintrop, H. (1996). Teachers and changing authority patterns in eastern German schools. *Comparative Education Review, 40*, 359–376.

Mitter, W. (1992). Educational adjustments and perspectives in a united Germany. *Comparative Education, 28*, 45–52.

Pritchard, R. M. O. (2002). Was East German education a victim of West German "colonisation" after unification? *Compare, 32,* 47–59.

Rommelspacher, B. (1995). *Dominanzkultur* [Culture of dominance]. Berlin: Orlanda.

Rust, V., & Rust, D. (1995). *The unification of German education.* New York: Garland.

Streitwieser, B. (2000a). Memory and judgment: How East Berlin schools and teachers have been regarded in the post-reunification decade. In D. Phillips (Ed.), *Oxford studies in comparative education* (pp. 57–80). Oxford: Symposium Books.

Streitwieser, B. (2000b). *Negotiating transformation: East Berlin teachers in the post-unification decade.* Unpublished doctoral dissertation, Columbia University, New York.

Tillmann, K.-J. (1996). *Von der Kontinuität, die nicht auffällt—Das ostdeutsche Schulsystem im Übergang von der DDR zur BRD* [The unnoticeable continuity: The East German school system in transition from the GDR to the FDR]. In W. Melzer & U. Sandfuchs (Eds.), *Schulreform in der Mitte der 90er Jahre* (pp. 13–22). Opladen, Germany: Leske & Budrich.

Tyack, D., & Cuban, L. (1995). *Tinkering toward utopia: A century of public school reform.* Cambridge, MA: Harvard University Press.

Weiler, H. N., Mintrop, H., & Fuhrmann, E. (1996). *Educational change and social transformation: Teachers, schools and universities in eastern Germany.* London: Falmer.

Chapter 8

The Politics of Constructing Scientific Knowledge: Lysenkoism in Poland

William deJong-Lambert

In 1948, Professor Stanisław Skowron, of the Academy of Medicine in Cracow, frantically searched stores in the city to buy every single copy of his own recently published book on genetics (Bikont & Zagórski, 1998). A week earlier, on August 7, at the Lenin All-Union Academy of Agricultural Sciences in Moscow, a speech had been given by a Soviet biologist, Trofim D. Lysenko, in which he declared that genetics was Western, imperialist science, created by servants of Wall Street to justify the injustices of capitalism according to natural processes. Lysenko insisted that "fascist distorters of Darwinism" had developed their erroneous gene theory simply because they didn't understand how heredity actually functioned, and sought to reinforce social inequality through notions such as "survival of the fittest" (Amsterdamski, 1989, p. 14). Lysenko himself articulated his own theory, "Michurinism,"[1] which insisted that through the inheritance of acquired characteristics, any species could effectively be "taught" to survive in any environment, and argued for the necessity of science to serve the needs of the working class. The outcome was a ban on genetic research in the Eastern Bloc that would exist in Poland until the late 1950s.

The fact that Lysenko's speech had been edited by Iosif Stalin (Rossiyanov, 2001) was evidence of the degree to which the natural sciences— as much as every other facet of Soviet society and culture—were required to play a part in the construction of a communist utopia (David-Fox &

Péteri, 2000). Meanwhile, the paranoia of Polish academics, such as Stanisław Skowron, is evidence of a recognition in Poland that, by the late 1940s, the social, artistic, and scientific implications of Marxism-Leninism were to be as central to the consolidation of power by the Communist Party in their country as they had been in other "People's Democracies" and the Soviet Union.

In 1949, an academic conference was organized by the Polish Society of Marxist Biologists and the editors of *Nowe Drogi* ("New Ways"—the principal theoretical journal of the Polish Communist Party), to introduce Michurinism as the only acceptable approach to the study of evolutionary biology in Poland. During the same year, numerous other conferences were held, including the National Party Meeting of Architects and the Polish Writers' Union, which served the purpose of establishing Party control over various disciplines. Thus, we see how the infiltration of the academic community was part of a general process by which every facet of Polish society was forced into the Party monopoly on power, as managed from Moscow.

The notion of a revolutionary transformation of capitalist society, according to formulas grounded in the natural sciences, was a fundamental characteristic of Stalinization, and Lysenko's Michurinist theory of evolutionary biology became the primary model of this "transformist" thinking. In 1949, the Stalin regime also produced the *Stalin Plan for the Transformation of Nature*, which described the conversion of Russia into a "blooming garden" through a process of irrigation and forestation (Rigby, 1966, p. 58). This plan, closely linked with industrial schemes designed to achieve technological parity with the West, signaled the formal integration of the Lysenkoist program into official Soviet policy. Stalin chose to support Lysenko because his theory provided a scientifically rational description of evolutionary processes in the natural world in Marxist-Leninist terms. Lysenko, meanwhile, deliberately formulated his theory in the requisite language of Marxism-Leninism to achieve the support necessary to replace genetics with Michurinism. Thus, we see how scientific and political goals may coincide in the context of a theory whose content was dictated by a social philosophy that enlisted the language of "objective" science to represent its own rationality.

The theory of self-referential systems provides further insight into this process. Social systems typically operate according to internal references. However, in moments of crisis or as part of a project of instituting reform, references may be sought in systems existing externally, understood to be endowed with the necessary authority to enact change. Luhmann and Schorr (1979) describe references to principles of scientific rationality as an "external authority" according to which reforms may be justified. However, the case of Lysenkoism provides us with an example of how competing scientific theories may make references to political authority in order to provoke a "paradigm shift" (Kuhn, 1962). Lysenko used the terminology necessary to acquire the political authority he required to replace genetics by defining a scientific quandary in social and political terms.

The degree to which Lysenko's success was a product of influences external to the scientific community has made Lysenkoism one of the most frequently cited examples of the negative effect of communist totalitarianism upon scientific development (Graham, 1998). However, it is important to recognize that the influence of Marxism did allow for the understanding that science, like every other discipline, is socially and politically determined. This same notion received its first formal treatment outside of the Eastern Bloc nearly 15 years later, after Lysenko established his theoretical monopoly in the Soviet Union. Therefore, although we may criticize Lysenkoism as a circumvention of academic channels to promote a scientific theory, we must acknowledge that it did allow for a more sophisticated conception of the relationship between the social, political, and scientific, well before this same conclusion was reached in the democratic West.

This is in no way to insist that Lysenko's role in the history of evolutionary biology necessarily conforms to Kuhn's definition of a paradigm shift, particularly as even the possibility that Darwinism may be so described is by no means definite (Greene, 1981). What I am pointing out, however, is that the notion that scientific knowledge is created, the product of a process, to a certain reductive degree no different from the production of music or steel, was apparent in the Soviet Union decades before Kuhn published *The Structure of Scientific Revolutions* (1962). Kuhn's work represents the first attempt, philosophically, to describe the process by which scientific knowledge is constructed (Golinski, 1998; Greene, 1981); however, if we account for what was taking place in the Soviet Union during the Stalinist period, we see evidence of an as yet unrecognized precursor.

THE RISE OF TROFIM DENISOVICH LYSENKO

To understand Lysenko's success it is necessary to take into account the social and political climate within the Soviet Union during the Stalinist era. Lysenko fit the model of the "proletarian intelligentsia," which the regime sought to establish as part of the belief that knowledge and scientific advancement should serve the needs of the working class, thus wresting Russia from "her inveterate backwardness" (Malia, 1994, p. 186). The first mention of Lysenko by the Soviet press, in the September 7, 1927, issue of *Pravda*, evinces this notion of communal, peasant simplicity triumphing over isolated bourgeois intellect.

> Stingy of words and insignificant of face is he; all one remembers is his sullen look creeping along the earth as if, at very least, he were ready to do someone in. Only once did this barefoot scientist let a smile pass, and that was at mention of Poltava cherry dumplings with sugar and sour cream. . . . The barefoot Professor Lysenko now has followers, pupils, an experimental field. He is visited in the winter by agronomic luminaries who stand before the green fields of the experiment station, gratefully shaking his hand. (Medvedev, 1969, p. 12)

The disastrous and deadly results of collectivization in the first Five Year Plan, as well as a dispute between Lamarckists and geneticists over how best to describe evolution in terms of Marxism-Leninism, frame the context in which Lysenko began his career. Jean Baptiste Lamarck was a scientist working in France in the late eighteenth and early nineteenth centuries, famous for overemphasizing the influence of the external environment on the internal development of the living organism. Well-known examples of mistaken notions attributed to Lamarck include the idea that the elongated neck of the giraffe is the result of repeated stretching to eat the leaves from trees, and that snakes lost their legs because they preferred to slither along the ground (Barthélemy-Madaule, 1982; Bowler, 1983). However, it's important to keep in mind that Lamarck did have an important influence on Darwin with reference to the idea that change in the natural world, rather than being the result of miraculous intervention, could be understood in terms of natural laws. Although Lamarck's ideas had long been discredited, Lamarckists in the Soviet Union cited Engels's theoretical study of the role of work in the evolution of ape into man, based on the transmissibility of characteristics through food and exercise (Medvedev, 1969). This fallacy concerning the "inheritance of acquired characteristics" came to be the primary academic criticism of Lysenko's work, within the more general condemnation concerning his manipulation of the Stalinist totalitarian system to have those who disagreed with him sent to labor camps and mental hospitals, and even murdered.

Geneticists also sought to give credibility to their work by citing Marx and Lenin; however, they were hindered by the fact that Lysenko proved more successful in gaining Stalin's support, in large part because much of the work being done in genetics at that time was taking place in the laboratory, with little apparent utility. The focus of research among geneticists was a fruit fly, *drosophila melanogaster*, which later would provide the information for a number of important innovations in agriculture, such as hybrid corn (Graham, 1998). Lysenko, however, aided by the fact that most professional biologists came from bourgeois backgrounds, had great success portraying geneticists as "fly lovers and people haters" (Amsterdamski, 1989, p. 14). When asked what genetics could offer as a scientific approach to deal with the famine produced by brutal collectivization and a string of severe winters, N. I. Vavilov, the leading Soviet geneticist, replied that it would take 10 years to produce varieties of wheat more resistant to frost. Lysenko meanwhile claimed that he had discovered a method, "vernalization," of transforming spring wheat into winter wheat, a solution that could be applied immediately (Bikont & Zagórski, 1998). Lysenko substituted demagoguery for academic debate when providing an explanation for continued shortages even after his methods had been applied.

> Tell me comrades, was there not a class struggle on the vernalization front? In the collective farm there were kulaks and their abettors who kept whispering (and they were not the only ones, every class enemy did) into the peasant's ears. . . . This is the way it was, such were the whispers, such were the kulak and saboteur deceptions, when, instead of helping collective farmers, they did their destructive business both in the scientific world and out of it; a class enemy is always an enemy whether he is a scientist or not. (Medvedev, 1969, p. 17)

This speech, given at the Second All-Union Conference of Collective Shock Workers, was attended by Stalin, who at the conclusion applauded: "Bravo Comrade Lysenko, Bravo!" (Bikont & Zagórski, 1998, p. 13). By this time geneticists were beginning to lose their jobs, be sent to the gulag, or simply disappear (Huxley, 1949). As for Vavilov, he was arrested in 1940 and sentenced to death, and died 2 years later in a prison camp in northeast Siberia (Huxley, 1949). It was later revealed that the director of the All-Union Agricultural Institute, appointed by Lysenko, was working for the NKVD (predecessor to the KGB) and had conducted an investigation against Vavilov (Amsterdamski, 1989).

World War II temporarily interrupted the dispute between the geneticists and the followers of Lysenko, but the controversy was revived quickly as the ideological divide between East and West deepened after World War II. The conference held at the Lenin All-Union Academy of Agricultural Sciences in 1948, from July 31 to August 7, became the model for various other ideological discussions in scholarly disciplines, meant to bring them under the control of the Party (Kojevnikov, 2000). Frequently invoking the names of scientists whose work had been fundamental in the development of genetics,[2] Lysenko and his followers declared:

Bourgeois genetics has become the fashionable "science" abroad, propagandizing "eugenics" and race politics. Weismannist (Mendelist-Morganist) genetics is a spawn of bourgeois society, which finds the recognition of the theory of development unprofitable because, from it, in connection with social phenomena, stems the inevitability of collapse of the bourgeoisie. . . . This is why this pseudoscience is such a useful tool in Hitler's hands for the promulgation of his monstrous racist theory. (Medvedev, 1969, pp. 117–118)

On the last day of the conference Lysenko announced that he had the backing of the Central Committee of the Communist Party, as well as that of Stalin himself. The geneticists present at the conference were forced to renounce their convictions and engage in self-criticism. Some found the situation to be more than they could bear. Dr. Sabinin, a professor of plant physiology at Moscow University, and an early supporter of Lysenko's, who only recently had come to recognize him as a charlatan, shot himself.

Meanwhile, the personality cult surrounding Lysenko grew. His portrait was hung in scientific institutions, stores sold busts and reliefs of his image, and in some cities monuments to him were erected. The repertoire of the Moscow Philharmonic was enhanced with a hymn composed for Lysenko (Medvedev, 1969).

LYSENKO'S MICHURINISM

Unifying Lysenko's ideas into a general "theory" could be criticized as an attempt to apply a false methodology to an "unscrupulous quack" (Brooks, 2000, p. 97; also see Malia, 1994, p. 329). Lysenko's Michurinism was, however, essentially Marxist. Like many of his fellow Romantics, Marx believed that the various sciences and philosophies were part of a totalizing system that ultimately would provide a true image of the universe and man. Marx believed that evolution was teleological, driven by human rationality, and operating according to scientific laws (Marx & Engels, 1964). Lysenko was able to translate the political language of Stalinization into a scientific methodological approach to understanding the natural world.

Lysenko also argued against Darwin's theory of natural selection, the practical result of which was his proposal to plant trees in "clusters" to alter the climate of the dry, southern regions of the Soviet Union. He insisted that the trees would cooperate, rather than compete for light and nourishment (Amsterdamski, 1989, p. 11). In fact he even claimed that the weaker trees would sacrifice themselves for the stronger, thus substituting "survival of the fittest" with the notion of individuals sacrificing themselves for the collective good. It would not be until 1954, after the loss of billions of rubles, that this particular method would be abandoned.

The anticipated consequences of the Lysenko campaign, transferred to the satellite nations, can be seen in the fate of Polish biochemist Jakub Parnas. Parnas was a professor at the University of Lwów (L'viv) before the war, and during the occupation, the Soviets offered him the opportunity to work in Moscow at the Institute of Molecular Biology. He remained in Moscow after the war ended, and his position brought him into contact with Lysenko, whom he had the misfortune of contradicting during a session of the Academy in 1949. After Lysenko stated, *"Gienow niet"* ("Genes do not exist"), Parnas lifted his head from the paper he had been reading and stated, *"Kakoj durak. Gieny suszczestwujut"* ("What an idiot. Genes do exist"). Parnas was arrested the next day and taken to the notorious Lubyanka prison. He was diabetic, and his wife attempted to visit him in prison to bring him his insulin, but she was not allowed. Parnas died shortly thereafter (Bikont & Zagórski, 1998).[3]

THE NEW BIOLOGY: LYSENKOISM IN POLAND

The framework within which one should consider the transfer of Lysenko's Michurinist theory to Poland is determined by the effect of World War II on education in Poland, as well as the nature of the Polish socialist regime and circumstances in which it took power. It is important to note, however, that the resistance of the Polish academic community, or "professorate" (Connelly, 2000), was unique. The Polish Communist Party was never able to infiltrate the universities in Poland to the same extent as in neighboring East Germany and Czechoslovakia. Polish professors proved quite adept at maintaining an atmosphere of relatively free inquiry among one another, and at protecting themselves from the worst excesses of political persecution (Connelly, 2000).

The conference enforcing Lysenko's doctrine among the Polish academic community took place in Warsaw in March 1949. Afterwards a book was produced entitled *O Nowej Genetyce* (*On the New Genetics*), which contained the contributions of Polish academics who had spoken at the conference, giving strong support to Lysenko. One of the participants was Stanisław Skowron, mentioned at the beginning of the chapter. Having removed the published evidence of his background in genetics, Skowron now proved the degree to which he himself had "acquired the necessary characteristics" to survive in the new environment by speaking in support of Lysenko (see Bikont & Zagórski, 1998, p. 13).

The reaction of Polish academics to the "Soviet genetics" was varied. Szczepan Pienizek studied genetics in the West before the war. Like many other biologists in Poland, he was sent to Moscow to become acquainted with Lysenko's work. Although he admitted to having had serious doubts about Lysenko's ideas, he ended up as the director of an agricultural institute north of Warsaw, established for the purpose of conducting Michurinist research. He explained his cooperation with Lysenko by stating, "Propagating his ideas in Poland was my compromise with power. I didn't return to Poland to sit in prison" (Bikont & Zagórski, 1998, p. 13).

Wacław Gajewski may be distinguished as one of the few academics who remained openly and unrepentantly critical of Lysenko. When asked by the Council of the Faculty of Biology at Warsaw University to conform his teaching and research to the new Michurinist doctrine, he refused. When offered as a compromise the option of teaching both the "old" and the "new" genetics, Gajewski responded that this was impossible as they were mutually contradictory. He was therefore forbidden from teaching at all and sent to Moscow to meet Lysenko. As Gajewski (1990) later described it:

> The meeting was quite strange. I was taken into a big office, where along one wall several gentlemen were seated in complete silence. They remained as mute witnesses of my visit until it ended. I have no idea why they were there. Lysenko greeted me with the statement: "If you will not believe in what I am going to say then your visit is pointless."
>
> As he spoke his mouth frothed, his voice became more and more aggressive, even though no one had contradicted him. I sat silently, since any polemics would have been pointless.
>
> Lysenko seemed to pronounce revealed truths, to be possessed like Rasputin, and with the fanaticism of Savonarola to be ready to send his opponents to death on the pyre. He impressed me as having some sort of mental illness, and to believe fanatically in what he was saying without any need to explain such completely unorthodox ideas. (pp. 426–427)

As Gajewski met with Lysenko's assistants at the Academy in Moscow, he encountered an atmosphere reflective of Lysenko's irrationality. The conditions of experimentation allowed for the production of whatever truth was necessary: "I was invited to look at the slides. The microscope preparations shown to me were so poor that, in fact, nothing could be seen. One could imagine whatever one was supposed to see" (p. 427). Despite his open advocacy of "reactionary Mendelism-Morganism," Gajewski was present at numerous conferences on Lysenkoism. A graduate student during the period recalled having him pointed out to her, and although surprised that he didn't look "particularly vicious. . . . I never thought that he ought to be allowed to present his point of view" (Putrament, 1990, p. 440).

EXTERNALIZATION: THE POLITICS
OF SCIENCE AND EDUCATION

Stalin's death on March 5, 1953, set in motion a process that ultimately would be described as the "crisis" of de-Stalinization. An important event in the de-Stalinization process in Poland was a conference held in Warsaw in April, organized by the editors of *Po Prostu* (*Straight Talk*), a magazine whose frank analysis and relatively uncensored coverage were recognized as part of the new political climate. Once again, a book was published based on the conference, in which it was announced that until that time, criticism of Lysenko had taken place only "in corridors," but now "young scientists want to end the pact of silence" (Płudowski, Turski, Kuczyński, & Sroka, 1957, p. 11).

Gajewski soon was allowed to receive a passport and traveled to the United States, Great Britain, and France, where he renewed scholarly contacts and gathered materials on the role of DNA in heredity. The first courses in genetics finally were offered in Poland in 1958, simultaneous with the publication of new textbooks. In some schools, however, the textbooks were not changed until many years later.

The competition between Lysenko and the geneticists was initially a competition between two alternative scientific theories. It was only when Lysenko was able to lay unquestioned claim to the political support of Stalin, that Michurinism could replace genetics as the paradigmatic approach to the study of evolutionary biology. Thus, the case of Lysenkoism provides us with an example of how political ideology may serve as an external referent, determining the development of scientific knowledge.

The degree to which Lysenko's success was a product of influences external to the scientific community has made "Lysenkoism" one of the most frequently cited examples of the notion that scientific knowledge is socially constructed (Graham, 1998). However, as insalubrious as the mutually reinforcing scientific-political referencing may have been in this instance, we must recognize that it enforced an essential understanding that in the Western capitalist system took place only in 1962, with the publication of Thomas Kuhn's *The Structure of Scientific Revolutions* (Golinski, 1998). Kuhn was the first to attempt to describe the process according to which scientific theories are constructed, changed, and developed (Greene, 1981). Of course, this labor- and outcomes-oriented conception of scientific knowledge appeared only well after the Stalinist era in the Soviet Union had concluded.

The irony of this is that once the pressure of the party hierarchy on the scientific community was significantly reduced during the process of de-Stalinization, Soviet historians of science tended to separate the scientific from its social and political context, preferring to emphasize the isolation of its inner logic. And in fact, the legitimate examples of scientific achievement in tsarist Russia, recovered amid the clutter of nationalist absurdities (such as the claim that the radio, electric lighting, the airplane, as well as the parachute, were all invented in Russia [Heller & Nekrich, 1986]), were used as arguments against socioeconomic determinism. If scientific knowledge is indeed socially constructed, then how could it have existed at all in despotic, backward tsarist Russia (Gerovitch, 1998)? Therefore, at exactly the same time as scientists and historians in the West were arriving at the conclusion that scientific development is determined by external factors, this same community in the Soviet Union was, as a reaction to excesses such as Lysenkoism, arriving at the opposite conclusion.

The overt attempt to determine scientific development according to ideology was the logical outgrowth of a perspective from which everything was understood as political. Thus, although the conclusion that scientific knowledge is socially constructed may have been arrived at by different avenues, we may say that evidence of this understanding, as a result of the influence of Marxism-Leninism, was first explicit in the Eastern Bloc. It has been pointed out that the dream of mass utopia, achievable through modernity, was shared by both the East and West during the twentieth century (Buck-Morss, 2000). It is interesting to note how in both instances this pursuit often has been, and continues to be, described simply as "research."

NOTES

1. The term was a reference to Ivan Michurin, an agronomist who was purported to have created several hundred different types of apples through grafting techniques, and was celebrated by the communists as the model of the peasant scientist, working in the fields among the people rather than in the laboratory. Even geneticists referred to themselves as "heirs to Michurin" as a way of gaining credibility.

2. August Weismann, nineteenth-century evolutionist; Gregor Mendel, Austrian monk who did fundamental research in selection and heredity; Thomas Hunt Morgan, who did work on selection, mutation, and adaptation.

3. All translations from sources published in Polish were made by the author, unless otherwise noted.

REFERENCES

Amsterdamski, S. (1989). *O Patologii życia naukowego: Casus T. D. Łysenko* [Pathology in science: The case of T. D. Lysenko]. Warszawa, Poland: Niezależnie Oficynie Wydawnicza.

Barthélemy-Madaule, M. (1982). *Lamarck the mythical precursor.* Cambridge, MA: MIT Press.

Bikont, A., & Zagórski, S. (1998). Burzliwe dzieje, gruszek na wierzbie. [Stormy times, pears on a willow tree]. *Gazeta Wyborcza, Sierpnia 1–2,* 12–15.

Bowler, P. J. (1983). *Evolution: The history of an idea.* Los Angeles: University of California Press.

Brooks, J. (2000). *Thank you Comrade Stalin! Soviet public culture from revolution to cold war.* Princeton, NJ: Princeton University Press.

Buck-Morss, S. (2000). *Dreamworld and catastrophe.* Cambridge, MA: MIT Press.

Connelly, J. (2000). *Captive university: The Sovietization of East German, Czech and Polish education, 1945–1956.* Chapel Hill: University of North Carolina Press.

David-Fox, M., & Péteri, G. (2000). On the origins and demise of the communist academic regime. In M. David-Fox & G. Péteri (Eds.), *Origins, transfers and transformations of the communist academic regime in Russia and Central Europe* (pp. 3–35). Westport, CT: Bergin & Garvey.

Gajewski, W. (1990). Lysenkoism in Poland. *Quarterly Review of Biology, 65,* 423–434.

Gerovitch, S. (1998). Writing history in the present tense: Cold war-era discursive strategies of Soviet historians of science and technology. In C. Simpson (Ed.), *Universities and empire* (pp. 189–228). New York: New Press.

Golinski, J. (1998). *Making natural knowledge: Constructivism and the history of science.* Cambridge: Cambridge University Press.

Graham, L. (1998). *What have we learned about science and technology from the Russian experience?* Stanford: Stanford University Press.

Greene, J. C. (1981). *Science, ideology, and worldview: Essays in the history of evolutionary ideas.* Berkeley: University of California Press.

Heller, M., & Nekrich, A. (1986). *Utopia in power: The history of the Soviet Union from 1917 to the present.* New York: Summit Books.

Huxley, J. (1949). *Soviet genetics and world science.* London: Chatto & Windus.

Kojevnikov, A. (2000). Games of Stalinist democracy: Ideological discussions in Soviet sciences, 1947–'52. In S. Fitzpatrick (Ed.), *Stalinism: New directions* (pp. 142–175). London: Routledge.

Kuhn, T. (1962). *The structure of scientific revolutions.* Chicago: University of Chicago Press.

Luhmann, N., & Schorr, K. E. (1979). *Reflexionsprobleme im Erziehungssystem* [The problem of reflection in educational systems]. Stuttgart, Germany: Klett-Cotta.

Malia, M. (1994). *The Soviet tragedy: A history of socialism in Russia, 1917–1991.* New York: Free Press.

Marx, K., & Engels, F. (1964). *The communist manifesto.* New York: Washington Square Press.

Medvedev, Z. A. (1969). *The rise and fall of T. D. Lysenko.* New York: Columbia University Press.

Płudowski, J., Turski, R., Kuczyński, J., & Sroka, M. (1957). *Bilogia i polityka: Materiały narady biologów zorganizowanej przez "Po prostu"* [Biology and politics: Materials from a meeting of biologists organized by "Po prostu"]. Warszawa, Poland: Książka i Wiedza.

Putrament, A. (1990). How I became a Lysenkoist. *Quarterly Review of Biology, 65,* 435–445.

Rigby, T. H. (1966). *Stalin: Great lives observed.* Englewood Cliffs, NJ: Prentice Hall.

Rossiyanov, K. (2001). *Stalin as Lysenko's editor: Reshaping political discourse in Soviet science.* Retrieved June 15, 2001, from http://www.eserver.org/cyber/stalin.txt.

Chapter 9

The Referential Web: Externalization Beyond Education in Tanzania

Frances Vavrus

Out of the accumulation of relations of cross-system observation and externalization of this kind emerges a web of reciprocal references which takes a life of its own, moving, reinforcing, and dynamizing the worldwide universalization of educational ideas, models, standards, and options for reform.

—Schriewer, 2000, p. 334

One of the most important aspects of comparative education research today involves the process of externalization. Schriewer (1990, 2000, 2002) and Steiner-Khamsi (2002), in particular, have examined how the borrowing of educational models external to a country serves to legitimize controversial changes in the home country. In addition, they have considered how externalization occurs when policy makers use "language from elsewhere" to justify the solutions in the documents they produce.

The goal of this chapter is to analyze the externalization process in the United Republic of Tanzania as it relates to the growth of global interconnections during the past few decades. By examining reciprocal references in different social and economic sectors within Tanzania and across international boundaries, I hope to highlight a form of externalization that is intimately connected to the intensification of global movements of policy actors and ideas. Up to now, the process of externalization has been considered primarily from an international perspective that looks at how educational models and policy language in one state are appropriated by another. However, at a time when supranational institutions are expanding their influence over "national" policy making, especially in the third world, an equally compelling approach to the study of borrowing and lending explores how the language of policy—in education and in other sectors—is externalized without reference to a specific lending country or agency. Thus, I argue that the intensification of global networks in recent years has contributed to the universalization of keywords related to "good" development policy that traverses different social sectors as well as national boundaries (Appadurai, 1996; Held, McGrew, Goldblatt, & Perraton, 1999).

In the pages that follow, I explore this increasingly important form of externalization in Tanzania through an analysis of policies in two critical sectors for social and economic development: education and agriculture. Although the policies under consideration were published by the Tanzanian government, I suggest that they are not solely of the Tanzanian state because they rely on "reciprocal references" that mark the texts as embedded in a "universalized" web of ideas about development problems and solutions in the third world (Schriewer, 2000, p. 334). Instead of framing the analysis as a chronological study of externalization from the World Bank to the Tanzanian government, I prefer to use Bourdieu's spatial metaphor of a field because it permits a reading of these policies in relation to the broader social context of international development, rather than reducing their similarities to a simple correspondence between two institutions (Bourdieu & Wacquant, 1992).

THE POSTCOLONIAL POLICY CONTEXT IN TANZANIA

Since independence from Britain in 1961, the political philosophy of the Tanzanian government has undergone several notable shifts. The first 6 years of the administration of President Julius Nyerere were marked by attempts to develop a capitalist economy, with farming and production for export remaining in private hands (Samoff, 1990). Despite the government's efforts to reduce the multiple disparities left in the wake of colonialism, it was clear by 1967 that the reforms of the first 6 years of independence had left regional, ethnic, and rural–urban inequalities largely intact. Thus, the Nyerere administration announced a critical shift in the country's development philosophy in a policy known as the Arusha Declaration. One of the central features of this policy was the promotion of *ujamaa* ("African socialism" or "familyhood"), a development strategy that included the nationalization of large segments of the industrial sector, the establishment of villages with collective agricultural production, and the provision of free or very inexpensive social services for the populace (Hyden, 1980). Social and economic policy making became highly centralized through the one-party state, even though *ujamaa* was intended to make rural villages the loci of development (Tripp & Swantz, 1996).

Since the early 1980s, Tanzania's socialist development policies have been drastically revised or eliminated (Vavrus, 2003). For a number of reasons, many of the programs for rural communities, implemented as part of *ujamaa*, began to decline significantly a decade or so after their implementation. The government initially blamed external forces for its serious economic woes, including bad weather, increases in oil prices, the war with neighboring Uganda, and unfavorable trade relations with some countries (Rugumisa, 1989). While these were certainly important factors fueling the crisis, there were also internal political and economic problems that the government slowly began to admit. As a result of the growing sense of crisis in the country, the Nyerere administration implemented a modest economic restructuring program in 1981. This was followed in 1986, after the resignation of President Nyerere in 1985, by an Economic Recovery Programme (ERP) designed by the World Bank Consultative Group and the government of the new president, Ali Hassan Mwinyi (Shao, 1992).

The ERP provides the foundation for current macroeconomic reform efforts in Tanzania. These structural adjustment policies, or SAPs, include trade liberalization, cost sharing for social services, eliminating consumer and agricultural subsidies, reducing civil service employment, and promoting the privatization of programs in many sectors, including education and agriculture (Ministry of Education and Culture, 1995; Ponte, 1998; Wagao, 1990). Despite their achievements in bringing down the country's inflation rate, SAPs have failed to alleviate Tanzania's debt burden and its dependence on aid from international financial institutions. Tanzania owes approximately $7 billion to different lenders, with its debt servicing payments at nearly $275 million per year, or roughly 35% of its earnings from exports (Oxfam, 1998). In terms of social services, this figure is approximately four times as much as the country spends on social services, such as basic education (Vavrus, 2000). With these historical changes and challenges to policy making in mind, I turn now to an examination of contemporary externalization in different social and economic sectors.

WEAVING THE REFERENTIAL WEB

Education policy-making in Tanzania is not a solely Tanzanian activity. Like their colleagues elsewhere in Africa, Tanzanian policy-makers look to the

North Atlantic for models, analyses and diagnoses, and approval. Often subtle, this deference to external authority conditions policies—from specifying what is problematic to designing intervention strategies to evaluating outcomes. Even more important, most new projects in education and even a portion of recurrent expenditures rely on externally provided funding. (Samoff, 1994, p. 143)

These comments highlight two important aspects of the externalization process in Tanzania: first, that references to "elsewhere" are often subtle, and second, that deference to models and discourses prevalent in the North Atlantic reflects Tanzania's dependence on external funding. Neither of these phenomena can be examined adequately using an approach in which the unit of analysis is solely the nation-state. Instead, as Schriewer (2000) suggests, contemporary comparative research needs to consider the interdependence of nations and the transnational field on which states, NGOs, and other institutions bandy ideas and models about development. This is not a level field, he notes, because players retain their differentiated histories within the broader world system: "Externalizations to world situations are not constructed in a vacuum. Rather, they are embedded in a global reality . . . which is characterized equally by differentiation into a multitude of territorially organized political systems and by multiple clusters of interrelations (of competition, rivalry, conflict, dominance, cooperation, or alliance) between these systems" (Schriewer, 2000, p. 334). Given the "global reality" of Tanzania's heavy dependency on foreign assistance, it should not be a surprise that its policies are, for the most part, consistent with the priorities of major international financial institutions. However, Schriewer's and Samoff's insights alert us to the possibility that externalization may be subtle and implicit, without explicit reference to a country or an organization from which ideas were borrowed.

TANZANIAN POLICIES IN EDUCATION AND AGRICULTURE

There are many questions that one might ask about how development policies in Tanzania have changed since the *ujamaa* era. The one on which my analysis focuses comes from Shore and Wright (1997): "How are normative claims used to present a particular way of defining a problem and its solution, as if these were the only ones possible, while enforcing closure or silence on other ways of thinking or talking?" (p. 3). One way that normative claims operate to curtail alternatives is through repetition of *similar* problems and solutions in policies directed at *different* social sectors. This process is evident in the two Tanzanian policies under review:

(1) the *Education and Training Policy* (ETP) (Ministry of Education and Culture, 1995); and (2) the *Agricultural Sector Development Strategy* (ASDS) (United Republic of Tanzania, 2001).

The introductory sections of these policies provide summaries of the arguments elaborated in the texts. In each one, different problems are identified that reflect the particular areas of concern for policy makers in these sectors, such as the disparate problems of the shortage of skilled Tanzanian professionals and applied researchers (ETP) and the dependence on hand hoes and rain-fed agriculture (ASDS). Despite these different problems, the policies lay out very similar solutions that reflect the country's current macroeconomic reform priorities to promote private investments and decentralization. It is worth looking in some detail at the solutions proposed in each document to identify the common references and assumptions that produce the "strategic formation" of developmentalism.

From the Education and Training Policy:
The new Government macro policy which emphasizes, inter alia, increased role of the private sector; continued liberalization of the economy; provision of essential resources to priority areas; increased investment in infrastructure and social sectors and the introduction of cost sharing measures, necessitated a review and restructuring of the education system. . . . The [ETP] intends to:
- decentralize education and training by empowering regions, districts, communities and educational institutions to manage and administer education and training;
- broaden the base for the financing of education and training through cost sharing measures involving individuals, communities, NGOs, parents and end-users. (Ministry of Education and Culture, 1995, Foreword)

From the Agricultural Sector Development Strategy:
The policy environment is key to agricultural development at two levels. First, a favourable and stable macroeconomic environment is a precondition to profitable private investment in agriculture. Second, sector specific policies have an important bearing on its productivity and profitability. . . . At the same time, the macroeconomic reforms rule out the possibility of profligate government expenditure or subsidies and limit the role of the Government to policy formulation, the establishment of a regulatory framework, and the provision of public goods and safety nets for the most vulnerable in society. Government is unlikely to be a major provider or funder of those goods and services that the private sector is capable of providing itself. (United Republic of Tanzania, 2001, pp. vi–vii)

The Local Government Reform Programme (LGRP) . . . is currently under phased implementation . . . and involves:

- Transferring political, financial and development planning authority from the central Ministries to LGAs [Local Government Authorities];
- District Councils taking responsibility for the delivery of social and economic services;
- Empowering local people by promoting their participation in decision-making on and, hence, ownership of local development initiatives. (United Republic of Tanzania, 2001, p. 15)

These excerpts from the education and agriculture sectors provide ample material with which to address Shore and Wright's (1997) question about how normative claims in policy define solutions and enforce closure on serious consideration of alternatives. There are several prescriptions for reform common to these documents that serve to reinforce the assumption that they are *the* solutions to development problems, regardless of whether the problems lie in the education or in the agriculture sector. For instance, each policy suggests that decentralization and community empowerment are linked in a causal chain, where devolution of financing and management will lead to greater local control. The ETP makes decentralizing education and empowering local institutions its very first objective, and the ASDS bases its entire Local Government Reform Programme on decentralization and empowerment.

Decentralization and community empowerment are not the only links in this discursive chain; there are also the processes of privatization and cost sharing for education and agricultural services. The ETP, for example, states clearly that one of the principal solutions to educational problems is "broadening the base" of educational funding through cost sharing with various organizations and "end-users," presumably meaning students. The ASDS is even more explicit about its priority to increase profitability in the agricultural sector by promoting privatization and transferring financial responsibility from the ministerial to the local level.

In addition to community participation and decentralization, the other common feature in these policies is the reduced role of the state as a provider of social services. In both sectors, one finds privatization and cost sharing favored over state-centered development. The role of the state in this framework is restricted to high-priority areas, such as basic education (ETP), and to services "that the private sector is unwilling to provide" (United Republic of Tanzania, 2001, p. 31). From this common perspective, the state should lead in the formulation of policy rather than in the provision of services to rectify the "profligate government expenditure" of the past (United Republic of Tanzania, 2001, p. vii).

The shift from service provider to promoter of privatization does not mean that the Tanzanian government has relinquished its development responsibilities. For instance, cost-sharing policies still require state investment, and decentralization does not necessarily mean the end of decision making at the ministerial or executive levels. Rather, the macro-level changes brought about through SAPs favor community management of social services, and household financing of a larger proportion of these costs. The point here is not to argue that centralized or decentralized development is superior because it is inherently more efficient or democratic; instead, my concern is with the normative claims about the flaws in state-centered development and the virtues of macroeconomic reforms since the mid-1980s that construct a consensus about the problems and solutions concerning development, and foreclose other ways of viewing the situation in Tanzania today. Indeed, to ask "what went right in Tanzania" during the *ujamaa* era, as Swantz and Tripp have done in their edited volume (1996), challenges current global ideas about "good" development policy.

WORLD BANK RECOMMENDATIONS FOR EDUCATION AND AGRICULTURE POLICY IN TANZANIA

Steiner-Khamsi (2002) has observed that externalization is particularly relevant during periods of social and political transformation when past domestic experiences may be cast aside in favor of models and ideas from elsewhere. This point is particularly relevant in the case of postsocialist Tanzania, where certain signifiers from the *ujamaa* period continue to coexist alongside the language of privatization, decentralization, and cost sharing. Tensions in some parts of the country between the current government embrace of privatization and its past state-centered development policies may explain the absence of explicit references to borrowed development models in the education sector and beyond: If such references were present, there might be political opposition to national policies that appeared too closely aligned with external forces, especially from the North Atlantic (see Halpin & Troyna, 1995). The Tanzanian case also illustrates how the global spread of certain models does not eradicate historically specific differences among nations; rather it shows how "*internationalization* and *indigenization*" are inextricable aspects of externalization (Schriewer, 2000, p. 327; emphasis in original).

Given Tanzania's heavy reliance on external funding, it is necessary to consider how the recommendations of international financial institutions, such as the World Bank (WB), compare with Tanzanian policies. There is not a direct correspondence between the Tanzanian policies considered above and the WB documents that follow, because national policy makers have maintained some locally relevant references and, in a few cases, expressed their discontent with certain reform initiatives. However, the following examples illustrate some common features of the field of development on which national policy makers in Tanzania and in international institutions make their moves.

The *Tanzania Social Sector Review* (TSSR), published by the World Bank (1999), lays out the overarching principles that are intended to guide the Tanzanian government's policy making in key social sectors, such as education and health. A coeval World Bank country study—*Agriculture in Tanzania Since 1996: Follower or Leader of Growth?* (2000)—provides comprehensive policy recommendations for this sector of the economy. The executive summary at the beginning of the TSSR explains that the work is "a product of the Government of Tanzania and The World Bank, plus experts and other interested parties from Tanzania, NGOs, and other bilateral and multilateral donors" (World Bank, 1999, p. 2). The summary also states that basic education and human capital investment in women should be the two major priorities for all social sectors. As the document proceeds, there is more detailed information about how macro-level reforms are intended to support these two priority areas. In particular, the section entitled "Current Era (early-1990s)" describes the "new thinking" regarding the provision of social services (p. 50). It states that the Tanzanian government "is liberalizing the environment for private-sector participation in high-demand services that provide individual benefits," such as services in education, health, family planning, nutrition, and water (p. 50).

As in the Tanzanian policies discussed above, in these WB documents the public sector—or the state—has a narrowly defined and limited role, while pride of place is given to the private sector and to decentralized (local) management of social services. For example, the TSSR states that the role of public-sector actors should be to serve "as agents to stimulate private investment, ensuring that basic services are adequately financed while not necessarily directly providing those services" (World Bank, 1999, p. 51). However, households and communities are given responsibility for "choosing" and "supporting" social services: "In the final analysis, it will be the consumers of social services themselves who must be satisfied with the quality and quantity of services and choices available to them. The means to do this is through further decentralization of authority and movement toward facility-based management" (p. 51).

The discourse of consumer choice and decentralized management that pervades the TSSR suggests, quite logically, that individuals will be more satisfied with social services if they support them in material and nonmaterial ways. However, the emphasis on choice in the text elides the materiality of everyday life in a country of more than 32 million people with only 174 hospitals and fewer than 500 secondary schools (World Bank, 1999).

Such conditions might suggest that construction of facilities rather than choice of providers ought to be the major priority for policy makers. The privileging of decentralized development in the document is also understandable because the underlying assumption is that it leads to more efficacious management of social services. While this may be the case in some communities, the shifting of financial responsibility for development from the government to households and individuals—some of whom are extremely poor—effectively may rule out social services for certain segments of the population. In short, decentralized development may be a preferable and a viable option in certain circumstances, but the consensus about its virtues in contemporary developmentalism should raise questions about its potential problems and about the alternative solutions that such widespread agreement may foreclose.

Taking a closer look at the externalization process in the education chapter of the TSSR, there are a number of recommendations for improving services that resemble national policy. For instance, the TSSR's proposals to improve basic education are quite similar to those found in the ETP: increasing the role of districts and school committees in the management and the provision of education; introducing more cost recovery programs to which parents must contribute; and reducing the role of the government in the provision of educational services but increasing its role in dispensing advice to schools (World Bank, 1999, pp. 82–83). Thus, the TSSR in general and its education chapter in particular illustrate the centrality of choice, decentralization, and limited state involvement in social service provision in contemporary developmentalism.

Similar to the TSSR, the WB's 1994 and 2000 studies of agriculture in Tanzania support the consensus about "good" policy reform. The 1994 report—*Tanzania: Agriculture*—recommends a number of short-term strategies for Tanzania that closely resemble those described in the ASDS policy. For example, state-directed development is viewed as inefficient, and priority is given to export-oriented and market-driven agricultural production. The more recent document—*Agriculture in Tanzania Since 1986* (2000)—presents a detailed assessment of agricultural liberalization during the past 15 years or so and also a forthright acknowledgment that macroeconomic reforms have not solved Tanzania's complex development problems. Nevertheless, there is little questioning of the benefit of moving from state-centered to market-driven development, despite the hardships the latter model has created: "The withdrawal of the state from Tanzanian agriculture has left a void in rural areas away from cities. This is a transitional problem in moving to a market-oriented system" (World Bank, 2000, p. 153). There is also no consideration of returning to a system where the state provides subsidies to farmers, but the document does make it clear that the government should encourage people to buy agricultural inputs themselves to improve their ability to grow profitable export crops. In sum, the WB's advice in the agricultural sector is quite consistent with the ASDS policy, compelling one to agree with and expand on Samoff's (1994) claim about education policy making in Tanzania: Policy making across different sectors—including but not limited to education—"is not solely a Tanzanian activity" (p. 143).

CONCLUSION

The consistency in Tanzanian policies and in World Bank recommendations regarding education and agriculture does not mean that there are no tensions among different groups of actors in these sectors and institutions. The differences, subtle as they may be, suggest that there is not a single vision of development emanating from Washington, DC or Dar es Salaam; instead, there is contestation amid consistency at national and international levels of policy making that should not be overlooked when engaging in comparative policy analysis.

Another caveat with which to conclude, concerns the role of local actors in the policy change process in Tanzania. The focus in this chapter has been on the national and international levels, but this does not mean that policy changes occur only because of externalization by Tanzanian policy makers or pressure "from above" by foreign financial institutions. Indeed, there is evidence to suggest that pressure on the Tanzanian government from urban dwellers during the economic crisis of the 1980s may have led the state to ease its restrictions on urban farming and on the transportation of crops from rural to urban districts (Tripp, 1996). Pressure "from below" in the cases of agricultural producers and cross-border traders also may have contributed to the government's decision to loosen its international trade and exchange rate policies during the same period of hardship for urban and rural residents (Ndulu, 1996). That some of the changes in government policy were consistent with the demands of key segments of the Tanzanian population makes it even more curious that the state engaged quite clearly in externalization rather than in "internalization," or the referencing of ideas and models from Tanzanian history, to justify its current changes in policy.

The "worldwide universalization" of options for "good" policy reform may be one of the reasons the Tanzanian government did not seek to construe its move to the market as consistent with some form of *ujamaa* or with another African-oriented development model (Schriewer, 2000, p. 334).

Instead, its broader goal may have been to minimize conflict with the external agencies that provide much of the country's social-sector funding by following their "cookie cutter approach" to development (Adelman, 2001, p. 118). The normative claims about privatization, decentralization, local control, and state-as-advisor illustrated in this chapter suggest, as Shore and Wright (1997) propose, that consensus in policy about problems and solutions enforces closure on alternative ways of thinking and acting. The tighter the referential web, the stronger the consensus, and the more difficult it becomes to speak up about "what went right" in development programs of the past or what might work in the future if radically different keywords and images begin to traverse global mediascapes and ideoscapes (Appadurai, 1996). Externalization in the context of globalization means that comparative education research needs to pay more attention to deterritorialized borrowing and lending that does not make explicit reference to a nation, a state, or an institution as the source of its "lessons from elsewhere." Exploring the circulation of "languages of elsewhere" in the education sector and beyond is one step toward accomplishing this goal.

REFERENCES

Adelman, I. (2001). Fallacies in development theory and their implications for policy. In G. Meier & J. Stiglitz (Eds.), *Frontiers of development economics: The future in perspective* (pp. 103–134). Washington, DC: World Bank.

Appadurai, A. (1996). *Modernity at large: Cultural dimensions of globalization.* Minneapolis: University of Minnesota Press.

Bourdieu, P., & Wacquant, L. (1992). *An invitation to reflexive sociology.* Chicago: University of Chicago Press.

Halpin, D., & Troyna, B. (1995). The politics of education policy borrowing. *Comparative Education, 31,* 303–310.

Held, D., McGrew, A., Goldblatt, D., & Perraton, J. (1999). *Global transformations: Politics, economics and culture.* Stanford: Stanford University Press.

Hyden, G. (1980). *Beyond Ujamaa in Tanzania: Underdevelopment and an uncaptured peasantry.* Berkeley: University of California Press.

Ministry of Education and Culture. (1995). *Education and training policy.* Dar es Salaam, Tanzania: Author.

Ndulu, B. (1996). Economic stagnation and the management of change: Reducing macro–micro conflict of interest. In M. L. Swantz & A. M. Tripp (Eds.), *What went right in Tanzania: People's response to directed development* (pp. 26–42). Dar es Salaam, Tanzania: Dar es Salaam University Press.

Oxfam. (1998). *Debt relief for Tanzania: An opportunity for a better future.* Retrieved October 30, 2002, from http://www.oxfam.org.uk/policy/papers/tanzdebt/nature.htm#profile.

Ponte, S. (1998). Fast crops, fast cash: Market liberalization and rural livelihoods in Songea and Morogoro districts, Tanzania. *Canadian Journal of African Studies, 32*, 316–348.

Rugumisa, S. (1989). *A review of the Tanzanian economic recovery programme.* Dar es Salaam, Tanzania: TADREG.

Samoff, J. (1990). "Modernizing" a socialist vision: Education in Tanzania. In M. Carnoy & J. Samoff (Eds.), *Education and social transformation in the third world* (pp. 209–273). Princeton, NJ: Princeton University Press.

Samoff, J., with Sumra, S. (1994). From planning to marketing: Making education and training policy in Tanzania. In J. Samoff (Ed.), *Coping with crisis: Austerity, adjustment and human resources* (pp. 134–172). Paris: UNESCO.

Schriewer, J. (1990). The method of comparison and the need for externalization: Methodological criteria and sociological concepts. In J. Schriewer (Ed.) in cooperation with B. Holmes, *Theories and methods in comparative education* (pp. 25–83). Frankfurt/M, Germany: Lang.

Schriewer, J. (2000). World system and interrelationship networks: The internationalization of education and the role of comparative inquiry. In T. S. Popkewitz (Ed.), *Educational knowledge: Changing relations between the state, civil society, and the educational community* (pp. 305–343). Albany: State University of New York Press.

Schriewer, J. (2002). *Inter-societal relations and the construction of reference societies: Externalisation in processes of modernisation.* Unpublished manuscript.

Shao, I. (Ed.). (1992). *Structural adjustment in a socialist country: The case of Tanzania.* Harare, Zimbabwe: Sapes Books.

Shore, C., & Wright, S. (1997). *Anthropology of policy: Critical perspectives on governance and power.* London: Routledge.

Steiner-Khamsi, G. (2002). Re-framing educational borrowing as a policy strategy. In M. Caruso & H.-E. Tenorth (Eds.), *Internationalisation—Internationalisierung* (pp. 57–89). Frankfurt/M, Germany: Lang.

Swantz, M. L., & Tripp, A. M. (Eds.), *What went right in Tanzania: People's response to directed development* (pp. 26–42). Dar es Salaam, Tanzania: Dar es Salaam University Press.

Tripp, A. M. (1996). Urban farming and changing rural–urban interactions in Tanzania. In M. L. Swantz & A. M. Tripp (Eds.), *What went right in Tanzania: People's response to directed development* (pp. 98–116). Dar es Salaam, Tanzania: Dar es Salaam University Press.

Tripp, A. M., & Swantz, M. L. (1996). Introduction. In M. L. Swantz & A. M. Tripp (Eds.), *What went right in Tanzania: People's response to directed development* (pp. 1–25). Dar es Salaam, Tanzania: Dar es Salaam University Press.

United Republic of Tanzania. (2001). *Agricultural sector development strategy.* Retrieved November 15, 2002, from http://www.tzonline.org/pdf/agricultural sectordevelopmentstrategy.pdf.

Vavrus, F. (2000). In pursuit of schooling: Girls' education and economic "reform" in Tanzania. *Cultural Survival Quarterly, 24*(3), 56–59.

Vavrus, F. (2003). *Desire and decline: Schooling amid crisis in Tanzania.* New York: Lang.

Wagao, J. H. (1990). *Adjustment policies in Tanzania, 1981–1989: The impact on growth, structure and human welfare* (Innocenti Occasional Papers No. 9). Florence, Italy: UNICEF.

World Bank. (1994). *Tanzania: Agriculture*. Washington, DC: Author.

World Bank. (1999). *Tanzania: Social sector review*. Washington, DC: Author.

World Bank. (2000). *Agriculture in Tanzania since 1986: Follower or leader of growth?* Washington, DC: Author.

Chapter 10

Timing Is Everything:
The Intersection of Borrowing
and Lending in Brazil's Adoption
of *Escuela Nueva*

Thomas F. Luschei

In their study of educational performance of poor children in Brazil's rural Northeast, Harbison and Hanushek (1992) described the effects of widespread poverty on the region's schools.

> There is not even a guarantee of a building, however modest and minimally maintained, built to serve as a school. Existing buildings are often missing water service and sanitary facilities or desks and chairs for the students and teachers. Direct educational inputs such as a blackboard, chalk, and other instructional materials . . . can be missing or inadequate. As a simple example, fewer than 70% of students have a desk or a chair. Coupled with this, too many of the teachers are untrained and unprepared for teaching. (p. 190)

In the time since Harbison and Hanushek published their study, educational access has expanded dramatically in Brazil's Northeast. Between 1994 and 1998, lower primary enrollment grew by 24%, while enrollment in grades 5–8 increased by 34%. By 1998, net primary enrollment in the Northeast had reached 90%. Yet low levels of school quality continue to plague the region, as manifested by high repetition rates and acute age–grade distortion. In 1998, 64% of primary school children in the Northeast were older than the appropriate age for their grades (Ministry of Education, 2000).

With assistance from the World Bank, Brazilian policy makers have adopted Colombia's promising *Escuela Nueva* model in Brazil's poorest rural regions. Since Colombia instituted the multigrade primary school program in 1975, *Escuela Nueva* has received considerable attention for its apparent ability to provide high-quality instruction in poor rural settings (Colbert, Chiappe, & Arboleda, 1993; Psacharopoulos, Rojas, & Velez, 1993; Schiefelbein, 1992; World Bank, 1995).

In 1998, under the World Bank-financed Northwest Basic Education Project III (NEBE III), seven of Brazil's nine northeastern states piloted a program called *Escola Ativa* (*Active School*), which is nearly identical to *Escuela Nueva* in terms of pedagogy, curriculum, and organization. After NEBE III ended in 1999, *Escola Ativa* continued to grow under its successor, FUNDESCOLA I. By 2000, *Escola Ativa* had expanded to more than 500 schools in all 19 states of Brazil's North, Northeast, and Center-West regions. The program continued to grow under FUNDESCOLA II, and project documents for FUNDESCOLA IIIA, which began in 2002, call for the implementation of *Escola Ativa* in 2,500 or more schools (World Bank, 2002a).[1]

As Brazil transplanted the Colombian program in the rural Northeast, the *Escuela Nueva* trademark seemed almost as important as the program itself. For example, the "Lessons Learned" section of the World Bank's FUNDESCOLA I Project Appraisal Document (PAD) describes the influence of international experience on project planning, noting that *Escuela Nueva* had "achieved effective results in the modular use of textbooks, capacity-building of teachers, student-centered learning, evaluation of student attainment, and community participation for multi-grade schools" (World Bank, 1998, p. 17). The PAD also contained a reference to the "specially designed teacher's professional development program" known as "Active School (*Escola Ativa, Escuela Nueva*)" (World Bank, 1998, p. 47) as if the two programs were interchangeable. The Brazilian Ministry of Education also drew a clear link between the Colombian and Brazilian programs. For instance, the Ministry's *Escola Ativa* teacher training manual referred to "*escola nova, escola ativa*" five times in a four-page introduction, without once referring simply to *Escola Ativa*. The manual's introduction also listed 12 Latin American countries that had implemented programs based on *Escuela Nueva* (FUNDESCOLA/Ministry of Education, 1999).

It is not surprising that Brazil looked to its neighbor to borrow a promising solution to a long-standing problem in its remote rural regions. Yet the problem of low educational quality in the Northeast had persisted for so long that the timing of Brazil's "loan" is curious. Colombia developed *Escuela Nueva* in 1975; by the early 1990s, several reports had noted the program's success (Colbert, Chiappe, & Arboleda, 1993; Levin, 1992; Lockheed & Verspoor, 1991; Schiefelbein, 1992). In fact, by 1992, Peru,

Paraguay, Argentina, and Chile had implemented adaptations of the *Escuela Nueva* model (Schiefelbein, 1992). Yet Brazil did not adopt *Escuela Nueva* until the late 1990s, as questions regarding its implementation began to appear in educational research journals (Benveniste & McEwan, 2000; McEwan, 1998).

In this chapter I will explore the political incentives and timing behind Brazil's adoption of the *Escuela Nueva* model. First, I will outline the history and apparent success of the Colombian program. Second, I will trace briefly the history of World Bank educational projects in the Brazilian Northeast. Finally, I will place Brazil's borrowing of *Escuela Nueva* in the political context of the time. I also will discuss possible incentives for the administration of Brazilian President Fernando Henrique Cardoso, in conjunction with the World Bank, to adopt the internationally acclaimed program.

THE NEW SCHOOL APPROACH

Escuela Nueva had begun to receive international accolades several years before the creation of *Escola Ativa*. For example, Colbert, Chiappe, and Arboleda (1993) described the program as a "system of primary education that integrates curricular, community, administrative, financial and training strategies" in a way that made it "possible to provide complete primary education and to improve the effectiveness of the nation's rural schools" (p. 54). Strengths of the program included the use of "active instruction, stronger relationship between the school and the community, and a flexible promotion mechanism adapted to the lifestyle of the rural child" (p. 54).

As evidence of *Escuela Nueva*'s success, Colbert, Chiappe, and Arboleda (1993) cited higher test scores, increased levels of student creativity and self-esteem, and a 1988 study indicating that 89.3% of Colombian teachers believed *Escuela Nueva* to be superior to other rural school programs. However, tracing the expansion of *Escuela Nueva* from 500 schools in 1978 to 27,000 in 1992, the authors acknowledged that such rapid expansion did not come without a cost, as "the numerous problems that emerge in implementation result in losses of effectiveness and efficiency" (p. 63).

Schiefelbein (1992) reported that students in *Escuela Nueva* schools had lower repetition and dropout rates and higher test scores in math and Spanish than students in traditional rural schools. Additionally, the program was able to accomplish these results with only a 5 to 10% increase in costs over traditional rural school programs. According to Schiefelbein, more than half of Colombia's 37,678 rural schools had adopted the *Escuela Nueva* model by 1992. Additionally, Honduras, Venezuela, Ecuador, and Bolivia had attempted to implement parts of the program, but, as Schiefelbein noted, "not one of these countries has followed the sequence of steps that seem to explain the success of the Colombian experience" (p. 85). Schiefelbein cautioned those in other countries attempting to replicate *Escuela Nueva*: "Planners must realize that the term replication does not mean mechanical reproduction, but rather adaptive implementation that remains true to the project's core philosophy and central strategies" (p. 95).

Benveniste and McEwan (2000) challenge earlier positive reviews of *Escuela Nueva*. Estimating a linear regression model to measure the effects of *Escuela Nueva* training on teachers' "core teaching practices," Benveniste and McEwan found that only one of three *Escuela Nueva* teacher workshops had a positive and statistically significant effect on the use of more student-centered, active pedagogy. Moreover, the independent variables in their model explained only 4% of variation in teaching practices. Benveniste and McEwan conclude that improving capacity is only one part of the implementation equation. Another element is local will, which they describe as the "motivation and commitment of micro-level actors who participate in the restructuring of core educational practices" (p. 40). Benveniste and McEwan suggest that the negative stigma frequently attached to multigrade models, especially in places where one teacher–one grade is the norm, could lessen teachers' will to implement *Escuela Nueva*.

Large variation in teachers' use of *Escuela Nueva* pedagogy prompted Benveniste and McEwan (2000) to caution educational planners: "Even if the requisite program inputs are developed and capacity is provided, the core of educational practice may remain only slightly altered" (p. 40). Furthermore, although many educational development experts "assume that multigrade schooling programs are easily transferable to a variety of contexts" (p. 33), transfer is actually quite difficult.

Even *Escuela Nueva*'s supporters acknowledged difficulties in large-scale implementation and transfer of the program to other settings. Colbert, Chiappe, and Arboleda (1993) found that expansion reduced program effects. Schiefelbein (1992) outlined the challenges of transferring the program to other countries and cited examples where such attempts had failed. Benveniste and McEwan (2000) suggested that even in its original setting, the *Escuela Nueva* program had not been fully implemented. Ironically, Brazil's interest in adopting *Escuela Nueva* grew in tandem with increasing doubts about the Colombian program.

WORLD BANK EDUCATION PROJECTS
IN NORTHEAST BRAZIL SINCE 1980

Escola Ativa was not Brazil's first attempt to combat school failure in the Northeast. In 1980, the government and the World Bank undertook the

7-year, $92 million Northeast Basic Education Project (EDURURAL) to improve and expand primary schooling in the region's poorest municipalities (see Table 10.1).

EDURURAL also commissioned a 7-year longitudinal study to answer two questions: (1) Did the project positively affect student achievement? and (2) In general, which school inputs were most likely to increase student achievement? The results of the study were published as Harbison and Hanushek's *Educational Performance of the Poor: Lessons from Rural Northeast Brazil* (1992).

Addressing the first question, Harbison and Hanushek found mixed results. While EDURURAL schools enjoyed more resources than control schools, these resources did not appear to raise student achievement. In fact, Harbison and Hanushek found evidence that students in EDURURAL actually lost ground relative to students in control schools (p. 209). Harbison and Hanushek also alluded to possible problems with project administration.

> The EDURURAL program was designed to expand resources at local schools. It did this by making extra funds available to state education secretariats for the purchase of incremental learning resources. These agencies then distributed the extra resources to the local schools. This arrangement permits substantial leakage—resources that never reach their intended destinations. (p. 208)

With respect to their second question, Harbison and Hanushek identified several strategies to improve educational performance, including the use of multigrade schooling: "If anything, achievement appears to be higher in multigrade settings than in graded classrooms. . . . There is little argument for incurring the additional expense involved in splitting a multigrade class into smaller graded classes, especially since the smaller classes per se offer no apparent achievement gains" (p. 202). In a footnote to this point, Harbison and Hanushek cited the example of Colombia's *Escuela Nueva*, which had "produced academic performance superior to that of schools operating in the traditional graded classroom mode" (p. 338).

Two years after the publication of Harbison and Hanushek's study, the Brazilian Ministry of Education and the World Bank initiated NEBE II and NEBE III, projects with identical components and objectives but different target states (see Table 10.1). The two projects were to be executed almost entirely by state secretariats, which would receive and administer 97% of project funds (World Bank, 1993).

The NEBE III *Staff Appraisal Report* (SAR) made only brief mention of the project's predecessor, EDURURAL. The report did not offer specific strategies for remote, rural settings and made no mention of multigrade instruction. Moreover, the training of teachers under the dual projects was

Table 10.1. World Bank Projects in Northeastern Brazil, 1980–2010

Project	Objective	Duration	Projected Cost, $US Millions
EDURURAL	Improve rural primary education	1980–1987	Total: 92 Loan: 32
NEBE II	Improve rural primary education in the states of Ceará, Maranhão, Pernambuco, Sergipe	1994–1999	Total: 370 Loan: 212
NEBE III	Improve rural primary education in the states of Alagoas, Bahia, Paraíba, Piauí, Rio Grande do Norte	1994–1999	Total: 367 Loan: 207
FUNDESCOLA I		1998–2001	Total: 125 Loan: 62.5
FUNDESCOLA II	Improve primary education in North, Northeast, and Center-West Regions	1999–2004	Total: 402 Loan: 202
FUNDESCOLA IIIA		2002–2006	Total: 320 Loan: 160
FUNDESCOLA IIIB		2006–2010	Total: 453 Loan: 226.5

Source: Harbison & Hanushek, 1992; World Bank, 2002b.

to be performed largely by state secretariats of education. Identifying possible risks to the project, the NEBE III SAR concluded that the most "deep-seated and persistent" of these risks concerned the fact that

> public school systems in the Northeast have traditionally served political, and not only educational, ends. . . . A significant share of school finances has been historically absorbed by politicians' needs to provide jobs, award construction contracts, and dole out scholarships. Given the tenacity of this so-called "clientelism" in the Northeast, the project's goal of rationalizing education management may be undermined. (World Bank, 1993, p. ii)

The results of NEBE II and III were mixed. Despite Harbison and Hanushek's (1992) criticism of state secretariats, the projects retained EDURURAL's strategy of targeting resources and responsibilities to states. This approach did not change until FUNDESCOLA I, which relied on a "microregional planning model," in which planning and implementation occur at a regional level. According to the FUNDESCOLA I PAD, this model "permits a more rational and effective managerial option than the traditional dispersion of resources to state governments chronically biased toward the state-run school system" (World Bank, 1998, p. 11).

The objective of FUNDESCOLA I was to strengthen primary schools in the North and Center-West regions of Brazil, with extension to the Northeast planned for FUNDESCOLA II and III. The last of the project's four components, strengthening education management and project administration, contained five subcomponents, including "providing specialized teaching and learning improvement programs." The objective of this subcomponent was to "focus on the improvement and provision of specially designed teachers' professional development programs such as 'Active School' (*Escola Ativa, Escuela Nueva*)" (World Bank, 1998, p. 47).

The FUNDESCOLA I PAD identified *Escola Ativa* as a "response to well-identified problems faced by schools and teachers at the earliest stages of children's schooling, particularly in the poorest and rural areas." Underscoring the significance of the new program, the PAD cited the "need for teaching improvement in very specific knowledge areas," the "low-performance profile of unskilled teachers," and the "documented difficulties that teachers have in taking advantage of innovations embedded in new educational paradigms, technologies, and approaches" (World Bank, 1998, p. 47).

THE POLITICS OF EDUCATIONAL BORROWING

Given earlier administrative problems, many changes in the design of FUNDESCOLA I appear logical. To begin with, the microregional approach attempted to bypass state secretariats in order to involve municipalities in decision making. *Escola Ativa*—with its predesigned curricular modules and its well-defined teacher training sessions—could have been an attempt to diminish the role of state secretariats in teacher training. That is, the more intact and scripted the program was, the less discretion state or even municipal secretariats had over its resources and design.

Numerous positive reports also provided compelling pedagogical reasons for Brazil to adopt multigrade schooling in the rural regions of the Northeast. But why did Brazilian policy makers and the World Bank choose to borrow the *Escuela Nueva* program in particular? According to Harbison and Hanushek (1992), at least some multigrade schools already existed in Brazil's Northeast, and these schools were at least as effective as traditional graded schools. Why not replicate and expand these native-grown models instead of going through the trouble and extra costs of borrowing a foreign model?

In their discussion of educational policy borrowing, Robertson and Waltman (1993) quote from Plato's *Laws*: "It is always right for one who dwells in a well-ordered State to go forth on a voyage of enquiry by land and sea, if so be that he himself is incorruptible, so as to confirm thereby such of his native laws as are rightly enacted, and to amend any that are deficient" (p. 21). Robertson and Waltman challenge the platonic notion of policy borrowing, arguing, "in contrast to Plato's ideal state, most nations resort to copying others' solutions when easier alternatives are in short supply" (p. 22).

According to Robertson and Waltman, decision makers first search for policy solutions in their own past; if an organization's policy legacy is not strong enough to solve current problems, then they look abroad for answers. Additionally, "when serious conflict erupts among policymakers (as in such labor market issues as wages, working conditions or the prerogatives of management and labor), they are likely to search for solutions that can achieve a consensus among the participants" (p. 24).

Seen through Robertson and Waltman's lens, Brazil could have borrowed *Escuela Nueva* in response to extreme dissatisfaction with a series of expensive and flawed projects in the Northeast. According to Harbison and Hanushek (1992), EDURURAL had suffered in part because state secretariats exercised excessive control and drained project resources. More fundamentally, the program apparently had failed to raise student achievement. One of the key elements in this failure, according to Harbison and Hanushek, was the absence of highly skilled teachers. Around the same time as the publication of Harbison and Hanushek's study, other researchers (Colbert, Chiappe, & Arboleda, 1993; Schiefelbein, 1992) published endorsements (along with some cautions) of *Escuela Nueva*. This would have been the prime moment for Robertson and Waltman's (1993) conception of borrowing—as the result of failed attempts at home. Instead, the NEBE III SAR made no mention of either *Escuela Nueva* or multigrade instruction. Curiously, while Brazil waited to adopt *Escuela Nueva*, evidence of teacher resistance to multigrade models grew (Benveniste & McEwan, 2000; Little, 1996; McEwan, 1998). Clearly, if there was a possibility of teacher resistance to *Escuela Nueva*, it could not have been borrowed as an "easy" solution or one that was likely to achieve consensus at home.

Schriewer's (1990) theory of externalization is more helpful in understanding the timing of Brazil's adoption of *Escuela Nueva*. According to Schriewer, governments borrow policies at times and in situations when an external reference is needed to bolster the legitimacy of the government and its policies. Steiner-Khamsi and Quist (2000) explain: "It is at the precise moment when a current practice becomes contested or the need for reform becomes publicly questioned that educational systems turn to externalized references to help justify the continuation of current practices or to legitimize the need for a reform" (p. 293).

Why did the Brazilian Ministry of Education and the World Bank seek an external model from Colombia when at least some examples of multigrade instruction already existed at home? From the World Bank's perspective, new loan agreements often can generate protest in borrowing countries. Considering the millions spent on EDURURAL—with questionable results—the external reference to *Escuela Nueva* could have been one element of a strategy to both discredit previous projects and make FUNDESCOLA look like something very different and new. That is, to secure popular and political approval of a long-term, massive loan, the Bank had to distance itself from its past loans.

Jones (1998) cautions, "We cannot understand World Bank education policy independently of its position as a bank" (p. 152). In other words, just like any other bank, the World Bank aggressively seeks out loan possibilities, especially large and long-term loans such as the FUNDESCOLA project. The Bank's use of the *Escuela Nueva* trademark may have been a means to promote FUNDESCOLA while simultaneously distancing itself from previous projects. One element of this strategy was the consistent criticism of clientelistic practices in World Bank literature, such as Harbison and Hanushek (1992), the NEBE III SAR, and the FUNDESCOLA I PAD. Discussions of these corrupt practices suggest that project failure results not from faulty design, but from inappropriate use of resources by state- and municipal-level politicians.

The political corruption argument was even more important from the standpoint of the Brazilian Ministry of Education. Elections in 1994 brought a new president, Fernando Henrique Cardoso, to office. At the same time, new governors and mayors were elected throughout the Northeast. As he sought to distance his government from recent political scandals, including the 1992 impeachment of President Fernando Collor de Mello, it was important for Cardoso to make a clear break with the past. Signing the first major World Bank education loan of his administration (FUNDESCOLA I), Cardoso needed to signal the freshness of his government's approach. The Brazilian government's heavy use of the *Escuela Nueva* trademark can be seen as an attempt not just to justify a large loan, but also to appear to be undertaking a bold and fundamental reform.

Tyack and Cuban (1995) shed light on the policy maker's desire for fundamental, rather than incremental, reform. Although they devote their analysis to the United States, many of their insights apply to Brazil. For instance, they characterize the type of people who push "start-from-scratch" reforms as "technocrats, university professors, salespeople with products to push, politicians intent on rapid results before the next elec-

tion, foundation officers, and business leaders" (p. 112). Such leaders en-
dorse large-scale reforms because they are "impatient with the glacial pace
of incremental reform, free of institutional memories of past shooting star
reforms, and sometimes hoping for quick profits as well as a quick fix"
(p. 112). From this perspective, we can view *Escola Ativa* as a "start-from-
scratch," fundamental reform, aimed not so much at winning the next election, but instead at validating the most recent election while discrediting
the work of prior regimes.

Yet Cardoso's aim extended beyond discrediting prior regimes. In fact,
it is not difficult to argue that Cardoso sought to *restructure* and *replace*
corrupt and inefficient elements of the bloated Brazilian state. As the World
Bank documents cited earlier make clear, political clientelism impeded
many prior educational reforms in the Northeast. Reference to a new and
fundamental reform could have been an attempt to bypass corrupt state
bureaucracies and target local schools directly with a glossy new package
of "proven" reforms from Colombia. In the *Escuela Nueva* model, curriculum and materials are created centrally, while training and management
are local (Colbert, Chiappe, & Arboleda, 1993). This scheme reduces the
role of state politicians and bureaucrats—and presumably the potential for
patronage arrangements—in project administration. Of course, such a plan
was sure to meet resistance from those whom it displaced. *Escuela Nueva/
Escola Ativa* may have been an externalization strategy not so much to build
legitimacy, but to reconstruct internal political and power arrangements.
That is, the reference to *Escuela Nueva* may have allowed the Cardoso administration to silence and weaken the very interests it sought to replace.

Yet was political clientelism truly as endemic to Brazilian politics as
the World Bank documents suggested? A number of authors (Ames, 2001;
Evans, 1995; Plank, 1990, 1996, 2001) have argued that patronage schemes
have long been a feature of the Brazilian political landscape. Plank (2001)
documents the effects of clientelistic political practices on the provision of
public education in Brazil. Examining the period from 1930 to 1995, Plank
argues that public interests historically have been subordinated to private
concerns in Brazilian education policy, as educational resources are di-
verted from the needy to the politically powerful. One of the principal
mechanisms of this clientelism is the practice of *empreguismo,* or "jobism,"
in which administrative and bureaucratic positions are doled out as political rewards, making jobs "the principal medium of exchange in Brazilian politics" (p. 109).

As a federal senator during Brazil's transition to democracy, Cardoso
observed in a 1991 newspaper column that the "state is bankrupt, broken"
(Resende-Santos, 1997, p. 174). According to Cardoso, Brazil's "deformed
political system" (p. 174) led to pervasive clientelism and corruption that

made Brazil resemble Nigeria more than its Latin American neighbors in terms of the scale and persistence of political corruption.

Once elected president in 1994, Cardoso embarked on a nationwide program of institutional reform, including sweeping changes in public education. Educational reforms undertaken during Cardoso's administration included the passage of a new national education law in 1996; a constitutional amendment in 1996 that restructured Brazil's primary education finance system; the establishment of a new program, "Money Direct to Schools," in which school councils receive funds directly from the Ministry of Education to manage local school finances; and a general trend toward decentralization and municipalization. In the epilogue of Plank's (2001) book, Paulino Motter and Candido Gomes observe that these reforms reflect the "growing repudiation of clientelism by Brazilian society" (p. 222).

CONCLUSION

Schriewer's theory of externalization, combined with Tyack and Cuban's ideas of fundamental reform, provides a powerful theoretical framework to examine the politics of educational borrowing. According to this framework, governments borrow educational policies when homemade approaches are contested or unpopular. In such a situation, an incremental, around-the-edges reform will not assuage a questioning public. Instead, a large and fundamental reform must be borrowed. In other words, when governments borrow, they borrow big.

International acclaim for *Escuela Nueva*, as well as the multiple attempts of Brazil's Latin American neighbors to implement the program (regardless of their success), earned the Colombian program distinction as a "big" reform. By flying in the face of traditional teacher resistance to multigrade schooling, demanding a more child-centered pedagogy and a flexible approach to student promotion, and by involving the local community in administrative and pedagogical concerns, *Escuela Nueva* also qualified as a fundamental reform.

While the externalization of a fundamental reform legitimizes the current regime, it also can be used to discredit prior regimes and to justify a replacement of bureaucratic functionaries. Here, Plank (2001) provides a clear rationale, underscoring the pervasive and insidious effects of political clientelism, especially *empreguismo*, on the provision of public education in northeastern Brazil. Reference to *Escola Ativa* may have been part of an attempt to bypass or replace corrupt state bureaucracies and target local schools directly with a glossy new package of "proven" reforms from Colombia.

Finally, the worldwide cachet that *Escuela Nueva* had earned explains the World Bank's interest in transferring the program to Brazil. After 18 years of mixed educational results in the Brazilian Northeast, nothing less than an internationally acclaimed, brand-name reform would do as the Bank rolled out its massive new FUNDESCOLA project. In the creation of Brazil's *Escuela Nueva/Escola Ativa*, borrower and lender joined in a symbiotic relationship that may—if the *Escola Ativa* program makes good on its many promises—benefit the children of northeastern Brazil as well.

Acknowledgments. I want to acknowledge support provided by the William R. and Sara Hart Kimball Stanford Graduate Fellowship. Thanks are due to Diana Rhoten, Gita Steiner-Khamsi, and Karen Mundy for their helpful comments on various drafts of this chapter.

NOTE

1. In October 2002, Brazilians elected a new president, Luis Inacio Lula da Silva, or "Lula." The long-time leader of Brazil's Workers' Party, Lula is the first leftist president in Brazil's history. Although educational observers questioned whether Lula's administration would support Brazil's relationship with the World Bank and, more specifically, the continuation of the FUNDESCOLA program, as this book went to press FUNDESCOLA III was scheduled to continue through 2006. Additionally, the number of Brazilian schools using *Escola Ativa* methodologies had increased to more than 4,000 by the end of 2003, with expansion to an additional 5,000 schools planned for 2004.

REFERENCES

Ames, B. (2001). *The deadlock of democracy in Brazil*. Ann Arbor: University of Michigan Press.

Benveniste, L. A., & McEwan, P. J. (2000). Constraints to implementing educational innovations: The case of multigrade schools. *International Review of Education, 46*, 31–48.

Colbert, V., Chiappe, C., & Arboleda, J. (1993). The new school program: More and better primary education for children in rural areas in Colombia. In H. M. Levin & M. E. Lockheed (Eds.), *Effective schools in developing countries* (pp. 52–68). London: Falmer.

Evans, P. B. (1995). *Embedded autonomy: States and industrial transformation*. Princeton, NJ: Princeton University Press.

FUNDESCOLA/Ministry of Education. (1999). *Escola ativa: Capacitação de professores*. Brasília: Ministry of Education.

Harbison, R. W., & Hanushek, E. A. (1992). *Educational performance of the poor: Lessons from rural northeast Brazil*. New York: Oxford University Press.

Jones, P. (1998). Globalisation and internationalism: Democratic prospects for world education. *Comparative Education, 35*(2), 143–155.

Levin, H. M. (1992). Effective schools in comparative focus. In R. F. Arnove, P. G. Altbach, & G. P. Kelly (Eds.), *Emergent issues in comparative education* (pp. 229–248). Albany: State University of New York Press.

Little, A. (1996). Globalisation and educational research: Whose context counts? *International Journal of Educational Development, 16*, 427–438.

Lockheed, M. E., & Verspoor, A. (1991). *Improving primary education in developing countries*. New York: Oxford University Press.

McEwan, P. J. (1998). The effectiveness of multigrade schools in Colombia. *International Journal of Educational Development, 18*, 435–452.

Ministry of Education. (2000). *Education for all: Evaluation of the year 2000*. Brasília: Ministry of Education.

Plank, D. N. (1990). The politics of basic education reform in Brazil. *Comparative Education Review, 34*, 538–559.

Plank, D. N. (1996). *The means of our salvation: Public education in Brazil, 1930–1995*. Boulder, CO: Westview Press.

Plank, D. N. (2001). *Política educacional no Brasil: Caminhos para a salvação pública* [Education policy in Brazil: Paths to public salvation.]. Porto Alegre, Brazil: Artmed Editora.

Psacharopoulos, G., Rojas, C., & Velez, E. (1993). Achievement evaluation of Colombia's Escuela Nueva: Is multigrade the answer? *Comparative Education Review, 37*, 263–276.

Resende-Santos, J. (1997). Fernando Henrique Cardoso: Social and institutional rebuilding in Brazil. In J. Domínguez (Ed.), *Technopols: Freeing politics and markets in Latin America in the 1990s* (pp. 145–194). University Park: Pennsylvania State University Press.

Robertson, D. B., & Waltman, J. L. (1993). The politics of policy borrowing. In D. Finegold, L. McFarland, & W. Richardson (Eds.), *Something borrowed, something learned? The transatlantic market in education and training reform* (pp. 21–44). Washington, DC: Brookings.

Schiefelbein, E. (1992). *Redefining basic education for Latin America: Lessons to be learned from the Colombian Escuela Nueva*. Paris: UNESCO, International Institute for Educational Planning.

Schriewer, J. (1990). The method of comparison and the need for externalization: Methodological criteria and sociological concepts. In J. Schriewer (Ed.) in cooperation with B. Holmes, *Theories and methods in comparative education* (pp. 25–83). Frankfurt/M, Germany: Lang.

Steiner-Khamsi, G., & Quist, H. O. (2000). The politics of educational borrowing: Reopening the case of Achimota in British Ghana. *Comparative Education Review, 44*(3), 272–299.

Tyack, D., & Cuban, L. (1995). *Tinkering toward utopia: A century of public school reform*. Cambridge, MA: Harvard University Press.

World Bank. (1993). *Staff appraisal report: Third northeast basic education project* (Report No. 11959-BR). Washington, DC: Author.

World Bank. (1995). *Priorities and strategies for education: A World Bank review.* Washington, DC: Author.

World Bank. (1998). *Project appraisal document on a proposed loan for the school improvement project—FUNDESCOLA I* (Report No. 17402-BR). Washington, DC: Author.

World Bank. (2002a). *Project appraisal document on a proposed loan for the third school improvement project—FUNDESCOLA IIIA* (Report no. 23297-BR). Washington, DC: Author.

World Bank. (2002b). *Project performance report: Brazil* (Report No. 24433). Washington, DC: Author.

PART III

The Politics of Educational Lending

When we deal with globalization and transnational transfer processes in education, it is necessary to always keep the actors in mind. There is no such thing as "agency-free" dissemination or reception, lending or borrowing, export or import. Throughout this book, the authors identify not only the process and the politics of educational borrowing and lending, but also the agencies involved in the transfer. Naturally, international organizations come to mind as facilitators, and at times initiators and administrators, of transnational policy borrowing and lending. Several scholars in comparative education point to the role of these multilateral organizations (e.g., UN organizations, World Bank, etc.) and international nongovernmental organizations (e.g., Save the Children, Open Society Institute/Soros Foundation, etc.) in advocating for a particular approach to educational reform that they subsequently fund and disseminate to every corner of the world. Given the success of their strategies of educational transfer, the processes by which these international agencies exhibit their influence on domestic educational reform merit special attention.

It would be wrong to assume that the World Bank, the largest lender in the education sector, is alone in disseminating (its) best practices, as well as (its) particular views on how education should be reformed across the globe. The Jomtien conference of 1990 ("Education for All") brought together, for the first time in the history of international cooperation, a motley blend of governmental and nongovernmental organizations. Among its many resolutions, the design and implementation of "development assistance programs" became the responsibility of a large coalition of governments, multilateral organizations, and international nongovernmental organizations. The "Education for All" action program of 1990 set out to accomplish its goals by the year 2000, and the "Millennium Development Goals" of 2000 by the year 2015. The Fast-Track Initiative of 2002 deserves scrutiny for it constitutes the most recent program of international cooperation to be initiated by the small group of G-8 countries (United States, Germany, France, United Kingdom, Italy, Japan, Canada, Russia) and a few of their allies, but implemented by the international coalition previously mentioned. Of all the countries in need of economic assistance, the "international community of donors" agreed to select 18 countries to put on the "fast track" for development. These countries, in turn, are envisaged to function as exemplars of successful development for other low-income countries. Researchers of education policy borrowing and lending keep their eyes wide open for such developments and initiatives. What appears to be unfolding is an unprecedented exercise in transferring reform models from one context to another: the "lessons learned" from the Fast-Track Countries are meant to be eventually borrowed by countries that have scored on the "slow track" for development. Moreover, it is important to bear in mind that these transferable reform models have been internationally agreed upon. In other words, they have not been developed locally. For scholars in development studies, this recent development comes with little surprise. After all, the national education sector reviews of the 1990s have been "strikingly similar" (Samoff, 1999, p. 251) and prescriptive in nature, with very little input from local experts. Nevertheless, through an internationally consolidated effort, the Fast-Track Initiative is likely to advance an international model of education designed exclusively for low-income countries.

The two chapters presented in this part of the book deal with different lenders in education and explore the political dimensions of policy lending. In reading Chapter 11, we wonder at first what parent–teacher associations (PTAs) have to do with civil society building. Any parent in the United States would attest that there is no apparent connection, but there is a tendency for international NGOs to create them nonetheless, particularly when they seek funding from U.S. donors. In recent years, PTAs, or "associations without members" (Skocpol, 1999), also have attracted considerable interest from political scientists and sociologists. Dana Burde observes a preschool reform project in Bosnia-Herzegovina from its glorious beginning through its deplorable demise. The particular international NGO that she studies was successful in securing funding for the project by promising U.S. donors to enhance not only parental involvement in the preschools, but also civil society building in postconflict Bosnia-Herzegovina at large.

The idea that voluntary associations are the most visible signs of civil society is a strongly held belief among many international donors, including USAID and the Open Society Institute/Soros Foundation. Perhaps of all the bilateral aid agencies, USAID uses the most pragmatic approach: It counts the number of local NGOs and associations to assess the degree of civil society building in a country (Mandel, 2002). Burde explains that international NGOs often regard associations such as PTAs as a substitute for local partners. In particular, in postconflict situations, it is common for international NGOs to invest in and cooperate with these "associations without members" rather than with local NGOs or local institutions. There is also a specific project logic that accounts for the global dissemination of the practice: The expectation is that these associations will carry on with the project once the funding has "dried up."

In Chapter 12, Phillip Jones focuses on the dual meaning of the World Bank's portfolio in education: the Bank's portfolio with regard to *loans* and its portfolio with regard to the *lending* of ideas about educational reform in low-income countries. Jones presents several considerations faced by the Bank in its operations in the education sector, not least of which is the interplay between providing finance and seeking to influence policy directions in borrowing countries. While the Bank has emerged as the largest single provider of external finance in the education sector, more compelling is the Bank's self-image as the world's leading purveyor of ideas about the dynamic relationship between economic, social, and educational change. Although using finance as a means to drive policy change is hardly new, the scale and global reach of the World Bank's education program prompts key questions of substantial interest for education theory, policy, and practice.

Jones takes us through the various stages of the World Bank's loan and lending policies, ranging from the "McNamara Bank" (1968–1980) to the "Knowledge Bank" of the early twenty-first century. He presents a detailed account of the various tools that the World Bank utilizes for influencing educational reforms in borrowing countries. Jones's depiction of the World Bank forces us to stop and consider its seemingly imminent future role as a "Knowledge Bank" in which the Bank sees itself more as an education policy lender than a loan-providing bank.

REFERENCES

Mandel, R. (2002). Seeding civil society. In C. M. Hann (Ed.), *Postsocialism: Ideals, ideologies, and practices in Eurasia* (pp. 279–296). London & New York: Routledge.

Samoff, J. (1999). Education sector analysis in Africa: Limited national control and even less national ownership. *International Journal of Educational Development, 19*(4), 427–438.

Skocpol, T. (1999). Associations without members. *The American Prospect, 14*(45), 66–77.

Chapter 11

International NGOs and Best Practices: The Art of Educational Lending

Dana Burde

Workers in international aid and development organizations often feel they are "damned if they do, and damned if they don't" in choosing education program approaches to alleviate poverty, to create positive social change, or to further a variety of other development missions. In the world of education development, the international worker must navigate among the multiple, overlapping, but often conflicting goals of organizations, financiers, and program "beneficiaries," as aid recipients or development participants often are called. On the one hand, international workers must adhere to "best practices" that are established based on the previous experiences of international agencies and generally accepted by program funders. Relying on these best practices can be a way to justify, or legitimize, transferring an educational model from one region to another (Halpin & Troyna, 1995; Luhmann, 1990; Schriewer, 2000; Steiner-Khamsi, 2002; Steiner-Khamsi & Quist, 2000). On the other hand, according to the organizations' own internal mandates, international workers must include local representatives in critical decisions about program design and implementation in order to encourage genuine local "ownership" of externally supported projects. Professional aid and development workers try to combat this difficulty by "animating" a community—sending locally hired representatives to communities to help them identify their needs and take steps accordingly to address these needs. The tension between the emphasis placed on local versus international decision making remains, however, and it is not clear whether or how the process of promoting best practices is compatible with promoting local actors in the global polity.

These unresolved, practical dilemmas re-emerge in the theoretical debate among comparative social scientists regarding the role of international development nongovernmental organizations (INGOs) in the process of transferring education reforms and civil society institutions. World polity institutionalists identify INGOs as transnational bodies that "enact cultural models," setting in motion specific processes that link the global with the local and increasingly penetrate "even the most peripheral social spaces" (Boli & Thomas, 1999, p. 5). These INGOs act as a "global civil society," perpetuating education reform models around the globe (Mundy & Murphy, 2001). Other scholars warn, however, of the need to question the empirical reality beneath globalizing discursive tactics and program models. They claim that INGOs' discourse leaves a significant portion of potential participants out of the global dialogue or, conversely, may activate some to participate in ways that challenge notions of convergence (Jones, 1998; Popkewitz, 2000; Schriewer, 2000; Steiner-Khamsi, 2002). These scholars argue that it is essential to distinguish between language and practice in studying the convergence of educational reform in order to determine what actually is converging—action or discourse (Schriewer, 2000; Steiner-Khamsi, 2002).

In brief, with respect to the political space that international institutions occupy, I concur with the world polity institutionalists: Insofar as INGOs' burgeoning presence in the world and increased influence on civil society have allowed, they have been able to promote world-cultural principles that have "shaped the frames that orient other actors, including states" (Boli & Thomas, 1999, p. 15). At the local, community level in non-Western countries, however, these frames break down. In other words, after INGOs complete their missions and move on, local actors may recycle this discourse, using the same old labels for new purposes, or new labels for old purposes, depending on the context and perspective. Or they may abandon the reform altogether, or feel that the reform has abandoned them. At the same time, international actors (INGOs and bilateral organizations) continue to use discursive tactics to satisfy the multiple agendas of conflicting political interests, giving the appearance of convergence.

In light of these theoretical positions, this chapter explores the role of international development nongovernmental organizations in the process of transferring, or "lending," educational models internationally. INGOs often implement education reform models that are composed of a collage of best practices, frequently underwritten by U.S.-based theories. Using data collected from an INGO-managed education program in Bosnia-

Herzegovina,[1] I argue that, at a local level, rhetoric converges more than action, and the way that INGOs implement education reform models often de-fangs conflicting political impulses, failing ultimately to link local actors to global processes. In addition, this chapter argues that, with a policy of educational lending, INGOs may be successful at satisfying the short-term emergency needs of their program beneficiaries, but the long-term goals of social mobilization and transformation will continue to elude them. There are a variety of explanations for these outcomes, including the contradictions that face nondemocratic, nonprofit, service-delivery organizations in trying to achieve empowerment goals; the complexity of the discourse regarding parent–teacher associations (PTAs) and their international transfer; and the global "aid superstructure" (Smillie, 1998) within which INGOs operate.

The chapter is divided into three sections. The first section addresses particular aspects of the aid superstructure: why the role that INGOs play in transferring educational reforms is important, why parent-teacher associations—such seemingly insignificant organizations—are also important in the context of international development and civil society building, and what constitutes an "educational lender." The second section analyzes the data from the education program in Bosnia-Herzegovina (BiH), describing the program model, the contradictions in its implementation, and its ultimate failure to engage local actors on a global or long-term basis. The conclusions highlight the complex factors that contribute to the weak or nonexistent social mobilization of local actors.

THE AID SUPERSTRUCTURE: CIVIL SOCIETY BUILDING, PTAs, AND EDUCATIONAL LENDERS

Both the role of nongovernmental organizations (NGOs) in international development and the importance placed on civil society have expanded dramatically in the past decade (Boli & Thomas, 1999; Edwards & Hulme, 1996; Vakil, 1997). The effect of these changes on humanitarian aid and development work with respect to education is apparent in the reliance on local "partner organizations" to implement reforms that have their roots elsewhere. When suitable local partners cannot be identified, INGOs promote new types of civic associations to implement projects.

In the spirit of civil society building, the act of fostering local civic associations itself has, in some cases, become a major reform goal among INGOs. In this context, PTAs, parent–school partnerships, and other types of parental involvement in education have moved into the spotlight because they are considered excellent examples of local civic organizations (Putnam, 1993, 2000). Because an interest in education is believed to motivate civic engagement among parents, particularly women, committed to improving their children's welfare, it is seen as a focal point for building civil society. Indeed, social scientists and humanitarian aid practitioners alike consider small civic associations such as PTAs to be ideal building blocks of civil society and to hold particular promise for repairing the social fabric that has been damaged by conflict. As a result, many international organizations administering aid promote PTAs or similar organizations as providers of multiple benefits for school and society.

These are high praises for small organizations. Although few studies have examined whether PTAs provide the benefits to civil society abroad in the ways that prominent theorists claim that they should, they remain a popular educational reform to lend to countries emerging from conflict. Whether or not they work, PTAs provide a vehicle for INGOs to claim increased local participation in poverty alleviation and social mobilization programs. Both the content (benefits to students) and process (community participation) of the PTA reform model satisfy requirements of best practices, and, as a result, the policy of lending them may legitimize INGO work.

In order to better understand the argument outlined in this chapter, it is important to discuss the structure of international educational development. In the literature describing nongovernmental organizations, civil society scholars have written numerous essays regarding the definitional problems of NGOs and the categories among them (Chabbott, 1999; Esman & Uphoff, 1984; Korten, 1986; Lewis & Wallace, 2000; Salamon & Anheier, 1992; Vakil, 1997). The type of NGO that I focus on in this chapter is an international development nongovernmental organization that is primarily a service-delivery organization, as opposed to a membership or advocacy agency. Membership organizations generally recruit members across class and race lines; they hold regular local meetings and convene assemblies of elected leaders at local, national, and international levels. Advocacy agencies usually rely on professionally led campaigns to shape public opinion, reform politics, and influence legislation via policy lobbying and public education (Skocpol, 1999). It is important to note that unlike membership or advocacy agencies, service-delivery organizations generally are not equipped to address political claims of disenfranchised groups; instead, they provide services that respond to the social or physical needs of these groups.

In the case presented below, the INGO[2] that designed and managed this emergency education program in the Balkans falls into the category of large, multinational, aid or development, service-delivery organizations that operate internationally via satellite offices but are based in the United States. In general, their annual budgets are over $100 million, and their work focuses on humanitarian relief (food distribution, medical supplies, shelter, emergency education) and development (health care, education, micro finance, general community development projects).[3] The particular INGO in this study works in over 40 countries, with satellite offices, called field or country offices, directed by an expatriate. The expatriate usually works with a handful of foreign (international) staff in management or technical positions, and with 20 to 200—or more depending on the size and funding of its operations—local (national) staff working in management, technical, and operations positions.

For the purposes of this chapter, two categories of educational lenders are defined here: financing organizations (e.g., bilateral aid agencies) and implementing organizations (e.g., international development nongovernmental organizations). On the one hand, although bilateral aid agencies such as the United States Agency for International Development (USAID) often carry out their work indirectly, they remain a powerful force among lenders since their requests for proposals frequently set agendas for reforms. On the other hand, international development nongovernmental organizations (e.g., Catholic Relief Services, International Rescue Committee, Save the Children Federation, World Learning, and World Vision, to name a few) that apply for and win these grants have a more direct impact on educational lending and program results than does the funding organization, since they implement the educational reforms that are designated by the requests for proposals. In applying for these grants, the INGOs usually use the same discourse designated by the funder to signal that they understand the parameters of the work involved. During implementation, the lending process enters another stage as INGOs add their own perspectives to the reform once the grant has been won from USAID.

In order to understand the characteristics that made the PTA a best practice with the INGO, and to examine the convergence of discourse, we should note the theories and popular notions associated with parental involvement in educational management.

Parent–teacher associations are unusual and interesting because they are expected to "double-task": They are expected to fulfill the purpose they were created to serve (improve local schools) and simultaneously provide a vehicle to produce add-on benefits that may relate to larger issues affecting education. As the association functions, it creates two by-products. One is the organization itself, which can serve as a vehicle for other purposes in addition to what it originally was intended to do, and the other is the benefits of the public good that the PTA creates (i.e., improvements in school working hours, or in the curriculum), which are available to all parents whether or not they participate in the association (Coleman, 1990).

The goals of the INGO programs that lend and promote parental involvement in education abroad, in the case study described in this chapter, state that the broad principles of the education program are meant to provide community members with "a nation-wide network" and "significant nation-wide capacity building" ([INGO], 1996, p. 4). In describing the role of parent volunteers in preschools, the INGO says:

> Parent volunteers in the classroom assist the teacher in supervising small groups and providing individual care and in the process acquire better parenting and communication skills. Parent/citizen involvement in and commitment to the operation of a local, non-governmental institution is a practical and necessary step in the development of civil society. This program provides a large number of citizens with the opportunity and experience. ([INGO], 1996, p. 22)

Thus, the INGO education program emphasizes parents' education, decision-making skills, and participation in local organizations that will lead to a wider impact on national education policy, and, following Putnam, on civil society.

THE CASE: LENDING PTAS TO THE BALKANS

The data for this chapter are drawn from a study of a preschool program sponsored by an international NGO in Croatia and BiH from 1993 to 2000. The case study focuses on how an INGO used PTAs to increase parental involvement in education in BiH in order to reach multiple humanitarian and development goals, and how local actors reacted to the concept of parental involvement, including the goals meant to arise from it. I collected data and conducted interviews with parents, teachers, trainers, and representatives of the INGO in BiH beginning in 1999 and continuing until the end of 2000, for a total of 10 months. In the following pages, I trace the transfer of the best practice of encouraging parental involvement in education, embodied by parent–teacher associations, to countries emerging from conflicts and examine whether and how local actors were linked to global processes.

The INGO staff promoted the preschool program described here in the midst of war-torn Yugoslavia because they believed it would provide multiple services to communities in crisis and critical protection to small children. Specifically, the aims of the designers were as follows:

- To provide high-quality, inexpensive early childhood education via a new and innovative program for the former Yugoslavia
- To offer a return to normalcy that provided increased stability in a war-torn society
- To provide income generation for women

- To increase civic participation resulting in increased civil society
- To translate community initiatives into education policy reform ([INGO], 1996)

The INGO provided funds to support the first 9 months of preschool operations, including, among other things, teachers' salaries, food for the children, and small renovations for the space. After 9 months of funding for each preschool, the INGO withdrew its financial support. According to the INGO, terminating the funding enabled the international organization to use its grant to continue to open new preschools in other areas. When preschools continued to function without these funds, they were considered "sustainable." The INGO's funding for its own management paid for staff salaries, operations, and overhead costs in the United States. Thus, in relation to the preschools, the INGO essentially functioned as a grant-disbursement agency, providing communities with start-up and operating costs, and training in order to establish preschools and the associated local organizations. According to the INGO, the program promoted over 100 parent associations, begun in the early to mid-1990s, that continued to operate without continued foreign funding, and it provided a goal during and after conflict that united parents and promoted ethnic reconciliation ([INGO], 1996).[4]

This educational reform sponsored by the INGO in BiH was based on a general understanding of best practices in education and community development, although the designer (the first field office director of the INGO in the former Yugoslavia) did not have a background in educational reform or international education. Starting preschools with engaged parents simply seemed like a good idea (interview with [INGO] first field office director, 1999).

In line with many development INGOs, the INGO featured in this case study believed that community commitment was the cornerstone to its preschool program's success. Community ownership and local participation were essential ingredients to any work that it conducted. Thus, although the education goals were important, the program was also a civil society-building project that hinged on the best practice of creating parent–teacher associations. To this end, the INGO designed an elaborate management and training system to establish three levels of associations (parent, municipal, cantonal) to support the preschools. The most basic level was called "parent support groups" and had a similar functional and operational definition to a local American PTA chapter. These nascent groups were given training in organizing, fund raising, and management, with the aim of increasing parents' participation, helping them to advocate and fund raise for themselves, and ultimately to sustain the preschools independently of the INGO. The international organization reasoned that bringing concerned parents and teachers together to care for and educate children, would create the proper conditions for community mobilization and for enduring social change.

Simultaneously, the community-building efforts appealed to donors: More than half of the funds received during the life of the program were secured because of explicit references to community development as an add-on benefit gained from parental involvement in the preschool program. Thus, the program was flexible enough to accommodate both USAID's and the INGO's interests.

CREATING NATIONAL NETWORKS

As noted above, creating national networks was meant to strengthen civil society. Starting in the Federation of BiH (Federation) in 1994 and relying on a structure similar to that in U.S., the INGO intended to encourage parental and teacher involvement in school management by organizing communities in several ways and at four distinct levels. This involved the following activities:

1. Training for individual parents in early childhood development
2. Organizing parents into parent support groups (PTAs) and providing training for these associations
3. Organizing association members into municipal level organizations (MLOs) and providing training to the MLOs
4. Bringing MLOs together to form a cantonal level organization (CLO) and providing training to the CLO.[5]

The INGO employed local facilitators, mentors, and sustainability trainers to organize parents into parent support groups, to provide support to teachers, and to help local associations access funds. Motivated parents from the parent support groups were invited to attend a community organization training session run by INGO staff, which usually was held at the end of the 9 months of material support to the preschool, in preparation for forming MLOs. The MLOs were meant to pursue and supply funds to PTAs in order to maintain the preschools. Members received training in techniques such as conducting needs assessments and proposal writing. There were 16 INGO-sponsored MLOs in BiH at the height of the program. Nine continued to function in one canton in the Federation until 1999, with the help of the INGO team of three trainers who provided training, seminars, and networking support to these associations. Three other organizations existed in some capacity without INGO support, and four were defunct as of Summer 1999.

In practice, in pursuit of finances, some MLO leaders used innovative ideas to support the program. For example, one received a van donated from Italy to drive children to and from preschools. However, this was the exception to their activities rather than the rule. Although all established working connections with international agencies for material donations, and used personal connections for local institutional support, institutional funding was not forthcoming. One MLO leader, for example, showed me several proposals she had written in response to donors' requests for applications. The objectives were in line with the donors' request, budgets were reasonable, and the organizational structure was sufficient, but each proposal had been declined. Without INGO representatives to facilitate the process, the nascent local associations could not bridge the divide between the local activities and global funding. These MLOs did not remain active for long after they stopped receiving funds or training from the INGO.

CONTRADICTIONS AND LEGITIMACY

Attempting to animate communities with short-term commitments and inconsistent interventions produced the intended discourse but did not produce the intended results. Given that INGOs are accountable ultimately to their donors, it is difficult for a service-delivery organization such as the INGO described here to operate between opposing political paradigms. Donor requirements can conflict with, and significantly hamper, an INGO's mission to create "lasting, positive changes" ([INGO], 2002). Or, in other words, INGOs are not always in the best position to support the political interests of their program beneficiaries.

In BiH, conflicts emerged in the lending process between the INGO and USAID when the INGO was set to begin work in the Serb Republic (RS) and USAID tied conditions to its grant making there.[6] If the INGO agreed to accept funds in this situation, it was meant to manage the expectations of the donor by actively enforcing the donor's political conditions. The INGO accepted the funds, although the decision subsequently created difficulties for the organization's credibility with the new communities in which it was planning to work[7] (Interview with former staff member, 1999).

But the U.S. government was not the only governing body that required conditions from the INGO. Local government officials also requested that the INGO compromise on its long-term goal of social mobilization. Although sustainability and community development were critical issues for the INGO in representing the program to donors funding the program as

well as for its own internal standards that emphasized the importance of
parental involvement, it was not critical or even important to local government officials. After the peace agreement was signed in 1995 and the
government systems began to reassert themselves, the INGO revised its
community approach to education in order to appeal to the local educators with whom it had to work, and to secure funding and government
space for the preschools. Aspects of the education reform program that
clashed with government education philosophy were modified or eliminated. For example, in the Federation, the INGO downplayed its use of
paraprofessional teachers and reinforced the educational value of the program. In negotiating program administration in the RS, the program was
inserted into government kindergartens, thereby generally eliminating
problems with space, but also placing the program back into the hands of
ex-socialist, government workers. Neither PTAs, nor parental involvement
of any kind, was a priority for the local government, and the INGO did
not advocate for supporting them.

As a result, after a short time of implementing the preschool model with
its strong, original emphasis on parental involvement, almost all traces of
the best practice promoted by the INGO vanished into the vortex of government bureaucracy. From the perspective of local actors—government
officials, teachers, and parents—ultimately there was little convergence
between the international model and the locally implemented program.

LONG-TERM GOALS AND "SUSTAINABILITY"

Conflicting demands placed on INGOs in implementing their programs
affect their ability to promote model reforms, but, at the same time, the
internal structure of the INGO itself may compound this dilemma in the
attempt to create sustainability. There is confusion among donors and
implementing agencies alike about the definition and importance of sustainability, particularly during or after an emergency. International donors
use the word *sustainability* to describe the potential of their investment
to be adopted by the local community, managed and for the most part
funded by local nonprofit, for-profit, or government groups. In the case
presented here, sustainability was central to the program design from the
outset, and it was the evidence used to back the INGO claims of success at
civil society building. Instead of creating sustainability, however, the INGO
seemed to create layers of professionals, isolating local actors from the
global polity.

The INGO tracked and judged sustainability on several levels. First,
numbers were critical in assessing a sustainable program. Important indi-

cators were, for example, the number of preschools that remained in existence after the foreign funding was withdrawn, the number of parent support groups established, and the number of teachers trained. Second, recording community action that asserted rights to services was considered an important representation of systemic change. In addition, cost was linked directly to sustainability. The program was meant to be inexpensive without sacrificing quality so that "community members will both want it and can afford to own and operate it" ([INGO], 1996). Included in the support were the teachers' manual, classroom consumable kits, hygienic kits, teacher remuneration, mentoring, and seminar costs. According to the first field office director, "If a preschool is able to operate one month after [foreign] funding has ended, then [the INGO] considers it sustainable." The international organization limited the definition because "we didn't want the responsibility of continuing to monitor something that we didn't have the time or resources to track" (interview, 1999).

These criteria only satisfied the short-term education goals of the program; they did not promote social mobilization or provide parents with direct access to shaping "the frames that orient actors, including states" (Boli & Thomas, 1999, p. 15). If the INGO preschool program aimed only to provide a service, it did so. If, on the other hand, the INGO aimed to reach its long-term mission of creating lasting change, the program did not. It did not leave behind an extensive network of community associations that supported and advocated for innovative preschools, and that introduced into the nationwide preschool system child-centered learning, shorter education programs, and learning through play. Instead, it trained and funded a layer of local professionals who worked between local communities and international institutions until the funds ended and they sought jobs elsewhere. Thus, after the funding for the program ceased, the link between parent members of associations and broader structures was severed.

CONCLUSION

In the world of international development, INGO model education reforms do seem to be converging on an international level—most INGOs and bilateral development organizations share model program interventions and best practices. According to this case study, even among the local staff of INGOs, there is a convergence of professionals, their training, and certainly their rhetoric. Program beneficiaries, however, seem to either participate in old ways that are familiar to them, eschewing the new models, or are left out of the process altogether. Thus, the global polity does not appear to be stretching to isolated communities, including the inhabitants of the outermost limits of marginal spaces, as some scholars believe.

It is not surprising that committed and altruistic development workers feel "damned if they do, and damned if they don't." Although their good intentions may be genuine, INGOs, like the one described above, must cater to donors and other interested parties in order to realize their programs. The resulting mixture of inconsistent activities and priorities and short-term projects prevents INGOs from engaging their local counterparts in lasting community mobilization. Making deals with donors and restricting themselves to prescribed timeframes decrease the INGOs' legitimacy in the eyes of the program participants. In the case of education reform models that focus on community participation, if decentralization occurs without empowerment, without links to the global polity, it poses a real danger for local communities. When INGOs move on to the next project, an entire layer of local field staff facilitators (animators, sustainability trainers, fund raisers) may disappear along with them, leaving isolated, autonomous community members, without lasting links to functioning networks, frustrated, and often devoid of resources.

The aid superstructure is difficult to change, and educational lending on the part of INGOs plays a powerful role in perpetuating it. INGOs justify their educational lending primarily through rhetoric and slogans (Joshi & Moore, 2000; Lewis & Wallace, 2000; Lynch, 1998). In the case discussed here, justification occurred by proclaiming program principles of "parental involvement," "community participation," "community ownership," and "nationwide networks." The PTAs in Bosnia-Herzegovina provided a vehicle for INGOs to claim that they were adhering to these principles, but the structure of service delivery organizations is ill-suited to establish networked, membership-based associations. Best practices continue to be transferred for what they represent, or for their potential achievements, but INGOs are hemmed in by their own constraints and cannot provide an effective and stable strategy to simultaneously critique the problems with these reforms and address them. Since accountability lags significantly behind programming, there are few incentives to change the system.

The Putnam assumptions about the importance of the type of civic association that parent–teacher associations represent, underpin their design in most humanitarian and development programs. This case study in BiH shows, however, that emphasizing parental participation without including locally rooted advocates in the networking process, does not link the local to the global. The process is as critical as the content. Fostering an organization from outside that is focused on providing a service, is not sufficient to produce the multiple benefits described above because links to political power also must be maintained. In the case study example discussed here, when the layer of professional INGO staff was removed, the remaining PTAs were not nationally linked. Thus, parents lacked a mechanism through which they might advocate for the education of their children.

These points are critical in analyzing the lending of PTAs to countries emerging from conflict. An effective PTA advocates for community interests and mobilizes members, thereby shaping local, state, and national legislation (Skocpol & Fiorina, 1999). However, parental involvement that is transferred piecemeal, without taking into consideration the importance of broad national or international participation, will not increase civic engagement. Nonetheless, civil society theories such as Putnam's continue to provide persuasive arguments for supporting the loan of this best practice, while sidestepping larger questions of resource distribution and the kinds of participation that define civic engagement in particular local contexts.

Finally, long-term social change and local participation that is linked beyond the confines of a single village are not accomplished by outsiders organizing brief training sessions to train poor, disenfranchised people to create civic associations. Some INGOs are beginning to change their work style. Instead of building field offices abroad and promoting educational lending and best practices, they form lasting, rooted partnerships with local citizens and organizations. These local educators may request innovative approaches to education from their foreign counterparts. Linking local educators and organizations to international actors can be a powerful advocacy tool for local groups to use to promote their own vision of their educational systems. Networks among international and national NGOs can provide local educators with essential information to form future educational policy. It is not beyond the scope of possibility to foster the equivalent of highly functioning PTAs and increase social mobilization as a result, but it requires conditions different from the ones illustrated by this case. Until structural conditions change, INGOs' practice of lending and their dependence on funding agencies will continue to leave local actors isolated and will continue to shift INGOs' priorities away from their long-term goals.

NOTES

1. The Dayton Agreement preserved Bosnia-Herzegovina as one country but divided it into two entities with largely distinct administrative processes: (1) the Federation of Bosnia-Herzegovina (Federation), and (2) the Serb Republic (RS). The Federation is divided into 10 cantons (three Croat, five Muslim, and two mixed) that are subdivided into municipalities. The RS is divided into municipalities, but has retained a highly centralized administrative structure similar to that of the former Yugoslavia.

2. The international development organization featured in this case study is referred to as the "INGO" throughout this chapter (e.g., [INGO], 1996, 2002), not only to keep it anonymous, but also to highlight the similar structural characteristics, mission statements, and types of programs among the group of large, multinational aid and development organizations that it symbolizes.

3. The agencies launching these initiatives define education in humanitarian relief programs as "emergency education," with programs normally short-term, rapid intervention consisting of educational materials such as "educational toolkits" adapted to populations living in, or affected by, conflict. This is in contrast to longer-term "development education" programs that rely on established materials and try to address systemic changes at an education policy level. The former focus on particular themes, such as landmine awareness or recovery from trauma. Other substantive differences between emergency and development education programs are debated among critics and proponents.

4. Although this information is summarized from the INGO annual report from 1996, the INGO reiterated these points in 1999 at a conference on emergency education hosted by the World Bank.

5. This structure was for the Federation preschools; the organizations were formed in a different way in the RS because of the timing and structure of the program.

6. According to USAID representatives, conditions also were applied to the Muslim-Croat Federation; however, in the case of the INGO program, these conditions were not implemented in either entity until *after* the USAID grant had been terminated in the Federation.

7. One INGO staff member eventually resigned as a result of this decision.

REFERENCES

Boli, J., & Thomas, G. M. (Eds.). (1999). *Constructing world culture: International nongovernmental organizations since 1875*. Stanford: Stanford University Press.

Chabbott, C. (1999). Development INGOs. In J. Boli & G. M. Thomas (Eds.), *Constructing world culture: International nongovernmental organizations since 1875* (pp. 222–248). Stanford: Stanford University Press.

Coleman, J. S. (1990). *Foundations of social theory*. Cambridge, MA: First Harvard University Press.

Edwards, M., & Hulme, D. (1996). Too close for comfort? The impact of official aid on nongovernmental organizations. *World Development, 24*(6), 961–973.

Esman, M. J., & Uphoff, N. T. (1984). *Local organizations: Intermediaries in rural development*. Ithaca, NY: Cornell University Press.

Halpin, D., & Troyna, B. (1995). The politics of education policy borrowing. *Comparative Education, 31*, 303–310.

[INGO]. (1996). *Community development through educational support project: Second annual report* (October 1, 1995–September 30, 1996).

[INGO]. (2002). Mission statement. Retrieved January 5, 2002, from INGO website.

Jones, P. (1998). Globalisation and internationalism: Democratic prospects for world education. *Comparative Education, 34*(2), 143–155.

Joshi, A., & Moore, M. (2000). Enabling environments: Do anti-poverty programmes mobilise the poor? *The Journal of Development Studies, 37*(1), 25–56.

Korten, D. C. (1986). Micro-policy reform—the role of private voluntary development agencies. In D. C. Korten (Ed.), *Community management: Asian experience and perspectives* (pp. 309–317). West Hartford, CT: Kumarian Press.

Lewis, D., & Wallace, T. (Eds.). (2000). *New roles and relevance: Development NGOs and the challenge of change*. West Hartford, CT: Kumarian Press.

Luhmann, N. (1990). *Essays on self-reference*. New York: Columbia University Press.

Lynch, J. (1998). The international transfer of dysfunctional paradigms. In D. Johnson, B. Smith, & M. Crossley (Eds.), *Learning and teaching in an international context: Research, theory, and practice* (pp. 7–33). Bristol, UK: University of Bristol, Centre for International Studies in Education.

Mundy, K., & Murphy, L. (2001). Transnational advocacy, global civil society? Emerging evidence from the field of education. *Comparative Education Review, 45,* 85–126.

Popkewitz, T. S. (Ed.). (2000). *Educational knowledge: Changing relationships between the state, civil society, and the educational community*. Albany: State University of New York Press.

Putnam, R. (1993). *Making democracy work: Civic traditions in modern Italy*. Princeton, NJ: Princeton University Press.

Putnam, R. (2000). *Bowling alone*. New York: Simon & Schuster.

Salamon, L. M., & Anheier, H. (1992). *In search of the nonprofit sector I: The question of definitions*. Baltimore, MD: Johns Hopkins Institute for Policy Studies.

Schriewer, J. (2000). World system and interrelationship networks: The internationalization of education and the role of comparative inquiry. In T. S. Popkewitz (Ed.), *Educational knowledge: Changing relationships between the state, civil society, and the educational community* (pp. 305–343). Albany: State University of New York Press.

Skocpol, T. (1999). Associations without members. *The American Prospect, 10*(45), 66–77.

Skocpol, T., & Fiorina, M. P. (1999). Making sense of the civic engagement debate. In T. Skocpol & M. P. Fiorina (Eds.), *Civic engagement in American democracy* (pp. 1–23). Washington, DC: Brookings.

Smillie, I. (1998). *Relief and development: The struggle for synergy* (Occasional Paper No. 33). Providence, RI: Brown University, Thomas J. Watson Jr. Institute for International Studies.

Steiner-Khamsi, G. (2002). Re-framing educational borrowing as a policy strategy. In M. Caruso & H.-E. Tenorth (Eds.), *Internationalisierung—Internationalisation* (pp. 57–89). Frankfurt/M: Lang.

Steiner-Khamsi, G., & Quist, H. O. (2000). The politics of educational borrowing: Reopening the case of Achimota in British Ghana. *Comparative Education Review, 44*(3), 272–299.

Vakil, A. (1997). Confronting the classification problem: Toward a taxonomy of NGOs. *World Development, 25,* 2057–2070.

Chapter 12

Taking the Credit:
Financing and Policy Linkages
in the Education Portfolio
of the World Bank

Phillip W. Jones

The World Bank's work in education cannot remain innocent of the Bank's primary role—financing, the extension to governments of repayable loan funds for developmental and poverty reduction purposes. Any discussion of the Bank needs to acknowledge this fundamental purpose. At the same time, Bank education *loans* are bound up with the Bank's *ideas* about education, especially how education can relate to development and to poverty reduction. The purpose of this chapter is to provide a framework for understanding the interplay between the Bank's financial operations in education and the Bank's promotion of certain ideas about how education relates (or ideally should relate) to economic and social policy objectives. In brief, it addresses the financing–policy link in World Bank operations.

THE WORLD BANK AS POLICY ACTOR

It will cause no surprise to claim that enormous geopolitical changes have surrounded the World Bank in the years since 1990, and that the organization has made strenuous efforts to accommodate and adjust to them

(Gilbert & Vines, 2000). Since the end of the Cold War, the Bank has become genuinely global. It has sought to address economic growth strategies in an increasingly diverse and volatile global environment (Miller-Adams, 1999). It has championed the worldwide application of a clearly defined set of prescriptions for economic reform (Williamson, 1993). It has placed a premium on the perceived quality and relevance of its economic and social thinking, aspiring to become the "Knowledge Bank" (Wolfensohn, 1996). It also has invested much energy in shifting public perceptions of its being an inflexible, domineering, and uncaring institution to a responsive, collaborative, and open one (Fox, 2000; Fox & Brown, 1998). Yet despite all these changes, the World Bank requires analysis first and foremost as a bank, just as it always has. Raising the vast bulk of its loanable capital on global financial markets, the Bank continues to provide a window on what global capital has to say about economic and social policy. In particular, it illuminates those ideas that global capital is prepared to back with finance.

For the education sector, it is important to recall the continuous interplay throughout Bank history between its own education financing criteria and those educational ideas the Bank wants others, not least of which are governments, other international agencies, and aid providers, to embrace (for a historical overview, see Jones, 1992). Whether as freestanding projects (e.g., school construction) or as more systematic program and reform packages (e.g., curriculum change or policy reform), the Bank's conventional instruments of financing have been accompanied from the outset by demands that borrowers adopt its preferred view of education futures. The crudest means are perhaps the best known—covenants attached to loan agreements, whereby borrowing governments "sign on" to certain policy prescriptions as a condition for receiving finance. In reality, loan covenants ("leverage" in Bank parlance) are among the most frequently ignored of the Bank's numerous ways of exerting policy influence. Nevertheless, there exists alongside individual loan covenants a wide range of strategies designed to ensure that world education systems conform to Bank preferences. Here, the Bank's preferred view of itself is not merely as the largest single source of external education financing for the world's governments; rather, it would see itself as setting the pace by asking the right questions about education's links with economic and social policy, and providing the most robust answers and prescriptions about educational reform. In this way, it seeks to fill the role of lead agency in the world of ideas about educational policy.

Very frequently, loan covenants have addressed issues of economic and social policy far broader than the scope of a project itself would suggest. The Bank, along with the International Monetary Fund (IMF), will always have a set of policy prescriptions at hand for any particular borrowing government—including fundamental matters of exchange rates, interest rates, government expenditure levels, public budget surplus and deficit prospects, privatization of government assets, and the like. When the Bank is ready to "invite" a government to embrace policy shifts in such fundamental areas, it is usually a matter of waiting for that borrower's next loan approval process. Thus, the loan in line might be for an education project, and it would be straightforward for that project to be approved by the Bank's Executive Directors in the context of the broader policy framework prescribed by the Bank and IMF. Borrowers, if they indeed want the loan funds to flow, have little option but to sign off on the attached loan covenants. This conditionality, it must be recalled, is an extremely blunt policy instrument: Borrowing governments are frequently skilled in ways of ignoring or delaying compliance, especially in the case of the larger and stronger economies. For weaker borrowers, there is little option but to comply, especially if prospects for future borrowing and retaining their credit worthiness are to be preserved. It is here that the fundamental sources of the Bank's and the IMF's sustained post-World War II influence and power can be discerned, by declaring the relative capacities of the world's governments to attract and absorb both public and private foreign capital. Without Bank and IMF sanctions, developing and transition governments lack borrowing capacity.

In addition, loan covenants might address broad themes *within* the project sector. In a sector like education, a project might have a sharp focus, but the attached loan covenants might address educational reform on a much wider front. Again, borrowers might have little option but to sign. However, in terms of how policies addressing educational change actually work in practice, such covenants are usually naive. A minister for education might issue an edict in terms of an agreed loan covenant, but rarely is this a dependable way of ensuring compliance or fostering educational change.

That the Bank is the keenest of participants in the battle of ideas is beyond question. Through the late 1990s, for instance, there were serious calls both inside and outside the Bank that it should pass its financing operations to the regional development banks, so that the World Bank might focus on influencing policy through the power of its ideas, rather than through its financial clout. The "Knowledge Bank" proposals have taken many forms, not just this one. But the fact that there have been serious arguments in favor of abandoning financing operations altogether points to the self-image of the Bank as a dynamic player in the world of ideas.

At the country level, Bank educational research and analysis are designed essentially to inform the production of education-sector strategies,

strategies to inform Bank lending in the narrow sense and to inform government policy formation in the broader sense. The power of sectoral research cannot be overstated at the country level. It is not only in the poorest countries that this is so, in those contexts with limited capacities for education-sector research and analysis. In many more places, the Bank has embarked on a remarkably successful strategy of aligning government policy processes with, and only with, those researchers and analysts whose products conform to Bank ways of thinking. In many a low- and middle-income country, the Bank has seen to it that education-sector work inimical to its interests has a more arduous route reaching the policy table.

FROM DEVELOPMENT TO GLOBALIZATION

I have argued elsewhere that despite apparent wild swings in its lending criteria for education, there nevertheless has been a relentless adherence in Bank education policies to human capital formation and to the broader economic and social policy framework in which human capital theory inevitably resides (Jones, 1992). While these policy shifts might point, for some, to a flexible and responsive Bank, for others they highlight the policy recklessness that can flow from dogmatism and ideological zeal. Many countries, it must never be forgotten, have had to struggle for years to pay off Bank loans for purposes since discredited by the Bank.

A broad view will see how Bank education policies were developed initially and applied over the 2 decades from 1962, with a clear focus on *development* (Jones, 1997). The human capital rationale underlying the Bank's entry into education lending was breathtakingly straightforward, however controversial, in-house. In contexts of poverty, the right knowledge and skills would be seen in time to increase worker productivity, their increasing output ushering in a period of development shaped by economic growth (Psacharopoulos & Woodhall, 1985). The economic, political, and cultural assumptions of focusing on the individual worker and his or her productivity were the hallmark of a way of thinking about development that was closely aligned with the modernist school of North American political sociology of the 1960s and 1970s (Apter, 1965; Fagerlind & Saha, 1989).

The McNamara Bank (1968–1980) is remembered in education circles as the period of rapid and dramatic "liberalization" of loan criteria (Ayres, 1983). A bigger, busier Bank was able to diversify its operations, and the scope of education lending was such that virtually all education subsectors were deemed "loanable," with the general exception of adult literacy and school textbooks (Jones, 1992). The McNamara years were also times when Bank education staff liked to portray themselves as development workers more than as loan officers. McNamara's much-heralded poverty focus, whereby redirecting investment to the poor was the basis of the "redistribution with growth" (RWG) strategy, has been much misunderstood. Within the McNamara Bank, RWG was in contention for policy dominance with a "basic human needs" (BHN) approach that demanded more fundamental understandings of poverty and its causes. While the McNamara Bank picked up much of the language of BHN—McNamara himself spoke tirelessly of the 40% of the world's poorest and their "needs"—it must be remembered that RWG constituted the softest redistributive policy option available. Put simply, it was a driver for reallocating the focus of investment in favor of the poor, while relieving itself of any need to reallocate resources within or across economies (Chenery et al., 1974; Kapur, Lewis, & Webb, 1997).

After McNamara's departure, nothing better symbolized the transition of the Bank from a development agency to a globalizing agency than the forced departure in 1983 of Hollis Chenery, the champion of RWG, a move linked by Stiglitz (2002) to the Reagan–Thatcher ascendancy. Bank President Clausen immediately set to work on "structural adjustment" policies and programs that, in tune with the IMF, Whitehall, and the White House, ushered in what is well known as the "Washington Consensus" on economic and social policy (Williamson, 1993). Through the 1980s and 1990s, the consensus provided an essentially ideological framework for guiding not only World Bank lending operations, but also the work of the IMF, U.S. Treasury, and the Organisation for Economic Co-operation and Development. This alliance sought to provide for policy makers everywhere a coherent and comprehensive framework for economic and social policy. Although complex, this neoliberal framework has been described as having three fundamental pillars: *stabilization* (of inflation and interest rates in particular), *liberalization* (of global markets, in the name of free trade), and *privatization* (including the shift of public assets and services to the private sector) (Stiglitz, 2002).

The essentially ideological basis of the Washington Consensus provided policy coherence to a global institution working in an astoundingly complex world. According to a stinging critique by Stiglitz, a former Chief Economist of the Bank, it also brought inflexibility and left the Bank and the IMF both open to charges that a "one size fits all" approach brought policy chaos through fundamental mistakes in timing and sequencing of consensus principles. Bank and IMF dogmatism and ideological zeal meant that governments were to implement all components of the consensus simultaneously and with vigor, even if technical judgments indicated risk. Whether addressing the protracted economic decline of sub-Saharan Africa, the transitions of Russia and other formerly communist states, the countries enmeshed in the Asian financial crisis of 1997, or the substantial indebtedness of many Latin American countries, the Washington Consensus was seen to provide a single set of economic and social solutions, policy prescriptions that as a whole provided little room for governments to move once they had adopted them (see also Gore, 2000).

The most explicit elaborations of the Bank as globalizer came, unsurprisingly, with the collapse of the Soviet bloc and the end of the Cold War. Those events ushered in a decade in which the Bank was quick to assert its worldwide role and influence, addressing the economic conditions not only of the poorest countries, but also of those "in transition"—especially the former socialist economies of Eastern and central Europe. The explicit character of the Bank's pro-globalization, neoliberal stances was patently evident in the 1995 education policy prescription, *Policies and Strategies for Education* (World Bank, 1995). Coming in the aftermath of the ambitious Education for All initiative of 1990, through which universal primary education was embraced as the decade's end goal and which led to a dramatic rise in Bank lending for education in the early to mid-1990s, the policy placed much less emphasis on "education and development" issues as on the economic and social policy environment in which the Bank's view of sound educational policies was supposed to flourish. Unlike its three predecessors of 1971, 1974, and 1980, the 1995 policy paper had little to say about educational processes themselves, or about education as a tool for poverty alleviation. Rather, it saw education as merely another sector subject to privatization and decentralization. For the first time, a Bank policy document on education was open and straightforward about the neoliberal basis of the Bank's work in education. At its heart was an overtly ideological commitment to rate-of-return analyses of educational benefits (and hence costs); the approach was grounded in human capital theory and silent on the subtleties of the wider benefits (and costs) of education, focusing as it did on individuals and households as the primary beneficiaries (and cost units) of educational provision. To be sure, the 1995 paper was hugely controversial among senior Bank education staff, and much subsequent Bank thinking and pronouncing about education should be seen partly as an attempt to project a softer, more inclusive, and less strident view of education and its benefits, even if no fundamental parameters of Bank operations had changed.

INCLUSION AT A PRICE

The new language of policy formation that followed the arrival in 1995 of James Wolfensohn as the Bank's ninth president has been associated with greater transparency; an increased sense of partnership with governments, nongovernmental organizations (NGOs), and aid agencies; and an explicit focus on poverty alleviation. At the same, the Bank's fundamental commitments remained intact, consolidating the pre-eminence of the marketplace through increased privatization, decentralization of public policy and service provision, and unrestrained structural reform along neoliberal lines.

Wolfensohn's first major change to the architecture of Bank policy came with his embracing of the concept "Knowledge Bank" in his March 1996 address to the Board of Governors (Wolfensohn, 1996). There are three major ways to interpret the term. First, Wolfensohn made much of the Bank's experience in development and poverty work, a "unique reservoir of development experience," enabling it to be seen as a lead development agency as well as a lead lending institution. Second, the term placed emphasis on knowledge work as a Bank planning goal—as the Bank moved progressively from capital infrastructure projects to sectoral work, policy advising, human capacity building, all with its focus on quality and efficiency, the Bank was turning much of its attention to promoting the "knowledge economy" as a pathway to prosperity. Third, the concept referred to an improvement in internal information management, with Wolfensohn wishing to improve knowledge transfer within the Bank and increase capacity for the Bank to share its knowledge with those outside through greater transparency and openness.

A year later, Wolfensohn's address to the Board of Governors, *The Challenge of Inclusion* (1997), was a groundbreaking attempt to redefine Bank operations. The speech frequently is referred to as the first comprehensive account of what the new Bank would be like when it put the Knowledge Bank concept into practice. Debate continues over the relative balance here between public relations hype and strategic policy and operational substance, but again it needs to be noted that nothing had changed in terms of the fundamentals of Bank lending operations. But what the speech ushered in were two approaches that were to have considerable impact on the style—at least—of Bank operations and the Bank's relationships with other actors: the Comprehensive Development Framework (CDF) and the Poverty Reduction Strategy Papers (PRSPs).

The CDF initiative by the Bank seemed to combine the elements of appeasing critics yet adopting a self-anointed leadership role in the donor and aid "community." Increasingly throughout the 1990s, calls became more strident for a more prominent role for nongovernment actors, seen to be more representative of "civil society." This democratic impulse sought to bring a greater sense of inclusiveness in both the planning and the execution of development strategies. First, the focus was on inclusion at the country level, with formal mechanisms put in place for governments (i.e., the Bank's borrowers, or clients) to consult with civil society organizations, local communities, opposition political parties, and other local "stakeholders" about Bank operations and the policy framework underpinning them. Second, the sense of inclusion involved closer collaboration and senses of partnership with other aid agencies—bilateral donors, multilateral and regional organizations, the UN, NGOs, and the private sector—the Bank's self-image undoubtedly being one of "lead agency," setting the agenda and retaining its position as top-ranking supplier of external finance.

The new language of inclusion, transparency, partnerships, and civil society participation did not necessarily lead to a dramatic shift in the politics of Bank operations. Rather, it was an expression of how complex development assistance and cooperation had become. For the Bank, the days of freestanding physical infrastructure projects were fading fast. Like many other players, the Bank was increasingly interested in capacity building, the soundness of the policy environment, the efficiency of aid delivery, and accountability. Important for the education sector, part of the rationale was a fresh emphasis on a multisectoral approach to development, a concept that has ebbed and flowed throughout the long history of colonial administration and development assistance. To succeed at school, children need to be adequately nourished and healthy. They need roads to get them there, well-trained teachers to teach them, and books and information technology to assist their learning. They need to be relieved of the need to work in order to have both time and energy to attend, something their parents need to be in a position to ensure.

For some, the restatement of multisectoral approaches has been little more than the structural adjustment approaches of the 1980s in new clothing. It enabled the Bank to extend its lending reach even further, an extension frequently seen as liberality. For the first time, the Bank was prepared to finance at the local level, adopting microfinancing approaches to community development initiatives. Joining its traditional critics and sparring partners—the NGOs—the Bank could project itself as a listening, responsive, flexible, and poverty-focused institution, increasingly aligned with poverty alleviation strategies on the ground and at local levels. A critic might muse, by contrast, that in order to stay in business the Bank has always had to find new, more expansive methods of lending. That critic also might suggest that the CDF dramatically extended the reach of the Bank, from the remoteness of government policy circles to hands-on involvement at the local level. Or, in the Bank's words, the CDF seeks "a better balance in policy-making and implementation by highlighting the interdependence of all elements of development—social, structural, human, governance, environmental, macroeconomic, and financial" (World Bank, 2000, p. 1).

Closely linked with the CDF were the Poverty Reduction Strategy Papers, intended as a means of putting CDF principles into practice. The intention was for all highly indebted countries seeking fresh loans and/or debt relief to prepare a PRSP in close consultation with national stakeholders. More important, PRSPs needed to display an overt policy and program concern with poverty reduction (and not merely economic growth), a key element in lending and debt relief under the Bank's Highly Indebted Poor Country initiative. Despite the inclusive intentions of the PRSP process, governments are nevertheless free to use their discretion in designing the consultative processes, a rationale likely to succeed in minimizing both domestic and foreign criticism of Bank and borrower alike.

It can be argued that the CDF and PRSP approaches have amounted, in practice, to little more than a repackaging of structural adjustment processes combined with fresh insistence on the reform of governance, efficiency, and quality. Such wide-ranging, all-inclusive multisectoral strategies demand of the Bank and its staff a hands-on, if not intrusive, relationship with the operations of national governments—a departure from earlier conventions of influencing governmental policies at arm's length.

It is important to consider the relevance for the Bank's education work of its CDF and PRSP commitments. Their multisectoral character and lack of discernible boundaries affect Bank education programming as profoundly as any other sector. The sectoral breadth of education lending in the 1990s, with its emphasis on privatization, cost recovery, decentralization, internal and external efficiency, good governance, and sustainability, means that education programming in the Bank is increasingly difficult to contain and quantify. By seeking involvement in virtually any and all of a country's policy environments, the Bank is insisting that its work have no bounds. This "mission creep" has been a hallmark of the Bank since its inception—a diversifying Bank becoming more likely to stay in business by opening up new avenues for borrowing. Increasingly common in Bank parlance are the catchwords "holistic" and "comprehensive," all in the name of greater openness, increased participation in programming by civil society, and programming flexibility and responsiveness. Such a Bank, to be sure, is a Bank extending its reach.

IDEAS FOR SALE: THE CRISIS OF LEGITIMACY

The public relations disaster of the 1995 education policy paper stemmed only in part from its overt neoliberalism, and only in part from its comprehensive failure to win support within the Bank from education sector managers. For external consumers, it appeared to sit uneasily with Bank commitments to Education for All so confidently embraced in 1990. Bank education-sector managers, by 1998–1999, were in a position to call up the language and style of the Wolfensohn leadership and of the CDF and PRSPs, and apply them to an *Education Sector Strategy* paper (World Bank, 1999). The paper was conventional in its attempt to portray a client focus, the starting point of any collaboration, in order to give careful consideration to country-specific factors and requirements. But the stance was pressed harder than usual, the Knowledge Bank also being the Listening, Caring, and Humble Bank, focused on sustainable development and poverty eradication.

> The mission we have set ourselves in education—to assist clients to identify and implement *their* next strategic steps in order to provide access for all to quality education—requires us to combine a number of different approaches and to resolve the tensions that may arise in doing so. First, we have to listen closely to our clients: what goals have they set for themselves? How have they analyzed their own situation? What variations exist across different constituencies? Second, we have to bring our global knowledge to bear on the particular issues each of our clients face: what kinds of interventions have worked well, and in what settings? (World Bank, 1999, p. iii; emphasis in original)

The 1999 *Education Sector Strategy* was very different from the earlier four education policy papers, being essentially devoid of substantive policy positions, with an unclear sense of purpose and conceivably directed internally at Bank staff as much as at the world beyond. Yet it set out four main areas of emphasis: basic education for all, especially for girls; early childhood education and school-based health programs; alternative delivery (e.g., distance education, open learning, IT); and system reform, not least of which were quality appraisal and decentralization. Quality outcomes, in addition to increased student access, were given particular emphasis. Holistic and comprehensive programming was seen as a key to Bank effectiveness: "[Bank] staff now look more at education as an integrated system, one part of which cannot function well if another is ailing. . . . The holistic approach is most clearly seen in projects that support sector-wide reform" (World Bank, 1999, p. 24). Importantly, the Bank acknowledged a decline in its own analytical work, remarking that "the decline in the Bank's role in research in education is inconsistent with the Bank's quest to become a 'knowledge bank' and with improving the impact of education operations" (p. 26).

The scale of Bank lending operations in education over the 1999–2001 triennium needs to be pitted against the language and pitch of recent Bank rhetoric. Lending over those 3 years was well down from 1990s averages, 4.5% as opposed to 8%. In 2000, education financing totaled $684 million, the lowest dollar amount since 1987. Even with a declining number of projects to manage, the percentage of Bank-classified problem projects rose, poorly managed projects in education being more numerous than in any other sector of lending (World Bank Education Sector Board, 2000b). By contrast, the 1999 *Education Sector Strategy* had looked to an expansion of Bank lending and project effectiveness, to be achieved largely through staff listening more carefully to its clients. The Education Sector Board noted, in early 2000, that in a review of education projects, 68% were classified as problem projects, the Board wondering "whether the Bank team has done enough listening" (World Bank Education Sector Board, 2000a, p. 1).

Not all would agree that the best indicator of Bank success is increased lending, or even increased project effectiveness. Yet, in terms of priority goals set for itself, the Bank's recent work in education has been a huge disappointment. In education, there had been a clear and decisive commitment to increase lending and expand operations. For the World Bank Education Sector Board (2000c), the explanation lay not so much with the Bank's relations with its clients (i.e., borrowing governments) as with the relations inside the Bank between its education policy staff and its loan officers, the latter charged with getting the money out (i.e., borrowed). Noting the decline, the Board was well aware of "the disconnect between rhetoric and reality" (p. 2) in the current capacity of the Bank to meet its education goals.

An explanation of some of the decline might lie in an overall decrease in investment lending and a rise in adjustment lending throughout the 1990s. There was a concern in adjustment lending that education—and human development more generally—was "receiving very little allocation on the whole. The strategic, corporate vision is not being shared [throughout the Bank]" (World Bank Education Sector Board, 2000c, p. 2). In addition, a new lending instrument—learning and innovation loans, capped at $5 million—became more popular. For the Bank, a loan of that size is trifling, seen as labor-intensive in the extreme.

The crisis of legitimacy, so frequently asserted across the range of multilateral organizations in recent years, has achieved no greater resonance than in the case of the World Bank and IMF (Coicaud & Heiskanen, 2001). In the case of the Bank at least, the push for efficiency, quality, and transparency may be little more than a reiteration of long-held Bank ideology. The push for greater inclusiveness, as seen in the CDF and PRSPs, may be little more than an attempt to lessen or temper the influence of national governments. The push for decentralized and privatized educational systems might be a clear attempt to limit central, political control of educational policy. A decreased state, an increase in consumer choice, and a broadening of competition in education are all consistent with long-held neoliberal Bank stances, not much more than a repackaging of 1980s-style structural adjustment policies and programs.

Is the Bank of the early twenty-first century significantly different from the Bank of the early 1950s? In many ways, yes. The size and scope of its lending, its global reach, and its intellectual imprint are considerably larger than its founders and early observers would have expected. Today's Bank also carries with it the weight of past disappointments, criticisms, and failures, a not inconsiderable political burden. Also, in many ways, the answer needs to be, no. Ideologically, the Bank has remained more or less the same. It has, indeed, remained a bank, despite attempts by both McNamara and Wolfensohn to recast it as a development agency or partner. As the first official historians noted of the early Bank:

> In the period before the mid-1950s . . . even a relatively small flow of funds could be justified as a contribution to development only if countries adopted sensible development policies. This meant in general settling outstanding external debt obligations, pursuing conservative monetary and fiscal policies, generating enough public savings to cover the local currency costs of necessary capital infrastructure, providing a hospitable climate for foreign and domestic private investment, and recognizing the management's boundary line between activities appropriate to the public sector and those appropriate to the private sector. (Mason & Asher, 1973, p. 464)

No one has found it a straightforward matter to sway the Bank from its chosen path.

REFERENCES

Apter, D. (1965). *The politics of modernization*. Chicago: University of Chicago Press.

Ayres, R. L. (1983). *Banking on the poor: The World Bank and world poverty*. Cambridge, MA: MIT Press.

Chenery, H., et al. (1974). *Redistribution with growth: Policies to improve income distribution in developing countries in the context of economic growth*. London: Oxford University Press for the World Bank and the Institute of Development Studies, University of Sussex.

Coicaud, J., & Heiskanen, V. (Eds.). (2001). *The legitimacy of international organizations*. Tokyo: United Nations University Press.

Fagerlind, I., & Saha, L. J. (1989). *Education and national development: A comparative perspective* (2d ed.). Oxford: Pergamon.

Fox, J. (2000). The World Bank inspection panel: Lessons from the first five years. *Global Governance, 6*, 279–318.

Fox, J., & Brown, L. D. (1998). *The struggle for accountability: The World Bank, NGOs and grassroots movements*. Cambridge, MA: MIT Press.

Gilbert, C., & Vines, D. (Eds.). (2000). *The World Bank: Structures and policies*. Cambridge: Cambridge University Press.

Gore, C. (2000). The rise and fall of the Washington consensus as a paradigm for developing countries. *World Development, 28,* 789–804.

Jones, P. W. (1992). *World Bank financing of education: Lending, learning and development*. London & New York: Routledge.

Jones, P. W. (1997). On World Bank education financing. *Comparative Education, 33,* 117–129.

Kapur, D., Lewis, J., & Webb, R. (1997). *The World Bank: Its first half century*. Washington, DC: Brookings.

Mason, E. S., & Asher, R. E. (1973). *The World Bank since Bretton Woods*. Washington, DC: Brookings.

Miller-Adams, M. (1999). *The World Bank: New agendas in a changing world*. London & New York: Routledge.

Psacharopoulos, G., & Woodhall, M. (1985). *Education for development: An analysis of investment choices*. New York: Oxford University Press for the World Bank.

Stiglitz, J. E. (2002). *Globalization and its discontents*. New York & London: Norton.

Williamson, J. (1993). Democracy and the Washington consensus. *World Development, 21,* 1329–1336.

Wolfensohn, J. D. (1996, October). *People and development*. Address to the Board of Governors, World Bank, Washington, DC.

Wolfensohn, J. D. (1997, September). *The challenge of inclusion*. Address to the Board of Governors, World Bank, Washington, DC.

World Bank. (1971). *Education sector working paper*. Washington, DC: Author.

World Bank. (1974). *Education sector working paper*. Washington, DC: Author.

World Bank. (1980). *Education sector policy paper*. Washington, DC: Author.

World Bank. (1995). *Policies and strategies for education: A World Bank review*. Washington, DC: Author.

World Bank. (1999). *Education sector strategy*. Washington, DC: Author.

World Bank. (2000). *Comprehensive development framework questions and answers*. Retrieved December 30, 2003, from http://www.worldbank.org/cdf/cdf-faq.htm#a1.

World Bank Education Sector Board. (2000a, March 6). *World Bank Education Sector Board minutes*.

World Bank Education Sector Board. (2000b, August 7). *World Bank Education Sector Board minutes*.

World Bank Education Sector Board. (2000c, October 2). *World Bank Education Sector Board minutes*.

Blazing a Trail for Policy Theory and Practice

Gita Steiner-Khamsi

Since its inception as an academic field, comparative education has been enamored with research on educational transfer. Whether we consider an old, albeit practical question, "What can we learn from the study of foreign systems?" (Sadler, 1900; reprinted in Bereday, 1964) or move on to a current topic of great academic concern such as, "Are national educational systems increasingly becoming similar as a result of borrowing?"—the range of questions dealing with educational transfer appears genuinely comparative. A few years ago, Robert Cowen (2000) revisited Sadler's hundred-year-old question and illustrated that, in practice, the comparative study of education has fueled a cargo-cult, that is, export and import of education across national boundaries.

Most introductory texts in comparative education treat educational transfer as a key research area of the field. There is no doubt that the study of transfer has helped to legitimize and sustain the comparative study of education. It is important to recall, however, that in addition to a long history of research on educational transfer, we also look back on a strong tradition of skepticism. Numerous warnings have been issued about borrowing and lending, whether wholesale, selective, or eclectic. Educational transfer implies isolating education from its political, economic, and cultural context. Given this particular concern with de-contextualization, it is not surprising that most research published thus far has focused on what has been transplanted from one context to another. However, there is much more to be explored in this area than simply mapping the trajectories of educational knowledge, policies, and reform strategies originating in one context, subsequently transferred to another, and, in some cases, disseminated globally.

The studies presented in this book depart from the traditional focus on the content of borrowing or lending, and draw attention to a host of unresolved mysteries and contradictions. Why was something borrowed never implemented? Why did policy makers refer to lessons from elsewhere, when similar experiences already existed in their own country? Why are controversial educational policies exported to other countries? In addition to scrutinizing the politics underlying policy borrowing and lending, several authors of this book also examined why the copy of a borrowed policy differed from the original, and analyzed how a policy, once borrowed, was locally adapted and re-contextualized.

In the Introduction I addressed some of the features of our interpretive framework and reflected on its application for globalization studies. The authors of the first two chapters take up the theme of globalization. Tilly (Chapter 1) refutes the myth of globalization as a twentieth-century phenomenon. He does so by illustrating several waves of globalization over the course of human history that were triggered by commerce, commitment, or coercion. Schriewer and Martinez (Chapter 2) take account of the most recent wave of globalization and confront the problematic assumption that globalization inevitably leads to an international convergence of knowledge. The findings from their comparative study of education journals in the Soviet Union/Russia, China, and Spain go against the grain of convergence theorists: Judging from what educational researchers read and to which authors they refer as their sources of educational knowledge, "internationality" in education scored highest during Dewey's time, in the 1920s and 1930s. Against all expectations of convergence theorists, educational knowledge in the three countries did not become internationalized after the mid-1980s, the period when all three countries opened their ideological boundaries and increased their international cooperation efforts. Dismissing globalization as the driving force for policy borrowing and lending invariably carries wider implications. One of them is to privilege an investigation of local policy tensions that, at a particular time, allow global pressure to become meaningful and powerful. The disproportion of case studies dealing with borrowing (Chapters 4–10) and lending (Chapters 11 and 12), respectively, mirrors our preoccupation with local policy contexts.

Several case studies in the book examined the local policy constellations at the time of borrowing and found a plethora of political and economic reasons why policies were imported from elsewhere. Educational transfer from one context to another not only occurs for different reasons, but also plays out differently. For example, despite all the political and economic pressure on low-income countries to comply with "international standards" in education, imported policies do not have homogenizing effects, that is, they do not lead to a convergence of educational systems.

IMPORT FOR CERTIFICATION

This is perhaps a good moment to recapitulate the externalization thesis mentioned several times throughout the book. Schriewer (1990) frames educational borrowing, in particular, the references to lessons from elsewhere, as an act of externalization, in which either an imaginary international community ("international standards") or a concrete other (e.g., national education systems, reform models, reform strategies, etc.) is evoked as a source of external authority for implementing reforms that otherwise would have been resisted. Or, phrased differently, the act of lesson drawing often is used as an effective policy strategy to certify contentious policies at home (Steiner-Khamsi, 2002).

The words *certification* and *decertification* best capture the mechanism of transnational policy borrowing and lending that we examined in this book. These terms were coined by McAdam, Tarrow, and Tilly (2001) to describe transnational interactions in social movements and other forms of political struggle. This is how they define them: "Certification entails the validation of actors, their performances, and their claims by external authorities. Decertification is the withdrawal of such validation by certifying agents" (p. 12).

Witnessing a boom in cross-national policy attraction and skeptical about policy makers' genuine interest in other people's educational reforms, we were curious to know what the political reasons and the policy impact were for policy borrowing. Several authors delved into the externalization thesis and found it to be especially applicable for analyzing policy borrowing in times of political change. This makes perfect sense given that all changes in political leadership imply a reorientation and recertification process. It is precisely during times of political change that retrospective references, that is, references to one's positive experiences from the past, are by necessity suspended. Instead, reform experiences are sought and borrowed from elsewhere. In times of political change, intro- and retrospection are not viable policy solutions, but externalization is. In post-socialist Latvia (Chapter 4) and post-apartheid South Africa (Chapter 6), for example, revamping the educational system in compliance with (what were perceived as) "international standards" led to the creation of a new "educational space," one that was within the radius of other market economies and simultaneously far removed from the previous space that the country inhabited (Nóvoa & Lawn, 2002).

It would be misleading to assume that the announcement of new, fundamental reforms, and the simultaneous decertification of previous reforms, occur only in countries that have undergone revolutions of sorts. For example, Smith, Heinecke, and Noble (1999) examine the "political spectacle" in Arizona, when the new state leadership signaled the beginning of a new political era by discrediting and abandoning the previous student assessment system. Similarly, Luschei (Chapter 10) sheds light on a planned side-effect of policy borrowing in Brazil: the disempowerment of local experts from the previous government, and their replacement with newly appointed experts and bureaucrats. Policy borrowing always goes hand in hand with a grand proclamation of fundamental reform, and yet, as Cuban (1998) has demonstrated convincingly, every fundamental reform is implemented gradually or incrementally, that is, if it is implemented at all.

In addition, for more than 10 years we have witnessed a policy transfer of a special kind: cross-sectoral policy transfer, specifically from the economic sector to the education sector. Given the amount written on the impact of neoliberal thought in current school reforms, there is no need to reiterate the evidence that the education sector is soaked in language and concepts borrowed from the economic sector (e.g., supply/demand, accountability, cost-effectiveness, etc.; see Henig, 1994). We also learn from Tyack and Cuban (1995) that the penetration of the education sector with principles typically applied to the market and the economic sector has been a recurring phenomenon, emerging cyclically every couple of years. Nevertheless, this phenomenon is striking from a sociology-of-knowledge perspective because it entails an interaction between two sectors that, by virtue of being different subsectors of society, manifest different epistemes and regulation mechanisms. From a policy theory perspective, it is a case of externalization that deserves greater attention. Most studies either examine the politics of cross-national attraction or scrutinize "globalization as an argument"[1] but, thus far, little has been written on the politics of "the economy as an argument" for fundamental reform.

EXPORT FOR SURVIVAL

Keeping in mind that the *raison d'être* for externalization is the existence of a legitimacy crisis in an educational system, we also suggest that the practice of policy lending should be seen in a new light. What do international organizations gain from exporting their experiences to elsewhere? The obvious will be addressed first.

There is no doubt that there are economic gains associated with educational trade. The education export business is a lucrative one. This applies especially to knowledge-driven economies, where typically two-thirds of all economic activities deal with the provision of services (Robertson, Bonal, & Dale, 2002). Drawing on the example of New Zealand's education industry, Robertson and colleagues contend that the export of education and training services from New Zealand to Asia generated larger economic gains than the export of New Zealand wines. This is not surprising for observers of transnational educational transfer who closely followed the global sojourn of the New Zealand outcomes-based education (OBE) reform. The profiteers are consulting firms, the textbook industry, and tuition-driven educational institutions.

What is the profit from transfer for nonprofits and international NGOs? Transferring an existing program from one context to another is not necessarily cheap. The high cost of local adaptation and implementation to make a borrowed model effective (Richardson, 1993) urges us to search for additional, noneconomic factors that account for dissemination and transfer. By now, virtually every international organization giving grants (Chapter 11) or loans (Chapter 12) has developed a portfolio with their "best practices," as well as a corresponding management structure that serves the dissemination and supervision of these practices. Given the high cost of transfer and local adaptation, I can offer three organizational reasons for international organizations to engage in educational lending.

First, international organizations need to mark their presence and demonstrate to their own constituents and donor(s) that their projects have an impact. They are concerned with survival in a policy environment that is increasingly crowded with other international organizations, each one seeking to exert the greatest influence on governments and education authorities. Having specific trademarks (best practices) enhances the visibility of an organization within the donor community. The trademarks undoubtedly differ. For example, Save the Children U.S. prioritizes community-based education; the Open Society Institute/Soros Foundation, critical thinking; DANIDA (Danish bilateral aid agency), student-centered learning; the United Nations Development Programme, micro-credits; and the World Bank, private-sector involvement in higher education.

Second, the transfer cost for North–South and West–East transfer might, after all, not be that high if we consider the division of labor in international organizations: The staff at the headquarters design, supervise, and evaluate, and those in the field offices adapt and implement. Hiring local staff (frequently more educated and experienced than headquarter staff) for adapting and implementing projects is cheap. The transplantation of (best) practices from the "center" to the "peripheries" needs to be added to the long list of practices in educational development that are, perhaps not in intent but certainly in effect, neocolonialist.

Third, prepackaged, modularized, and checklisted programs developed at the headquarters of international organizations and subsequently transferred to their field offices are easier to manage than locally developed programs. The design of best practices evokes associations with principles of efficiency, calculability, predictability, control, and "irrationality of rationality" that McDonalds and other commercial chains follow religiously (see Ritzer, 1996). One of the irrationalities of rationality in educational development is epitomized in the tireless insistence on the sustainability of funded projects and reforms on the one hand, and the exclusion of local experts on the other. The dependency on international experts and consultants who recycle and transfer educational reforms from one context to another is considerable, absorbing on the average one-third of all funds allocated to international cooperation projects (McGinn, 1996). One is no doubt curious how the great dependency on international consultants or the irrationality of rationality is rationalized. The explanation that international consultants are guarantors for "professionalism" (see Escobar, 1995) reflects a mind-set of redemption, which Popkewitz (1998) has demystified for other contexts. Popkewitz (1998) deconstructs the redemptive discourse of schools and characterizes the teacher as an individual who, in an attempt to "rescue" the child, pursues a mission of "pastoral care" (pp. 59–78; also see Popkewitz & Brennan, 1998). The mission of pastoral care provides schools with a much-needed justification for disciplining and normalizing the individual child. For our context, Popkewitz's concept of pastoral care brilliantly captures the redemptive relationship between the center (headquarters) and the periphery (field offices) in international organizations. On a larger scale, the concept is also suitable to describe the interaction between donors that are big-footed (e.g., World Bank, regional banks, and, to some degree, UN organizations) and the others that do the footwork (e.g., governments, international NGOs, and local NGOs).

What about governments? Why do they provide grants for researchers and bureaucrats to disseminate their reforms elsewhere? In high-income countries, there is competition over effective school reform strategies. Very often, the survival of a policy depends on whether it is borrowed by other educational systems. For example, the busy transatlantic trade of quasi-market school reform strategies between the United States and the United Kingdom in the 1990s was used politically to demonstrate international support for the reforms and to appease critics in the two countries (Halpin & Troyna, 1995). In a historical study, we analyzed why the Hampton–Tuskegee model of industrial and agricultural education was transferred from the segregated South in the United States to Achimota, British colonial Ghana (Steiner-Khamsi & Quist, 2000). We were intrigued by the fact that the U.S. export initiative of the Hampton–Tuskegee model (labeled "adapted education") to the British colonial empire was busiest in the 1920s. The timing for export coincided with the historical period, a time when the Hampton–Tuskegee model was under serious attack by W. E. DuBois and other leading African American scholars in the United States. For a variety of reasons, we interpreted the export of the model as follows (Steiner-Khamsi & Quist, 2000): The need for a stamp of approval by external authorities (in this case, the British colonial government) accounts for the wholesale export of the Hampton–Tuskegee model to colonial Africa. Interestingly, after only a few years, Achimota, the flagship school for adapted education in Western colonial Africa, was criticized by local elites; its survival, in turn, depended on whether other schools were willing to borrow its adapted education curriculum.

THE POLITICS OF LEAGUE TABLES AND
THE POLITICS OF COMPARISON

Perhaps more than any other two-column Excel spreadsheet, league tables that rank educational systems with regard to mathematics, science, reading literacy, and so forth, have the potential of turning ongoing educational reform upside down. The IEA-sponsored Third International Mathematics and Science Study (TIMSS), for example, which was sponsored by the International Association for the Evaluation of Educational Achievement (IEA), generated tremendous reform pressure in the United States and in the United Kingdom (Gorard, 2001; Rust, 2000). The poor results earned by students both in U.S. and U.K. schools were dramatically overstated in the media, but nevertheless it worked: The public "scandalization" of the educational system established tremendous reform pressure and served ongoing debates of the time to introduce standards, clearer accountability measures, and high-stakes testing. There are two features of OECD- and IEA-type studies that turn them into credible and respected "certifying agencies" (McAdam et al., 2001, p. 12): They are meticulous in methodology and international in scope. Having the clout of scientific rationality, these studies give impetus to the trend of evidence-based and outcomes-based education reform (Chatterji, 2002). Furthermore, drawing from an international pool of educational systems implies that the "comparative advantage" or "comparative disadvantage" of each system can be determined and politically and economically utilized.

Let us speculate about two possible political and economic implications of rankings, and then interject a third: Does a comparative disadvantage inevitably initiate a process of critical self-reflection and scandalization of an ongoing reform, enhance reform pressure, and eventually increase the likelihood of transnational policy borrowing? Alternatively, does a comparative advantage cause self-affirmation and glorification of an ongoing reform, relieve reform pressure, and eventually boost educational export and lending to other educational systems? These causal chains make sense, but the assumptions are incomplete. To complicate matters, we need to acknowledge that self-scandalization and self-glorification constitute only the more extreme policy responses to league tables. The most frequent policy response to OECD- and IEA-type studies is indifference. In fact, in most countries, international comparative studies pass unnoticed by politicians and the general public, and cause little excitement, either positive or negative.

A more convincing narrative is needed, one that accounts for the various policy responses to international comparative studies. David Phillips's theory of cross-national policy attraction (Chapter 3) is key for understanding the politics of league tables. In short, the potential of influencing educational reform depends on whether a controversy over educational reforms in a particular country already exists. In such instances, international league tables indeed are utilized as a policy tool to certify the demands of reform proponents. Thus, international comparisons are attractive to politicians and policy makers only if they are, at that particular moment, in need of additional, external support for their reform agenda. Two cases might help to clarify this argument.

The first case deals with the policy and media responses in Germany with respect to the following three studies: (1) Programme for International Student Assessment (PISA), conducted by the OECD, (2) Civic Education (CivEd), conducted by the IEA, and (3) Progress in International Reading Literacy Study (PIRLS), also conducted by the IEA. The results from PISA were released first, made the headlines of all major German newspapers in December 2001, and continued almost on a daily basis to attract public attention in the German press, television, and radio, and on the Internet. The below-average performance of German secondary school students not only was surprising, but was publicly framed as a scandal for the German educational system. Particular attention was given to the low performance in reading literacy. Not only did German students score significantly below the average of other OECD educational systems, but the distance between students performing in the top and bottom 5% was greater than in all the other 31 participating countries (Baumert et al., 2001). The great variation in reading literacy among students of the German educational system stimulated a major public debate on the need for fundamental educational reform demanding the introduction of standards, close and continuous quality monitoring, and a thorough reconsideration of the current highly selective educational structure, which tracks secondary school students into different performance levels.

A few months later, the results from the IEA CivEd study were released. CivEd was yet another prophet of doom. German 14-year-old students ranked lowest with regard to positive attitudes toward immigrants as compared with students from the other 27 participating countries (Oesterreich, 2002; Torney-Purta, Lehmann, Oswald, & Schulz, 2001). The media response? Virtually none. Given that the German students did far worse with regard to xenophobia in CivEd, why was there such a political fuss about their below-average reading literacy scores in PISA? Also, what explains the silence about the scandalous results in civic education? One could argue that civic education is not a core subject, and therefore draws less media and policy reaction. But why did the next reading literacy study, PIRLS, released 2 years later, elicit the same indifferent response as CivEd did?

The PIRLS report (Bos et al., 2003) was published in April 2003, and the fourth graders in German schools did relatively well, that is, they performed above the average score of other OECD countries. By the time the positive results from PIRLS were released, nobody seemed to be receptive to good news. German politicians and policy makers were already fully absorbed with finalizing the remaining details for a fundamental reform of the German educational system. After all the bad tidings regarding the below-average reading literacy scores of German secondary school students (PISA) 2 years earlier, nobody was prepared to turn the clock back and continue with incremental school reform. Politically speaking, PISA served as a much-needed certificate for accelerating a standards-based school reform that, for the past few years, had been in debate, but had little chance of passing due to skepticism and resistance among political stakeholders. "Timing is everything" (Luschei, Chapter 10) when it comes to the release of international comparative studies. Shortly after the release, study tours or "policy tourism" to countries that ranked top, especially to the league-leader Finland, blossomed in Germany.

The second case deals with the policy response in Japan after TIMSS was released. There are few signs that would suggest that the Japanese media celebrated or glorified, in any manner, its second international rank in mathematics and science in the third- and fourth-grade levels. Despite heightening concerns over the declining quality of education, it came as little news in Japan that the schools were performing well in these subjects. Nevertheless, TIMSS did have an impact on how Japan resituated herself in the international donor community. In 1994, for the first time in Japan's foreign aid history, the Japan International Cooperation Agency (JICA) published a policy paper that focused on the importance of basic education. The JICA report, entitled "Study on Japan's Development Assistance for Development and Education" (1994), suggested both a new aid focus (basic education) and a new aid approach (cooperation with other donors, community participation, etc.). Building on this historical cornerstone representing a stronger commitment to the education sector, Japan has been expanding foreign assistance in basic education. In 1994, the first basic education project, the Science and Mathematics Education Manpower Development Project, was launched in the Philippines. This is the first basic education project administrated by JICA to provide technical assistance by dispatching education specialists and volunteers as well as conducting in-country training. It incorporated both "soft-type" aid and traditional "hard-type" assistance such as school construction and equipment. The project had a specific objective and audience: building the capacity of teachers in math and science at the level of upper elementary and secondary education (JICA, 2003; Osumi, 1999). Since this kind of project first began in 1994, Japan has been delivering similar projects in math and science education in numerous developing countries (see Kijima, 2003). In 1997, a smaller-scaled project that dispatched Japanese experts in math and science was administered in Egypt. In 1998, two math and science projects were implemented in Kenya and Indonesia. In 1999, another math and science project was launched in South Africa. In 2000, Ghana and Cambodia were sites for Japan's education in projects in math and science.

The story is complex and there is no doubt that several factors account for Japan's reorientation toward external assistance (Kijima & Steiner-Khamsi, 2003). Nevertheless, TIMSS demonstrated to the rest of the world, and, in particular, to the international donor community, that Japanese experts do indeed have something to offer in mathematics and science education reform. TIMSS was released 4 years after the Education for All Declaration, when Japan agreed to coordinate its international development efforts more closely in line with the international donor community. Again, TIMSS was released at the right time, that is, when the reorientation in Japan's foreign assistance needed to be certified.

In this section, I drew from Phillips's theory of attraction (Chapter 3) and made a case for scrutinizing the local policy context so as to better understand the various policy responses that international comparative studies have evoked. Beginning in the 1990s, ranking and league tables in fact became such important policy tools to accelerate change and innovation in educational organizations (Kellaghan, 1996; Lowe, 2001; Robinson, 1999) that several researchers felt compelled to study the politics of comparison (see Steiner-Khamsi, 2003). Moreover, Phillips's theory lends itself to other cases of borrowing. For example, Vavrus's marked observations on the "referential web" in the Tanzanian policy context (Chapter 9) and Yariv-Mashal's fascinating study of the Israeli Black Panthers (Chapter 5) make it clear that any transferred discourse or policy needs to resonate with local groups. For transfer to succeed, groups of local protagonists benefiting from, believing in, and advancing a specific policy agenda are indispensable.

Attention to reasons for cross-national policy attraction, however, should not be approached at the expense of analyzing power relations. It is important to acknowledge the numerous cases of imposed policy transfer in which the policies from elsewhere resonated only with a tiny political elite exerting tremendous power over masses of people. deJong-Lambert's study of Stalinist indoctrination of the sciences in Poland (Chapter 8) and Streitwieser's analysis of the West German "culture of dominance" toward East German educators in the postunification period of the 1990s (Chapter 7) represent perhaps two extreme examples of policy imposition. In both cases the majority of scientists or educators, respectively, did not find the imported beliefs and reforms particularly attractive, and they did not voluntarily adopt what was transplanted from one political context to another. More subtle forms of policy manipulation do exist. They are objects of greater scrutiny in postcolonial, postdevelopment, and postsocialist studies of education.

LESS THAN SIX DEGREES APART:
THE MARIS O'ROURKE EFFECT IN EDUCATION

There are only a few research areas that capture our imagination more than studies dealing with the small world phenomenon (Watts, 2003). The fact that we all know the same herder in the province of Arkhangai (Mongolia) within six degrees of separation is at first mind-blowing. This is how I am connected to him: His daughter has a teacher whose sister works for an organization in Ulaanbaatar that is headed by the divorced husband of a former student of mine. Every now and then, we actually do meet those individuals whom we know within two, three, or more degrees of separation. After exchanging information about our acquaintances, we realize that we know the same people from totally different contexts and in far-flung places, and cannot help but be mesmerized by how small our world is. The calculation is simple. If everyone has on average 100 friends, and each of these friends has in turn 100 friends, one already is connected with 10,000 (100 x 100) individuals within two degrees. In five degrees, finally, one can reach out to 9 billion people. In other words, it only takes six steps to be connected to anyone in this world.

Actually, there are far less than six degrees of separation within professional networks. Conferences, publications, meetings, list-serves, and so on, make the world appear smaller for individuals within the same community. For the longest time, universities acted, notably with funding from governments and philanthropic organizations, as hubs for generating a policy network and for attracting and disseminating innovative ideas.

Teachers College, Columbia University, lends itself to a global network analysis for a variety of reasons. For more than a century, it has enrolled a large international body of students; it offers research, teaching, and projects with an international dimension; and it employs a considerable number of faculty members who work internationally. Not surprisingly, its role as a global disseminator of innovations in education has been an object of great academic curiosity and has been well studied (e.g., Cremin, Shannon, & Townsend, 1954; Glotzer, 1996). The list of professors with a global reach at Teachers College is long. It is surpassed only by the list of their students who have transplanted what they learned both to their own and to other countries. In 1924, William F. Russell, professor, co-director of the International Institute, and later dean of Teachers College, referred to the international students as "merchants of light" (see Bu, 1997), implying, in retrospect, nonflattering attributes of the international students' fellow-citizens, supposedly left behind in the dark. In today's terminology of network analysis, we would use a more neutral term and call these students the "early adopters" of an idea. Nowadays, we also would refrain from making judgments as to whether those ideas actually were always enlightening.

A less prominent research tradition at Teachers College deserves special mention here: research on the diffusion of innovation. According to Ross (1958), Teachers College alone generated 150 education diffusion studies. The majority of them were dissertations developed under the sponsorship of Paul Mort. The peak of education diffusion research was reached in 1959, when Teachers College received over a quarter million dollars, mostly from the Metropolitan School Study Council (public schools in New York) and from other school boards throughout the United States, to conduct research on adaptability, or innovativeness. Mort and his doctoral students were preoccupied with educational finance and management. They identified the lack of local control over school finance as one of the main causes for the "time lag" that existed between innovative ideas (referred to as "best practices") and their implementation in schools. Summarizing the main findings from Teachers College research, Mort (1946) contended that "the average American school lags 25 years behind the best practice" (p. 200).

The diffusion of innovation research tradition generated an abundance of studies on the barriers that prevent effective diffusion, and produced a wealth of publications on adoption, that is, the receptiveness toward innovations. The "adoption rate" or time lag, that is, how long it takes for an innovation to be diffused, was a matter not only of great fascination, but also of great concern for diffusion of innovation researchers (e.g., Mort, 1947). The greatest concern was that innovations do not spread fast enough. Rogers (1995) refers, for example, to a study conducted by Allen (1956), who compared the diffusion of driver training (promoted by safety groups and car dealers) with the idea of having students study their community. Rogers (1995) summarizes the findings of the study: "Sixty years were required for this idea to reach 90% adoption among 168 United States schools while only 18 years were needed for driver training to reach this level of adoption" (p. 41).

Rogers (1995) provides an excellent overview of this particular research tradition, which emerged first in anthropology, and then in sociology and education. At the core of diffusion studies were research questions related to "whether ideas were independently invented in two different cultures, or whether an idea was invented in one culture and diffused to the other, and how individuals and institutions 'adapt' or cope with innovations" (p. 24).

One may wonder whether this book is diffusion of innovation research in disguise, recycled, or revisited. Actually, it is not. The major bulk of diffusion of innovation research was published between the 1920s and the 1970s. It operated within a problematic research paradigm—modernization theory—advocating the diffusion of innovations made in metropolitan areas and in the Western hemisphere.

Publications on diffusion of innovation dramatically dropped in the 1970s, and the research field was buried a couple of years later. Elements of the research tradition, however, lived on in new research paradigms. One of the great strengths of diffusion of innovation research was its attention to "innovators" and "adopters" of new ideas. This important focus on agency became one of the core characteristics of social network theory. In the 1970s, social network theory dropped the ideological baggage of modernization theory and developed a sophisticated approach to the study of dissemination processes.

Contemporary research on borrowing and lending, reception and diffusion, or import and export, draws directly from social network analysis. As a corollary, our research field is also, within two degrees of separation, related to diffusion of innovation research. Our kinship to social network analysis is defined in terms of theory and methodology. At the theoretical level, research on educational transfer also views the social structure reflected in the interactions of individuals, organizations, and nations (Watts, 1999). Since social constraints, hierarchies, and inequalities characterize a social structure, they also are manifested in interactions. Shifting "attention away from seeing the world as composed of egalitarian, voluntarily chosen, two-person ties," and concentrating instead "on seeing it as composed of asymmetric ties bound up in hierarchical structures" (Wellman, 1983, p. 156), has important implications for studying interaction and transfer processes. In his succinct summary of the theory of social networks, Wellman (1983) reflects on some of these consequences.

> This shift has important consequences at all analytical scales. In studying communities, for example, it abandons spatial determinism and does not assume automatically that all communities are bound up in local solidarities. In studying world systems, it moves away from sorting countries into traditional or modern categories on the basis of their internal characteristics (such as level of industrialization) and leads to the categorization of units on the basis of their structural relationships with each other. (p. 156)

Along with cultural anthropologists (e.g., Appadurai, 1994; Comaroff & Comaroff, 2001; Hannerz, 1989), social network analysts invite us to abandon the concept of "spatial determinism" (Wellman, 1983, p. 156) of communities and networks, and replace it with spatial concepts that are more fluid and hybrid. As a consequence, the distinctions into two separate spaces—in particular, between local and global, internal and external—perpetuate erroneous dichotomies and need to be dismissed altogether in research on educational transfer.

Methodologically, research on educational transfer lags behind network analysis. Thus far, we can only speak of the importance of networks for disseminating educational reform, but we have not provided concrete empirical evidence. In an attempt to formulate the tacit network assumptions commonly held in research on educational transfer, I suggest that we address the phenomenon explicitly and label it the "Maris O'Rourke effect." In case you do not know a friend of a colleague of a former employee of Maris O'Rourke, the affirmation is the following: She is for real. O'Rourke was instrumental in the development of outcomes-based education reform in New Zealand in the 1980s, and she became instrumental for disseminating OBE in the 1990s to other parts of the world. In fact, some scholars would say that O'Rourke embodied OBE; with her move from New Zealand to the United States in 1995, OBE moved along with her. It spread like wildfire in all high-income countries as well as in countries receiving loans from the World Bank. In sum, OBE experienced a "global career" (Dale, 2001, p. 498). The tipping point for the "New Zealand model" going global coincided with Maris O'Rourke's tenure at the World Bank. Coincidence, or the power of global networks?

In network analysis, the dissemination of ideas and innovations often is compared to the spread of rumors or epidemics (Watts, 1999, 2003). In more ways than one, we can think of policy borrowing and lending in terms of epidemics. As I mentioned in the Introduction, epidemics start out with a few scholars; simple, lasting explanations designed to resonate over time are then generated; after a while, they burn out. The idea of comparing the rapid global dissemination of school reform models to epidemics is not new (see Levin, 1998). But it is novel to reflect on the profound impact it may have on explaining why, from a sea of school reform models, only a few (e.g., choice, vouchers, outcomes-based education, and standards) surface, with a time lag, in different corners of the world. In other words, which features enhance exportability, or account for the contagion of a specific school reform? Several factors come to mind.

De-territorialization helps. As with epidemics, there is a tipping point wherein the period of a policy epidemic spreads exponentially. Beyond that point, when several systems have already borrowed a particular policy, the source of the contagion becomes difficult to trace. The domino effect accounts for the fact that with time, when a substantial number of systems have borrowed a model from elsewhere, the reform model becomes de-territorialized. For example, OBE is no longer associated with the New Zealand school reform of the 1980s. A few reforms claim to be twins, triplets, or even quadruplets of the original reform idea. Most of them, however, are likely to claim to be improved versions of the original (see Spreen, Chapter 6). At such a stage of a policy epidemic, the model comes across as transnational and is in fact traded as a global model.

Numbers count, both for mobilization and for survival. As soon as a critical mass of educational systems has adopted a policy, "issue networks" (Mintrom & Vergari, 1998, p. 5) enter the scene. They share the same interest: the adoption of their reform by more educational systems. In educational policy, these issue networks are institutionalized in the form of associations, journals, newsletters, list-serves, and conferences. They export and expand the "issue," that is, a particular policy, for their own survival. The role of "policy entrepreneurs" brokering a particular reform is not to be belittled. Mintrom (1997), for example, investigated the sophisticated networking strategies of policy entrepreneurs who lobbied for school choice in 26 U.S. states. The pressure to continuously extend one's sphere of influence by generating new "markets" follows the logic of a (capitalist) world-economy, a process that Wallerstein (1990) refers to as "incorporation" (p. 96).

Furthermore, exposure is key. Some individuals (e.g., Maris O'Rourke) hold professional positions that make them exposed. Their ability to maintain "weak ties" to different clusters of stakeholders that are spread throughout the globe (Granovetter, 1973, 1983) elevates them to global players in school reform. Social network theory helps us to understand the role of institutions in disseminating educational policies. Institutional backing is an asset for the lending of education reform ideas, as it dramatically increases the number of stakeholders in other countries willing to hoist their "flag of convenience" (Lynch, 1998, p. 9) or engage in "phony borrowing" (Phillips, Chapter 3) or "policy mimicry" (Ganderton, 1996) mainly to attain international support and secure the financial resources attached to borrowed policy discourse. Policy network analysis, briefly illustrated above, has the potential of invigorating education policy studies. How global networks exert influence is as important a question as how educational policy makers and stakeholders are positioned in them.

In the beginning of this Conclusion, I pointed to the comparative nature of studies dealing with borrowing and lending, and convergence processes. Naturally, comparative education research is not alone in elaborating on these matters. In fact, it would be hard to imagine how comparative education could intellectually absorb matters of such complexity. For the past 2 decades or so, comparative sociology, comparative politics, and in particular comparative policy studies also have theorized policy convergence (e.g., Dierkes, Weiler, & Berthoin Antal, 1987). Our common ground becomes immediately apparent when we consider how policy convergence is explained in comparative policy studies. For example, in his review of the literature on policy convergence, Bennett (1991) distinguishes among four different processes that may account for convergence: emulation (state officials copying actions taken elsewhere), elite networking (convergence resulting from transnational policy communities), harmonization (advanced by international regimes), and penetration (initiated by external actors and interests).

These distinctions made in comparative policy studies are very much in concert with what this book has attempted to illustrate. Several comparative studies of education presented in this book focused on the process of emulation and found, in line with theories in comparative policy studies, that references to lessons from elsewhere usually have a salutary effect in a climate of protracted policy conflict. A few studies also examined the processes of networking, harmonization, and penetration. They paid special attention to the role of the World Bank, international NGOs, and other international organizations that function as global networks in education or, more precisely, as transnational policy communities, international regimes, and external actors. In particular moments, policy makers and stakeholders refer to these networks as quasi-external authorities and use them to either generate or relieve reform pressure on the education sector.

In conclusion, I have two propositions to offer, each directed to a different audience. My first proposition is that research on education policy borrowing and lending could move beyond the narrow focus of educational research and pay more attention to research in adjacent fields, in particular sociology of knowledge, policy network analysis, and comparative policy studies. My final proposition is that domestically oriented theorists and practitioners in education policy studies could enlarge their repertory by looking into "globalization" or "lessons from elsewhere" as effective policy strategies that increasingly are used as arguments for justifying the need for fundamental educational reform at home.

NOTE

1. Zymek (1975) coined the expression "Das Ausland als Argument" [foreign countries as an argument] to describe the politics of transnational references made in German educational journals of the Nazi period. In the late 1930s, Nazi educators and researchers provided all kinds of justifications as to why Jews, Roma, and all other groups deemed inferior should be removed from schools and later on deported to concentration camps. A popular justification strategy was to publish the positive experiences with segregation that educators and researchers from other countries, notably the United States, were reporting.

REFERENCES

Allen, H. E. (1956). *The diffusion of educational practices in the school systems of the Metropolitan School Study Council.* Unpublished doctoral thesis, Teachers College, Columbia University, New York.

Appadurai, A. (1994). Disjuncture and difference in the global cultural economy. In M. Featherstone (Ed.), *Global culture, nationalism, globalization and modernity* (pp. 31–55). Newbury Park, CA: Sage.

Baumert, J., Klieme, E., Neubrand, M., Prenzel, M., Schiefele, U., Schneider, W., Stanat, P., Tillmann, K.-J., & Weiss, M. (Eds.). (2001). *PISA 2000: Basiskompetenzen von deutschen Schülerinnen und Schülern im internationalen Vergleich* [PISA 2000: Basic skills of German students in international comparison]. Opladen, Germany: Leske & Budrich.

Bennett, C. J. (1991). What is policy convergence and what causes it? *British Journal of Political Science, 21*(2), 215–233.

Bereday, G. Z. F. (1964). Sir Michael Sadler's "Study of foreign systems of education." *Comparative Education Review, 7*(3). (Reprint of the notes of an address given at the Guildford Educational Conference, October 20, 1900, by M. E. Sadler, Christ Church, Oxford)

Bos, W., Lankes, E.–M., Prenzel, M., Schwippert, K., Valtin, R., & Walther, G. (Eds.). (2003). *Erste Ergebnisse aus IGLU* [First results from PIRLS]. Münster: Waxmann.

Bu, L. (1997). International activism and comparative education: Pioneering efforts of the International Institute of Teachers College, Columbia University. *Comparative Education Review, 41*(4), 413–434.

Comaroff, J., & Comaroff, J. L. (2001). Millennial capitalism: First thoughts on a second coming. In J. Comaroff & J. L. Comaroff (Eds.), *Millennial capitalism and the culture of neoliberalism* (pp. 1–56). Durham, NC: Duke University Press.

Chatterji, M. (2002). Models and methods for examining standards-based reforms and accountability initiatives: Have the tools of inquiry answered pressing questions on improving schools? *Review of Educational Research, 72*(3), 345–386.

Cowen, R. (2000). Comparing futures or comparing pasts? *Comparative Education, 36*(3), 333–342.

Cremin, L. A., Shannon, D. A., & Townsend, M. E. (1954). *A history of Teachers College, Columbia University*. New York: Columbia University Press.

Cuban, L. (1998). How schools change reforms. *Teachers College Record, 99*(3), 453–477.

Dale, R. (2001). Constructing a long spoon for comparative education: Charting the career of the "New Zealand model." *Comparative Education, 37*(4), 493–500.

Dierkes, M., Weiler, H. N., & Berthoin Antal, A. (1987). *Comparative policy research: Learning from experience*. Aldershot: Gower.

Escobar, A. (1995). *Encountering development: The making and unmaking of the third world*. Princeton, NJ: Princeton University Press.

Ganderton, P. S. (1996). Concepts of globalisation and their impact upon curriculum policy-making: Rhetoric and reality—a study of Australian reform. *International Journal of Educational Development, 16*(4), 393–405.

Glotzer, R. (1996). The career of Mabel Carney: The study of race and rural development in the United States and South Africa. *The International Journal of African Historical Studies, 29*(2), 309–336.

Gorard, S. (2001). International comparisons of school effectiveness: The second component of the "crisis account" in England? *Comparative Education, 37*(3), 279–296.

Granovetter, M. S. (1973). The strengths of weak ties. *American Journal of Sociology, 78*(6), 1360–1380.

Granovetter, M. S. (1983). The strength of weak ties: A network theory revisited. *Sociological Theory, 1*, 201–233.

Halpin, D., & Troyna, B. (1995). The politics of educational policy borrowing. *Comparative Education, 31*(3), 303–310.

Hannerz, M. (1989). Notes on the global ecumene. *Public Culture, 1*, 66–75.

Henig, J. (1994). *Rethinking school choice: Limits of the market metaphor*. Princeton, NJ: Princeton University Press.

Japan International Cooperation Agency. (1994). *Kaihatsu to Kyoryoku Bunya Betsu Enjyo Kenkyu-kai* [Study on Japan's development assistance for development and education]. Tokyo: Author.

Japan International Cooperation Agency. (2003). *Approaches for systematic planning of development projects* (Chapter 1: Basic education). Tokyo: Author.

Kellaghan, T. (1996). IEA studies and educational policy. *Assessment in Education, 3*, 143–160.

Kijima, R. (2003). *Uniquely Japanese? Strategic approaches to education aid, 1991–2001* (Monograph). Stanford: Stanford University School of Education, Program in International Comparative Education.

Kijima, R., & Steiner-Khamsi, G. (2003). The politics of educational lending: Japan's math and science education abroad. Unpublished manuscript.

Levin, B. (1998). An epidemic of education policy: (What) can we learn from each other? *Comparative Education, 34*(2), 131–141.

Lowe, J. (2001). International examinations, national systems and the global market. In K. Wilson (Ed.), *Doing comparative education research: Issues and problems* (pp. 355–370). Oxford: Symposium Books.

Lynch, J. (1998). The international transfer of dysfunctional paradigms. In D. Johnson, B. Smith, & M. Crossley (Eds.), *Learning and teaching in an international context: Research, theory and practice* (pp. 7–33). Bristol, UK: University of Bristol, Centre for International Studies in Education.

McAdam, D., Tarrow, S., & Tilly, C. (2001). *Dynamics of contention.* Cambridge: Cambridge University Press.

McGinn, N. (1996). Education, democratization, globalization: Challenges for comparative education. *Comparative Education Review, 40*(4), 341–357.

Mintrom, M. (1997). Policy entrepreneurs and the diffusion of innovation. *American Journal of Political Science, 41*(3), 738–770.

Mintrom, M., & Vergari, S. (1998). Policy networks and innovation diffusion: The case of state education reforms. *The Journal of Politics, 60*(1), 126–148.

Mort, P. R. (1946). *Principles of school administration.* New York: McGraw-Hill.

Mort, P. R. (1947). *A time scale for measuring the adaptability of school systems with an instrument, scoring method and standards for the measurement of such adaptability.* New York: Metropolitan School Study Council.

Nóvoa, A., & Lawn, M. (Eds.). (2002). *Fabricating Europe: The formation of an education space.* Dordrecht, Netherlands: Kluwer.

Oesterreich, D. (2002). *Politische Bildung von 14–Jährigen in Deutschland: Studien aus dem Projekt Civic Education* [Political education of 14-year-olds in Germany: Studies from the Civic Education Project]. Opladen, Germany: Leske & Budrich.

Osumi, N. (1999). Kongo no Kagaku Kyo-iku Kyoryoku no Mokuhyo- to Gijyutsu Iten no Ho-saku-Firipin no Risu-ka Kyo-iku Purojekuto Gijyutsu Kyoryoku no Keiken Kara [A discussion on the results of the Science and Mathematics Education Manpower Development Project (SMEMDP) in the Philippines (1994–1999)]. *Journal of International Cooperation in Education, 1*(2), 31–42.

Popkewitz, T. S. (1998). *Struggling for the soul: The politics of schooling and the construction of the teacher.* New York: Teachers College Press.

Popkewitz, T. S., & Brennan, M. (Eds.). (1998). *Foucault's challenge: Discourse, knowledge, and power in education.* New York: Teachers College Press.

Richardson, W. (1993). Employers as an instrument of school reform? Education–business "compacts" in Britain and America. In D. Finegold, L. McFarland, & W. Richardson (Eds.), *Something borrowed? Something learned? The transatlantic market in education and training programs* (pp. 171–192). Washington, DC: Brookings.

Ritzer, G. (1996). The McDonaldization thesis: Is expansion inevitable? *International Sociology, 11*(3), 291–308.

Robertson, S. L., Bonal, X., & Dale, R. (2002). GATS and the education service industry: The politics of scale and global reterritorialization. *Comparative Education Review, 46*(4), 472–496.

Robinson, P. (1999). The tyranny of league tables: International comparisons of educational attainment and economic performance. In R. Alexander, P. Broadford, & D. Phillips (Eds.), *Learning from comparing: New directions in comparative education research* (Vol. 1, pp. 217–235). Oxford: Symposium Books.

Rogers, E. M. (1995). *Diffusion of innovations* (4th ed.). New York: Free Press.

Ross, D. H. (Ed.). (1958). *Administration for adaptability: A source book drawing together the results of more than 150 individual studies related to the question of why and how schools improve.* New York: Metropolitan School Study Council.

Rust, V. D. (2000). Education policy studies and comparative education. In R. Alexander, M. Osborn, & D. Phillips (Eds.), *Learning from comparing: New directions in comparative education research* (Vol. 2, pp. 13–39). Oxford: Symposium Books.

Schriewer, J. (1990). The method of comparison and the need for externalization: Methodological criteria and sociological concepts. In J. Schriewer (Ed.) in cooperation with B. Holmes, *Theories and methods in comparative education* (pp. 25–83). Frankfurt/M, Germany: Lang.

Smith, M. L., Heinecke, W., & Noble, A. J. (1999). Assessment policy and political spectacle. *Teachers College Record, 101*(2), 157–191.

Steiner-Khamsi, G. (2002). Re-framing educational borrowing as a policy strategy. In M. Caruso & H.-E. Tenorth (Eds.), *Internationalisierung—Internationalisation* (pp. 57–89). Frankfurt/M, Germany: Lang.

Steiner-Khamsi, G. (2003). The politics of league tables. *SOWI, 1* (on-line journal).

Steiner-Khamsi, G., & Quist, H. O. (2000). The politics of educational borrowing: Reopening the case of Achimota in British Ghana. *Comparative Education Review, 44*(3), 272–299.

Torney-Purta, J., Lehmann, R., Oswald, H., & Schulz, W. (2001). *Citizenship and education in twenty-eight countries: Civic knowledge and engagement at age fourteen.* Amsterdam: International Association for the Evaluation of Educational Achievement.

Tyack, D., & Cuban, L. (1995). *Tinkering toward utopia: A century of public school reform.* Cambridge, MA: Harvard University Press.

Wallerstein, I. (1990). Culture as the ideological battleground of the modern world system. In M. Featherstone (Ed.), *Global culture, nationalism, globalization and modernity* (pp. 86–101). Newbury Park, CA: Sage.

Watts, D. J. (1999). Networks, dynamics, and the small-world phenomenon. *American Journal of Sociology, 105*(2), 493–527.

Watts, D. J. (2003). *Six degrees: The science of a connected age.* New York: Norton.

Wellman, B. (1983). Network analysis: Some basic principles. *Sociological Theory, 1*, 155–200.

Zymek, B. (1975). *Das Ausland als Argument in der pädagogischen Reformdiskussion* [Foreign countries as an argument in educational reform discussions]. Rattingen, Germany: Henn.

About the Editor and the Contributors

Gita Steiner-Khamsi is Professor of Comparative and International Education at Teachers College, Columbia University (New York). Steiner-Khamsi has written books and articles on policy borrowing and lending in the fields of multicultural education, citizenship/political education, and school reform. Her most recent book (with Judith Torney-Purta and John Schwille), *New Paradigms and Recurring Paradoxes in Education for Citizenship: An International Comparative Perspective*, was published in 2002. She is currently undertaking field research in Mongolia, where she is focusing on the role of international organizations in exporting particular school reforms to postsocialist countries. Her next monograph (forthcoming with Palgrave Macmillan Publisher) will deal with education policy borrowing in Mongolia.

Dana Burde is Visiting Assistant Professor of Comparative and International Education at Teachers College, Columbia University. Burde is the author of "Can Old Peace Movements Stand up to the New War?" (*Vacarme*, 2002) and has extensive experience with education program evaluation and assessment in conflict and postconflict regions. As a practitioner she also has worked for international humanitarian aid and development agencies in Latin America, the Caucasus, and the Balkans on education and civic development projects.

William deJong-Lambert is a Ph.D. candidate in Comparative Education at Teachers College, Columbia University. deJong-Lambert served as a Peace Corps volunteer in Poland from 1992–1994, and in Madagascar from 1994–1996. In 2003, he was awarded a Fulbright-Hays Doctoral Dissertation Fellowship, and returned to Warsaw to conduct archival research on Lysenko. In 2003 and 2004, he contributed book chapters to two other edited volumes: *Implementing European Union Education and Training Policy* (David Phillips and Hubert Ertl, Eds.), and *Re-imagining Comparative Education* (Peter Ninnes and Sonja Mehta, Eds.).

Phillip W. Jones is Pro-Dean of the Faculty of Education and Social Work at the University of Sydney. Jones is well known for his historical analyses of the education programs of major international organizations, including UNESCO and the World Bank. His current book projects include *Australia's International Relations in Education 1945–2000*, *Education and World Order*, and *Education and the New Multilateralism: The UN, Development and Globalization*.

Thomas F. Luschei is a Ph.D. candidate in International and Comparative Education at Stanford University. Luschei has lived and worked in São Paulo and Salvador, Brazil. His research interests include education policy borrowing, teacher preparation and professional development, and accountability and instructional improvement in public schools. In 2003, he contributed a book chapter, together with Richard Lemons and Leslie Siskin, to *New Accountability: High Schools and High-Stakes Testing* (Martin Carnoy, Richard Elmore, and Leslie Siskin, Eds.).

Carlos Martinez is Senior Researcher at the Comparative Education Centre of Humboldt University, Berlin (Germany). Martinez is completing his dissertation in the Department of History and Political Ideas at the Complutense University in Madrid. His dissertation examines the political implications of the theological concept of free will in the late sixteenth and seventeenth centuries. While he was writing his dissertation, he was granted a European Union fellowship that enabled him to collaborate in the Comparative Education Centre's research project "Constructions of Internationality."

David Phillips is Professor of Comparative Education and Fellow of St. Edmund Hall in the University of Oxford (England). Phillips was Editor of the *Oxford Review of Education* from 1983 to 2003 and serves on the editorial board of *Comparative Education* and the advisory boards of various other journals. He is series editor of *Oxford Studies in Comparative Education*, and the author of many publications on comparative topics, with a special focus on Germany. He is a member of the (UK) Social Sciences Academy and a Fellow of the Royal Historical Society.

Jürgen Schriewer is Professor of Comparative Education and Director of the Comparative Education Centre of Humboldt University, Berlin. A former Dean of Humboldt University's School of Education, he also served as President of the Comparative Education Society in Europe (1992 to 1996). Schriewer's particular research interests include the comparative social history of education, issues of globalization and world-system research, as well as the history and methodology of cross-cultural comparison in education and the social sciences. He is editor of the Comparative Studies Series (Lang); several of his articles and books have been translated and are available in German, English, French, Italian, Spanish, Portuguese, Chinese, and Japanese.

Iveta Silova is Visiting Professor at the American Studies Center at Baku State University, Azerbaijan (2004–2006). After completing her Ph.D. degree in Comparative Education and Political Sociology at Teachers College, Columbia University, Silova moved to Almaty (Kazakhstan) and worked as a research associate and education advisor for the Open Society Institute/Soros Foundation, UNICEF, and the Organisation for Security and Cooperation in Europe. Her research on globalization, educational reform, and minority policies in the transformation societies of the former Soviet Union has been widely published in academic journals and books.

Carol Anne Spreen is Assistant Professor at the University of Maryland, Department of Education Policy and Leadership, College Park. In 1998 Spreen was a Visiting Scholar at the University of Witwatersrand in Johannesburg, South Africa. Her dissertation research and her teaching in South Africa focused on curriculum policy development and international aid influences. Her principal research and teaching experiences are in the field of comparative education and international education policy, with an emphasis on international studies of school reform, curriculum planning, and instructional leadership.

Bernhard T. Streitwieser is Coordinator of Research and Evaluation for a Mellon Foundation study at the Searle Center for Teaching Excellence, Northwestern University, Evanston, Illinois. Streitwieser was a visiting researcher at the Max Planck Institute for Human Development and Education in Berlin, Germany, in 1998–1999, and recipient of a dissertation grant of the Alexander von Humboldt Foundation. His dissertation research on eastern German teachers after reunification resulted in a co-authored book (with Christa Händle; in German), several chapters in edited volumes (*Oxford Studies in Comparative Education, Educational Reconstruction and Transformation in Europe*) and the education journal *European Education*.

Charles Tilly is Joseph L. Buttenwieser Professor of Social Science, Columbia University, New York. An internationally known scholar in comparative history and sociology, Tilly is the author of several award-winning books, such as *Durable Inequality* (1998), for which he received the 2000

Distinguished Scholarly Publication Award from the American Sociological Association. His most recent books include *Stories, Identities, and Political Change* (2002), *The Politics of Collective Violence* (2003), *Contention and Democracy in Europe* (2004), and *Social Movements, 1768–2004* (2004).

Frances Vavrus is Associate Professor of Education at Teachers College, Columbia University. She holds a Ph.D. from the University of Wisconsin–Madison in Education and African Studies. Vavrus is also the recipient of a Foreign Languages and Area Studies Fellowship for Swahili, a Fulbright–Hays doctoral dissertation fellowship, and an Andrew W. Mellon Postdoctoral Fellowship in Anthropological Demography at Harvard University. Her current research focuses on the impact of structural adjustment policies on educational opportunity in Sub-Saharan Africa; AIDS, education, and orphanhood in Tanzania; and the politics of water privatization on Mount Kilimanjaro. In 2003 she completed a book on these matters entitled *Desire and Decline: Schooling amid Crisis in Tanzania* (Lang).

Tali Yariv-Mashal holds a Ph.D. in Comparative Education and History from Teachers College, Columbia University. Her research deals primarily with educational and political discourse, especially in relation to Zionist ideology and its educational implications in Palestine and Israel. She also writes on methodological issues of historical research in education. In 2003 she co-authored an article (with Antonio Nóvoa) entitled "Comparative Research in Education: A Mode of Governance or a Historical Inquiry?" which was published in the journal *Comparative Education*.

Index